Making Star Trek: The Next Generation Ev

ISBN: 9781520237411

First Published in 2016 by Petulant Po

Copyright 2016 by Steven Gordon.

This book of literary criticism unauthorized by the Star Trek people.

Dedicated to Nagelum from "Where Silence has Lease",
for giving us a few laughs.

Star Trek: The Next Generation had a lot of good things going for it. Visually, it was a treat: the colorful uniforms, the sets, the spaceships, Counselor Troi in certain outfits, etc. Some of the characters like Picard and Data were very interesting. The show also had a lot of intriguing ideas about time travel, parallel dimensions, clones, robots and other classic sci-fi themes.

But some of these ideas were either executed poorly, or weren't written as well as they could have been. Some episodes felt like they were dropped in from soap operas or Sesame Street and had little to do with Star Trek. At times the behavior of many of the characters simply was not realistic.

The purpose of this book is to show how much better The Next Generation could have been, critiquing both the plot and the characterizations.

A few things before we begin:

1) I am critical of episodes. A **lot** of episodes, especially in the declining sixth and seventh seasons, which were well stocked with episodes about rearing children, or Mrs. Troi going through Betazoid menopause, or episodes with endless technobabble. I analyze them and provide what is intended as constructive criticism. The fact is that TNG had a lot of good ideas, but a lot of poor execution. The purpose of this book is to show how it could have been better.

2) Many times you will see references to a "reset button". Bad TV writing typically features the "reset button", where at the end of the episode everything is resolved and absolutely nothing is changed from the beginning of the episode. If someone is injured, they are instantly healed, or we are told they will be instantly healed by the beginning of the next episode. If someone does something which viewers expect to have far reaching consequences, and we are told there will be no changes at all, that's another example of the reset button in action.

The reset button is bad writing. Actions should have consequences. If an episode ends with everything and everyone exactly the way they started, it does not feel real, and the drama suffers.

It shows timidity of writers afraid to change anything. You will see me frequently make reference to the reset button because it is used a lot in TNG.

Now we are ready to begin...

Encounter at Farpoint

The plot:

Captain Jean-Luc Picard takes command of the USS Enterprise. He and his crew are confronted by a hostile alien named Q who threatens to destroy them if they act "barbaric" on their Farpoint mission. At Farpoint, Picard discovers a society of white people wearing fake dreadlocks who are abusing a giant glowing space jellyfish. Picard helps free the space jellyfish from captivity after the space jellyfish's boyfriend arrives.

What works:

1) The general idea of bringing Star Trek back as a series.

2) Having a physically imposing first officer--Riker and his big chest.

3) Having a Captain who speaks with authority--Picard does, even when he says nonsense (which is often).

4) Troi has big frizzy hair that looks bad. On the other hand, she wears a miniskirt which is quite revealing, especially when she is sitting, and the miniskirt really works well with her gogo boots.

5) When Troi gives her very first "I sense something" line, she looks like she is having a painful but still quite erotic orgasm.

5b) Troi had some great lines throughout the episode "Pain... unhappiness... great joy and gratitude...." Amazing!

6) I wondered for a moment why they had an anonymous spanish man at the helm. Then when Q froze him I knew why. Minorities don't last long at the helm. Just ask the black guy who suddenly appeared to take Wesley's place right before Nagelum showed up in "Where Silence has Lease".

7) I liked it when Q freeze dried the anonymous spanish helmsman as well as Tasha. They were both sprayed with white paint mean to simulate cold which looked very funny.

8) I liked it when Q played the part of a future soldier in a big rubber suit with its own built in narcotics. He looked like a walking truck tire.

9) I liked it when Troi, asked for input about the situation, responded, "It's very different". Thanks!

10) The Battle Bridge looks more like a real bridge than the regular bridge, which looks like a lounge.

11) I liked the midget who repeatedly rang the bell at Picard's trial. A great freak show!

12) Q's judge outfit, his big pointed hat and screaming red gloves are very good. But why is he wearing lipstick? He also has a bad comb over. In later episodes, he uses the power of the Q to get a wig with much more hair that stands up.

13) I like how when one rubber suited guard is about to be executed, he snorts some narcotics first.

14) It was funny watching Data speak in Picard and then Q's exact voice.

15) It was also funny when Riker, showing up in Part II of this episode, is made to watch Part I on TV, like it was a TV episode... which it was!

16) I liked when Worf threatened to shoot Q's image on the viewscreen.

17) Data pulls Wesley out of the water one handed on the holodeck! But wouldn't Wesley be instantly dry when he exited the holodeck?

What doesn't work:

1) Picard is supposed to be French. But he has a British accent. I think Roddenberry did this because in the 1980's Americans didn't like the French and he wanted to irritate us by having a historic enemy command the ship in the future. But it was weird having an actor with a British accent play the part and the discrepancy is never explained.

2) Data's nipples conspicuously stick out of his uniform. Is that a special Dr. Soong touch? We never see Geordi's nipples or Riker's nipples doing the same. Do androids get cold easily?

3) Suddenly, the Klingons have head putty and are honorable instead of looking Mongolian and behaving treacherously. What happened?

4) Q starts out talking in middle ages language, saying things like "Thou art". Then he suddenly drops this style of speaking without explanation.

5) Q's moral equivalence of capitalism and communism was annoying: "You slaughtered millions in silly arguments about how to divide the resources of your little world"

6) Saucer separation never works, dramatically speaking. The Enterprise looks headless, like a chicken running around after its head as been cut off. Furthermore when the saucer section detaches, it doesn't have warp drive. How does it decelerate? How does it accelerate and meet them at Farpoint? There is never any explanation for this.

7) Guys wearing skirts. That never works.

8) Picard surrenders to Q without even being asked. He does that a lot. His favorite kind of surrendering is unconditional "State that we are not asking for any terms or conditions". One time I'd like to see him surrender without condition and have the aliens violate with an anal probe, and when he protests, have them say, "Well, you did insist on surrendering without conditions."

9) How can the dreadlocks people keep the jellyfish prisoner if it can create things out of thin air? Can't it just vaporize all the dreadlock people?

10) Old doctor McCoy speaks with a super thick southern accent. Did he just come from a Klan meeting?

11) Picard begs Q for help, saying he'll do whatever Q says. That makes Picard look very weak and needy.

12) When Space Jellyfish #2 attacks the city, Picard refuses to defend them, even as many dreadlocked people are being blown to pieces.

13) How does Picard know that phaser blasts will feed the space jellyfish rather than kill it? Why can't the other jellyfish send its own food beam?

14) The tender moment at the end, when the space jellyfishes hold hands, is very stupid.

How it could have been better:

Some parts of this episode work well. The introduction to the ship and the crew. Q as an adversary. But the space jellyfish part did not work well. There was no real antagonist, unless you consider Q an antagonist.

A better idea: instead of Q judging humanity, simply have him *warn* humanity. Warn them and foreshadow a difficult mission, and have him drop by during the episode to observe their progress and make witty comments.

Make the space jellyfish actively evil. Have it control the dreadlock haired white people, and when Riker and Crusher beam down, have it control them too. Have Picard figure out that the space jellyfish is controlling people and have him realize that phasers won't work. Have him use an antimatter bomb to destroy it.

That's compelling. That's excitement. That's not what the first episode was.

The Naked Now

The plot:

The crew become infected with the Original Series virus that makes men silly and women eager to be boned. They get cured, but not before Data scores some sex with Tasha.

What works:

1) Some people criticize this episode because it was a copy of the original Star Trek Naked Time episode. I don't see that as a problem as it was well done. Others say it was too soon to show the crew acting silly because we aren't very familiar with them yet. Also not a major problem.

2) I liked how Riker referenced the incident from the original Enterprise.

3) I liked how Data reads pages really fast--shows he's a robot--show not tell, very good! And no, I see no difference between an android and a robot, sorry.

4) When Tasha gets infected, she wiggles her ass at everyone and tries to smile goofy-like. It's bad acting, but it's funny.

5) When Dr. Crusher gets infected, she tries to get Picard to bone her, even starting to unzip herself on the bridge, an act that would not have been possible after the second season, when they moved their zippers to the back of their shirts. She says a great line, which is unintentionally made even more funny by her poor acting ability: Crusher unzips and says: "You owe me something. I'm a woman, I haven't had the comfort of a husband."

6) A great Wesley moment simulating Picard's voice saying: ""Attention all decks, effective immediately I have handed over control of this vessel to acting Captain Wcslcy Crusher" and then Wesley adding, "Thank you Captain thank you, and with that order comes a brave new day for the Enterprise!"

7) I like the Chinese guy with the bad hair who laughs like a retard when the Chief Engineer says, "These are control chips!" A great scene!

8) Great lines between Tasha and Data

"You are fully functional, aren't you Data?"
"Of course."
"How fully functional?"
"I am programmed in multiple techniques."

9) This is the very first episode that we get to hear about Tasha and the rape gangs. After this we hear her talk about it constantly.

10) Wesley saves the day! I used to hate Wesley, until I started watching the other Star Trek series and seeing the really boring kids there like Jake and Nog and realized, in retrospect, that Wesley wasn't so bad. He had a kind of goofiness that was amusing.

11) A great bit of tension with the collapsing star chunk coming towards them. Adds to the compelling nature of the story.

12) A very funny Picard line: "You have lost the capacity for self-judgment. Now alcohol does this, Wesley."

13) Great Tasha line to Data at the end: "It never happened!"

What doesn't work:

1) The Chief Engineer is a lady we haven't been introduced to (and never see again) who has a giant wart on her face.

2) Wesley cuts them off from engineering, and yet there is a simple pane of glass separating them. Why can't they phaser through the glass? Or why can't they just beam into the room? Never explained.

3) Realistically, this virus cannot affect Data. He's a machine.

4) Somehow, when the women get infected, they always want sex. It's not a problem, but it's also not very realistic. Already mentioned were Crusher and Tasha, and then Troi, who, when infected, presses her breasts against Riker and moans, "Let me into your mind...."

5) Picard got infected after Riker does, but showed symptoms before him.

6) Not one person got the idea to beam to the other, infected ship and use it to tow the Enterprise to safety. If Wesley is such a genius why didn't he think of it?

7) Data's nipples stick out of his uniform. Do androids feel cold?

How it could have been better:

Generally a very amusing episode. But it would have been more dramatic if instead of showing us an empty bridge of the contaminated ship, they actually showed the scene where they blew themselves into space, their bodies spinning around in the distance as little figures with special effects.

Inquiring minds also want to know how satisfied Tasha was to have sex with a robot. Was she sore down there afterwards?

Code of Honor

The plot:

Tasha gets kidnapped by the planet of the black people who bang sticks. She has to fight to the death with the wife of the leader of the black stick banging people. Picard arranges for the leader to be deposed.

What works:

1) Some people say this is a racist episode because it has black people banging sticks. I couldn't disagree more. In "Justice", we see a planet of blonde people having a lot of free sex and executing criminals. Is that discriminating against blonde people? I find it refreshing in the first season that they showed aliens being alien by ethnicity rather than by slopping putty on their foreheads, which became greatly overused in later seasons.

2) I liked it when the black people banged sticks. There's nothing wrong with that. They do it in Africa too.

3) I like Lutan's Jamaican accent. At one point he says "A coat of honor protects one like a magic chlooak" with an emphasis on the hard consonant sounds that is very amusing. This may be the only episode in Star Trek where we see black people not acting precisely like white people.

4) Picard gives Lutan a gift of a toy horse, like he's a retard, heh heh.

5) There actually was a Space 1999 episode called "The Rules of Luton"; here they are dealing with the rules of Lutan. Both involved a fight to the death.

6) When Tasha is kidnapped, why don't they just locate her on sensors and beam her out? They didn't even take away her communicator, she could have contacted the ship at any time.

7) The black lady who Tasha fights grunts, "Huh! Huh!" when she is fighting. It is comical.

8) Lutan's black assistant at one point yells, "No woman has challenged supercedence for over 200 years!" I have no idea what that means, but the urgency with which he said this nonsense phrase has always struck me as funny.

9) When the poison needle glove falls into the lap of one of the stick bangers, he looks at it stupidly like a retard right before he dies.

What doesn't work:

1) Troi's severe black outfit looks like it has a blood-red chastity belt built into it that goes down to her groin. Ug.

2) Picard having to beg Riker every time he wants to beam down is annoying. After the first season they stopped having these discussions.

3) Picard lets Wesley sit at ops. Why? No explanation. Does he let all the children on the ship have a turn? Or is he trying to get into Beverly's pants?

4) Picard seems almost eager to humiliate himself in front of Lutan and his colleagues, praising Lutan for kidnapping Tasha. Picard seems to lean rather heavily on the surrender button in the first season.

5) The Prime Directive sucks. If they need the vaccine so badly, they should take it by force.

6) Data has a very patronizing talk with Geordi where twice he calls Geordi "my friend". Friends don't talk like that. Is Data so insecure about having his first black friend?

7) I don't understand the ending at all. Men are in charge in this society. How does Mrs. Lutan suddenly become in charge once she is divorced from Mr. Lutan? Shouldn't he inherit? And one other little plot detail missing: once Mrs. Lutan is in charge, does she give the Federation the vaccine? Never addressed, and this was the entire point of the episode.

How it could have been better:

It was a very amusing episode, with a great antagonist. Unfortunately, after this episode, things start going downhill.

The Last Outpost

The plot:

The Enterprise and a Ferengi ship get immobilized by an ancient civilization. Riker gets morally judged by his alien superior and pleads guilty.

What works:

1) I really like the matte painting of the alien planet. And the set with plastic rocks reminds me of the original Star Trek.

2) I like how the Ferengi talk differently, it shows their alienness. In later episodes most putty headed aliens speak perfect English, relying on their putty heads to prove their alienness.

3) I also like the viewscreen close up of the Ferengi fangs and bad teeth.

4) There's a great scene of Riker on a cliff, staring out at an expanse, yelling, "Anyboooooody out theeeeere?"

5) A great Ferengi line, "You work with your females, force them to wear clothing."

6) I like how Ferengi move their heads back and forth and point their fingers, mannerisms like chimpanzees. As Riker and old axe man talk, they move back and forth in the background, like restless monkeys in a cage.

What doesn't work:

1) It's still early in the series, and I'm already tired of aliens passing moral judgment on humanity.

2) Riker, being judged by the old guy with the axe, admits all the terrible things the Federation has done. Someone trying to save himself would make a persuasive effort to make a good impression but Riker does his best to make a bad one--he feels so guilty, so immoral, for no reason. It's unrealistic and unpleasant to watch.

3) When old axe man spins his axe Riker stands very still, like a side of beef, even when the axe almost comes whistling down on his shoulder. That's not a realistic reaction at all.

4) The Enterprise is fired on twice by the Ferengi, but Picard won't fire back, saying "They're just responding to our close pursuit."

5) When the Ferengi talk on the viewscreen there is a blank white background. Is the interior of their ship a cloud?

6) The Ferengi are supposed to show how evil capitalist are. I hate this left wing propaganda. Where are the communist aliens? (The Borg, right?)

7) At one point Picard can't reach anyone in engineering... maybe because there is no chief engineer?

8) The scene where Picard talks about the French flag is goofy, and obvious padding for a thinly plotted episode. It's even odder for a man with a British accent pretend to be French.

9) Geordi says, "We shift out into warp 9 and come back fighting, woo wee!" It is goofy to say "Woo wee!"

10) At one point, Picard orders the Ferengi to return his stolen power unit, as if he is about to attack them. Then Picard orders the Enterprise to run away, and quotes Sun Tsu as if he is a genius. Picard is always running away or surrendering. In fact, Picard offers to surrender, again, in this episode, merely because Counselor Troi suggests it. Worf & Tasha want to fight, but Troi says, "They did fire on us, but we were chasing them."

11) The Enterprise gets very cold because of the power drain. Picard is not wearing a coat, and is the only one who doesn't look cold at all. They forgot to tell him to act like he was cold.

12) Old axe man has a very bad makeup job, his baldness cap looks very phony.

13) After Riker confesses all the vile things the Federation has done, the old axe man doesn't execute him. There is no explanation for his decision.

How it could have been better:

The first half of the episode, chasing the Ferengi ship and then figuring out that the planet has paralyzed the Enterprise, is very slow. Why not show more Ferengi interaction sooner? Show us more of Ferengi philosophy, don't simply call them bad capitalists. Show them trying to make a deal with the Federation that will cheat them. In other words, *show* us about the Ferengi, don't *tell* us about them.

As for Old Ax Man, try to think of something more original than having a superior alien culture judging our morality, again. Have Picard fool Old Ax Man into thinking the Federation destroyed Old Ax Man's empire and get him to self-destruct or surrender.

Where No One Has Gone Before

The plot:

The Traveler, the man in the striped pajamas who wears mitten claws, comes aboard and enables the Enterprise to travel intergalactically, to a place where thoughts become reality. Then the Enterprise goes home without doing much, the end.

What works:

1) Intergalactic travel, cool!

2) A touching moment: Wesley holds the Traveler's paw.

3) The idea of a place where your imagination becomes reality.

What doesn't work:

1) Lt Cdr Argyle is casually mentioned as "one of the chief engineers". How can a ship have several Chief Engineers? There are a long string of Chief Engineers in the first season. Why didn't Roddenberry simply have a casting call, run auditions, and make a choice? By the way, Argyle is a weak Scotty clone, very boring, no personality, not even an accent.

2) Wesley wears a shirt that looks like an orange tablecloth.

3) Wesley is a Mozart of starship operations? Really? What???? Well, at least we have some kind of rationale for having Wesley on the bridge, right?

4) When they get to the thoughts-become-reality galaxy/dimension, Picard doesn't want to explore, he wants Starfleet to send a "pure" science vessel. That's a lame excuse. The Enterprise is not a science vessel? What is it, a garbage scow?

5) Worf's Targ is a pig wearing a fur coat.

6) Tasha mentions the rape gangs. Only the second mention, but already getting old, fast. For all her talking about it, we never learn if the rape gang ever caught up with Tasha.

7) Goofy: Picard telling everyone "Everyone think happy thoughts!" Doubly goofy: Troi "I feel such an abundance of well being on this ship!"

8) In the galaxy of imagination, why can't they just think up another copy of the Traveler to help them get home?

9) A Chinese guy in a skirt! Stop that.

How it could have been better:

The most interesting part of the story was in the land of imagination. But it was not really explored.   We saw a guy playing the violin, a woman ballerina, and Picard talking to his dead mommie. Big deal. It felt very rushed and underexplored. What if most of the episode had focused on people getting trapped in their thoughts and having to fight their way out, having to figure out reality from fantasy? That would have been a lot more interesting than the first half (slow) and the second half, which gave short shrift to the imagination galaxy.

Lonely Among Us

The plot:

An electricity monster takes over various members of the crew, ending up with Picard. Then it leaves, taking Picard with it. They use the transporter to regenerate Picard and press the reset button.

What works:

1) The idea of alien takeover, if done well (here it was not).

2) I like how when Crusher and Riker confront Picard when he is controlled by the electricity monster, they act like gutless wonders. Picard forces them to back down and have themselves examined, hopefully with deep anal probes.

3) Worf screams when he gets mouth raped by the electricity monster. Very dramatic!

4) The Indian guy in engineering gets crotch raped by the electricity monster. Very dramatic!

4) While I don't like the B story with the furry/fish aliens who hate each other, I do appreciate the fact that they have light sabers.

What doesn't work:

1) Picard at one point admits to Crusher he is being controlled by the electricity monster. Beverly does nothing, even though she should call security and have him removed from command. Also the scene where Riker tells Picard he is concerned that Picard is being controlled by an alien is very goofy--why would Riker waste his time telling an alien controlling Picard that he is being controlled by an alien?

2) The Be story features guys in monster who hate each other, supposed to be humorous but is very boring.

3) Picard does the moral equivalency thing again with capitalism and communism: Picard, on past wars: "Even strangely enough... they fought over economic systems." Even more strangely, Communism killed and enslaved tens of millions of people. But, strangely enough, Picard never mentions that.

4) Riker: "We no longer enslave animals for food purposes." Animals enslaved? What? Then Riker says they only eat "transporter meat". What?

5) During Worf's medical exam, Crusher wears a cheap looking bald cap on her head.

6) They use the transporter to make a copy of Picard. Why does anyone need to die on Star Trek if they have a transporter pattern for them?

7) Geordi sees the electricity monster jump into Picard. He tells Beverly, she does nothing.

8) Data waves around a pipe like Sherlock Holmes and tries to talk like him. Not remotely amusing.

9) Picard asks Engineer Sing whether he has talked to Chief Engineer Argyle--Is the chief engineer too busy to attend the captain's meeting?

How it could have been better:

This was a very slow episode. It was also unrealistic because even with a ton of clues, the crew does not revolt against alien controlled Picard. When the electricity monster controls Worf and Crusher, it does absolutely nothing interesting.

So what if the electricity monster wasn't actually such a nice monster, and did bad things while it was controlling members of the crew? What if, for example, while controlling Worf, it stuck itself with pain sticks over and over? What if, controlling Crusher, it had her spank Wesley?

What if, instead of simply wanting to go home, the electricity monster had some evil plan. Maybe it wanted to go to a colony planet to take over the population there. Maybe the Enterprise crew wouldn't take most of the episode to figure out what was going on. Maybe they could try to figure out a way to fight electricity monster, maybe by draining its power. That would have made for a more interesting episode then watching electricity monster take over crew members who don't protest very much.

Justice

The plot:

I always thought of this episode as the Planet of the Scantily Clad Blonde People. Wesley gets sentenced to death on the blonde sex planet, and Picard has to give a speech and rescue him.

What works:

1) Blonde people having sex all over the place! I very much enjoyed the welcome of the away team. A big breasted blonde woman rubs Riker's chest and then hugs him. Then the same lady says to Worf, "I welcome this huge one". And then when the blonde guy hugs Tasha, you can see her grinning from ear to ear. And then the blonde lady says, "Please, enjoy what we have." It's just like Risa, except everyone is blonde and good looking.

2) When the voice of the space station speaks, the Enterprise shakes! Nice touch.

3) The Jr. hot blonde with bouncy breasts goes to Wesley, grabbing him, "I want to do something with you too. It's something you can teach me."

Wesley, "There are some games I don't quite know yet."

Ha!

4) When they learn that there is only one punishment for all crimes--death-- somehow everyone on the Away Team IMMEDIATELY realizes that this is all a setup for Wesley! Unintentionally funny.

5) The blonde guy who wanted to inject Wesley with poison said, "Now look what you've done, you've scared him!"

6) Crusher give a good cry when Picard says he won't let them execute Wesley.

7) One of the blonde kids seems to purposefully throw the ball into the forbidden zone. Wesley was getting a lot of attention from the junior hot blonde girl--was the guy jealous of Wesley and purposefully trying to get rid of him? Because, that would be interesting!

What doesn't work:

1) The very, very fake looking wigs the blonde women are wearing. They looked like they raided Thomas Jefferson's house for hair wear.

2) The guys are wearing some kind of strange alien bikini that makes their nuts stick out. It's very distracting. Those things aren't supposed to show. They looked like they are wrapped so tight that they are about to burst.

3) The episode features scantily clad blonde people constantly jogging around an advanced metal building and pools of luscious water. This is actually a sewage treatment plant in Los Angeles. The pools are filled with filtered shit and piss. What would have happened, I wonder, if they had tossed the ball to Wesley and it had gone into the water?

4) When they can't figure out the alien space station, they have Geordi go to a window and look out. Are Geordi's eyes better than ship sensors? It seems a little ridiculous.

5) Worf: "I am not concerned with pleasure, Commander, I am a warrior." Ridiculous.

6) If the flowers were in a forbidden zone, how do gardeners tend them?

7) Wesley, speaking in an artificially deep voice, says "I'm with Starfleet. We don't lie." GROAN!

8) Picard is very trusting letting them hold Wesley before the execution in another location! What if they had killed him? Well, there's always the transporter.

9) Why is Data being examined in sickbay and not engineering?

10) It's a sign of a slow episode when Picard literally says, "Let's have more talk, Data."

11) Picard gets the space station alien to let them beam up by saying, "Every rule must have exceptions"... that's it? It's kind of a low key climax.

12) Picard speaks to Riker as he's being dematerialized by the transporter. How can this be possible?

How it could have been better:

Generally, this was a pretty good episode, but even good episodes can be even better.

1) Let the blonde people execute Wesley to satisfy their justice system. Then make another copy of Wesley in the transporter.

2) How about showing Wesley being executed and deal with the aftermath, then show this to be a false reality made by the space station alien just to teach the crew of the Enterprise a lesson.

3) Have Wesley be executed not by lethal injection, but by a gun that explodes his head like a watermelon. Have pieces of Wesley's head splatter on Counselor Troi and Tasha.

4) Make a more realistic ending than the one that aired. "Every rule must have an exception."
Too weak. Have Picard convince the aliens that this particular punishment is disproportionate to
this particular crime.

The Battle

The plot:

A Ferengi Captain gives Picard a gift of his old ship, the Star Gazer. But then he uses a mind control device to try to get Picard to attack the Enterprise with the Star Gazer.

What works:

Not much. One funny line: "As you humans say, I'm all ears."

What doesn't work:

1) This is a very slow episode, with a very slow examination of the Star Gazer, and very slow replays of the original Star Gazer battle, and very slow Picard headaches.

2) Why do the Ferengi transmissions have no background, are they transmitting from a cloud?

3) Riker demands the truth from a Ferengi, "first officer to first officer", as if Ferengi would tell the truth because they were both first officers. Unbelievable.

3) The big climax to the episode--Picard shoots the glowing mind control ball. Very weak.

4) The Star Gazer was so badly damaged that it was abandoned. And the Ferengi spent a lot of money to repair it? That seems unlikely.

How it could have been better:

If Picard is under Ferengi mind control, why not get him to do something more interesting? Maybe have some of the Ferengi characteristics rub off on him--have Picard become mercenary, concerned with the Enterprise making a profit. Have him act selfish and greedy around the crew. Have him rub his ears a lot.

This is a classic revenge story but it is written in such a slow and boring way that it is a chore to watch. It either needs to be made humorous, or needs some drama added to it to make it a faster-paced story.

Hide and Q

The plot:

Q offers Riker the power of the Q. He puts the crew into dangerous situations to persuade Riker to use his new powers. Riker ultimately refuses, proving that he has had his balls cut off.

What works:

1) When Q says to Worf, "Macrohead... with a microbrain!", Worf responds by growling like a cocker spaniel.... showing Q is absolutely correct!

2) Tasha cries in fear because she's in an IMAGINARY penalty box. She's so weak. She's the security chief! Did she get her job because she's a girl?

3) a Funny scene where Q buys drinks for everyone, and Worf pours his drink on the ground, while Data staring incredulously at his, since he doesn't drink at all.

4) There was a great scene where Q turns into Data. Great makeup job!!!

5) Worf gets bayoneted and screams! Great scene.

6) And then Wesley goes to help and we see him impaled! Even better!

7) I like Riker's superior attitude once he gets powers of the Q. He stands there with his arms folded and chin raised, and calls Picard "Jean Luc."

8) It's goofy, but also funny when Riker offers gifts, widening his eyes and saying patronizing things like, "I know what you want, my friend."

9) It's very funny seeing a grown up Wesley, identical down to the same child like uniform! And it's even more bizarre to see the whore in Klingon pantyhose who grabs for Worf's penis.

What doesn't work:

1) After Wesley is bayoneted, Riker restores him to health.

2) Tasha cries when she is put in the penalty box. But Q told the crew about that AFTER Tasha was brought back to the Enterprise; how does she know she is in a penalty box?

3) Tasha is the security chief, and she is crying in Picard's arms like a little girl.

"Tasha, when one is in the penalty box, tears are permitted." She's weak!

4) "Incredible Worf, you came out of nowhere!" They try to build up Worf as some incredible warrior. In one scene he rushes out and orders everyone to drop their weapons. The problem is that there is no one there. Some warrior.

5) Why does Riker so freely kills vicious animal things? Doesn't he have any respect for all life forms? Why at least did he not set his weapon to stun?

6) It is very unrealistic that Riker rejects the power of the Q. What human being would reject such power?

7) It is also very unrealistic that the crew rejects their gifts. Geordi really wants to stay blind rather than thank Q for giving him his sight back. Really??? The crew are not acting like people here. They are acting like saints. It just makes you tune out the whole story because of the lack of realism of character.

8) Can Worf really have no interest in sex?

Geordi: "Worf, this is sex?" after he beats up Klingon sex girl.

"It is sex, but I have no place for it in my life!" Ridiculous.

9) Geordi to Tasha--"You're as beautiful as I imagined"--I laughed when I heard this. Tasha is a skinny girl with a boy's haircut.

How it could have been better:

The idea of the episode was interesting but the characters, especially Riker, did not act realistically. Normal human beings would not reject great powers. Blind people would not reject sight just to make a point.

I think Q's intentions were generally positive--he wanted Riker in the Q for cultural exchange, but Riker inexplicably acted like Q's generous gift was a painful castration.

And then we are shown Riker is corrupted simply because he calls Picard by his first name. Not very frightening.

It would have been more interesting if Riker had *really* gotten corrupted by his powers, and started treating the crew like playthings. Have him give Geordi giant scrambled egg eyes. Have him turn Tasha into a woman, complete with long hair and a dress. Have him remove Deanna's clothes and make her walk around naked. Have him force Picard on his knees, like Gary Mitchell did to Kirk. That's much more dramatic. Then when Picard should get Riker to come to his senses, it's more dramatic than watching a sensitive first officer who gives everyone fantastic gifts and calls his Captain "Jean Luc".

Haven

The plot:

Troi's mother sets her up for an arranged marriage. But the boy she's set up with wants to bone a plague girl instead. At the end, boy joins plague girl on leper colony ship and all is well, except for boy, who, of course, is now infected with the plague.

What works:

1) Mrs. Troi beams aboard a talking box with a face who yells excited things about Troi's coming wedding. It's bizarre and memorable.

What doesn't work:

1) Any appearance of Mrs. Troi. I know she had sex with Gene Roddenberry, but if that's enough to get her on the show, shouldn't Nichelle Nichols (Lt. Uhura) be a regular guest star too?

2) Mrs. Troi's assistant Mr. Hom never talks. He's there for physical humor because he is tall. It doesn't work.

3) Deanna's red chastity belt on her outfit looks like a giant used maxi pad.

4) If Deanna had a longstanding arranged marriage, how did she come to have a relationship with Riker? Unexplained.

5) At the party Tasha tries to do something with her lesbian hair, but ends up with a frizzy, weird punk rocker look.

6) The whole episode is slow, and boring. There's a slow party where in-laws talk to each other. There is conflict between the in-laws which is supposed to be amusing, but isn't. Deanna looks sad. Riker looks sad. And so on.

7) It is never explained how plague girl entered the guy's dreams. It's a "destined love story" but this isn't a harlequin romance, it's Star Trek and it makes no sense.

8) Why doesn't Picard simply tractor beam the plague ship at warp drive to another solar system far away?

9) On the plague ship we see their crew staring at giant swirly patterns on big screens that make no sense. It looks exactly like people pretending to be a bridge crew by looking at swirly patterns on big screens.

10) Picard says the tractor beam prevents the plague people from beaming down to the planet, but does not explain how.

11) It is not credible that dream boy would let himself be infected with the plague just to be with plague blonde. If he wanted a blonde he could have found one without the plague.

How it could have been better:

1) It would have funny if dream boy beams over to the plague ship and plague girl hits him with the news that she is already married to someone else and so he infected himself for nothing.

2) What if Deanna tried to get out of her arranged marriage by publically having sex with Riker? That would be an interesting twist.

3) This episode is meant to be romantic comedy. It is neither. No matter how good she was in bed with Gene Roddenberry, Mrs. Roddenberry is not funny. If they want romance, have two men compete for Troi--perhaps Riker and a very wealthy alien.

The Big Goodbye

The plot:

Picard gets trapped in the holodeck with the safeties off. This is the first time this happens, but not nearly the last. In fact, it happens over and over again.

What works:

1) The idea of playing out a story through the holodeck. But only once. Not 20 times.

What doesn't work:

1) The holodeck story is supposed to be exciting. But Picard spends much of the time admiring his office and the clothes people are wearing. We are supposed to be amused watching Dr. Crusher, Picard, and Data in old style clothing. It is cute, for a moment, but not enough to keep us interested for an entire episode.

2) Picard & Co are held hostage. Geordi should be able to cut power to the holodeck. It is a device that operates with electricity. It should have a switch to turn it off. It should be as simple as that.

How it could have been better:

The whole thrill of the holodeck is having an adventure in another time and place (simulated, of course). But in all the times the crew uses the holodeck, they never actually end up having such an adventure. As in this situation, they begin an adventure, but something goes wrong and someone gets held hostage.

As a hostage story this wasn't especially compelling. It could have been interesting if it had been what it set out to be--if Picard actually played the role of a detective and solved a mystery, with the aid of his friends. But this episode felt like a tease because not much happened until they got captured by the bad guys. If you want to have an episode showing the novelty of Captain Picard playing a 20th century detective, well, then, have an episode showing him actually playing a 20th century detective and actually solving a mystery.

Datalore

The plot:

Data meets his evil twin brother Lore, who impersonates Data and tries to feed the Enterprise crew to the crystalline entity.

What works:

1) Evil Data! Evil Data who can smile, and has a sense of humor! When you see Lore, you can see how much undeveloped potential there is for Data.

2) Exploring the scary, empty base where Data was built was filled with suspense. Well done.

3) The crystalline entity, though it never speaks, is a scary villain. It eats people!

4) A lot of great lines:

Picard: "Shut up, Wesley!"

Crusher: "Shut up, Wesley!"

Wesley: "Mom, I heard you know how to turn them (androids) on"

Lore, regarding the crystalline entity, "Can you imagine its gratitude when I give it the lives on this vessel?"

5) Lore makes a funny face when he beats up Worf.

6) Lore threatens to turn Crusher's "little man" into a "human torch"! Now that's a villain!

7) Lore sets fire to Dr. Crusher's blue bathrobe! Only time that happens in 7 years.

What doesn't work:

1) With the constantly rotating post of Chief Engineer, we get clumsy lines like this where Data says directly to Argyle: "I have been most anxious to hear the chief's engineer's opinion, Mr. Argyle," Which is like saying, "So, Commander Riker, I hear you are first officer. First officer of this ship. How are you today, first officer?" Argyle is Scotty-lite, a boring chubby white guy.

2) Why is Dr. Crusher involved in assembling Lore? Lore is a machine.

3) Lore gives Data a drink to knock him out. But Data doesn't digest drinks. What kind of liquid could deactivate him? Since Data doesn't drink or have a sense of taste, why would he put this liquid in his mouth?

4) Wesley tells Captain Picard not to trust Data, but never explicitly says why, he never says that he thinks Lore is impersonating Data. That's why Picard tells him to shut up, because he doesn't explain himself.

5) Data/Lore asks Picard permission to beam up a part of the crystalline entity and then beam it out into space to blast it. That makes no sense.

How it could have been better:

The episode was quite good. No improvement needed.

Angel One

The plot:

Riker is the perfect ambassador to a planet ruled by women. He bones the leader of Angel One. Some men try to revolt and we get a "happy" ending when they get sentenced to internal exile instead of death.

What works:

1) A planet ruled by sexy, domineering women who use men for sex and dress them like gigolos!

2) Riker dresses like a ridiculous gigolo as he gets ready to let himself be used as a sex toy by Mistress Biata. Sure enough, she orders him to have sex with her and he complies.

3) There's a great scene where Tasha and Troi laugh at Riker's outfit, with his enormous hairy chest sticking out like a side of beef.

4) The scene where Data is alone on the bridge due to the plague, and takes command, is very dramatic.

5) Mistress Biata rubs Riker's hairy chest like a magic lamp.

6) Riker gives her a gift--a fancy light bulb--but you can see she's more interested in the sex she is about to force him into. Nonetheless she responds, "Very impressive!"

7) The disintegration ray for the death penalty is fun to watch in action, as is Biata's explanation of it: "As you can see we are not without compassion. Your deaths will be swift and painless."

8) Mistress Biata's nemesis, Mistress Ariel is the actress who plays the cutie from "Knight Rider". It is vanilla versus chocolate, blonde versus brunette!

What doesn't work:

1) Picard says Angel One's position is vital, but doesn't say why. Then Picard says he wants Angel One to join the Federation, even though they enslave their men!

2) How can Wesley take a virus off the holodeck? Impossible.

3) How can holosnow survive off the holodeck? Impossible.

4) Riker can't make Ramsey & co., the rebellious men, leave the planet even thought they are members of the Federation? Only Starfleet is bound by the Prime Directive, not citizens of the Federation? That makes no sense.

5) Data claims he knows exactly how long the Federation outpost can last against 7 Romulan battle cruisers? What would that be, like two minutes? Data pretends an outpost and one starship can hold out for hours. It's ridiculous.

6) Tasha tells Ramsey they traced his location from orbit by the tiny platinum pin on his uniform. Not believable.

7) Ramsey is offered the chance to leave the planet with his women and he refuses. He's being entirely unreasonable. He says he likes it on Angel One, even though he is a fugitive. It's not believable, so since he can leave at any time with his girlfriend it is hard to have any sympathy for him.

8) Why does everyone on the ship except Crusher get sick?

9) Why is it whenever a ship wide illness breaks out Crusher suddenly acts like a bitch?

10) Crusher says no one can beam up because of the virus--but why couldn't they be confined to a sealed environment, like a shuttle craft?

11) Riker's lame speech about the impossibility of executing ideas is uncompelling.

12) The girl guards in this episode have long salad forks for weapons!

13) At the end Picard orders them to the Neutral Zone at Warp 6. Since they can go even faster, I presume there never was much of a hurry.

How it could have been better:

Despite its flaws, this was a pretty amusing episode. Having sexy women in charge can cover a lot of flaws of an episodes. But it could have been even better. What if instead of giving a lame speech, Riker convinced the blonde lady not to execute the prisoners by seducing her with more sex?

11001001

The plot:

Midget semi-robot eunuchs hijack the enterprise so they can borrow the ship's computer. They get rid of everyone on the ship except Picard and Riker, and distract the two of them with a holowhore.

What works:

1) The idea of Riker being seduced by a holowhore.

2) Data painting with advice from Geordi, and Riker observing: "A blind man is teaching an android how to paint!"

3) I like how Picard enters the holodeck while Riker is making out with the holowhore and Picard is all smiles. He enjoys watching.

4) Data takes command! He makes the decision to abandon ship. A wrong decision, but a very decisive one.

5) It is funny seeing Wesley on the transporter pad with little kids. Perhaps they are being beamed directly to daycare.

What doesn't work:

1) The holowhore is very uncompelling. First of all she is physically ugly, with a giant chin and small eyes. Secondly she simply flirts a little and that's enough to get Picard and Riker to marvel at how wonderful she is. Most of what we are hearing is Picard and Riker's admiration, not any actual tremendous conversational ability on the part of the holowhore. Because they didn't know how to write her part, her role as a seductress falls completely flat.

2) The Enterprise goes inside the starbase, a starbase with giant doors. Why would a starbase have giant doors for an indoor parking lot that is not pressurized? Why would it be indoors at all?

3) Why don't the Binars, who seem very technologically advanced, have their own computers and ships, thus obviating their need for the Enterprise?

4) It is unbelievable that the entire content of the Binar's planet could fit in the Enterprise's computer.

5) If the Binars are worried about solar flares, why can't they simply shield their own computers? An enormous plot hole.

6) What we are actually told is that one of the **b**inar's sun went *supernova*. If that really happened, their whole planet would be destroyed. Sloppy writing.

7) Listening to Picard speak in French is laughable, he sounds like he's talking in Klingon.

8) Picard drinks holowine. What is he drinking? Will it disappear from his stomach when he leaves the holodeck?

9) When the crew abandon ships, we see a Chinese guy in miniskirt running away. I hope he took the time to get some pants first.

10) The Enterprise is evacuated in four minutes. Can they really evacuate hundreds of people in 4 minutes? Not credible.

11) How do Data and Geordi get off the ship in 41 seconds? One moment they are in the turbolift, then beaming onto station--why not beam from the bridge?

12) There are no other ships on this giant starbase capable of pursuing the Enterprise?

13) The Enterprise computer at different points has both male and female voices. Is it transgendering?

14) They had a 5 minute countdown for self destruct, and Picard noted there was no option to change the destruct time... except a few episodes later when they encounter Nagelum and they set the time to destruct at whatever they like.

15) Why can't Picard take control of the ship from engineering? He didn't even try.

16) Why were the Binars unconscious if they were using the Enterprise's computer for their mental computer coordination?

17) Instead of beaming onto the bridge, why didn't Picard locate the Binars and gas them, or beam them directly to brig?

18) Why would the Binars have used a password to protect their program if they wanted Picard's help to complete their work?

19) The Binars remind me of a later episode where Riker gets a genderless girl/boyfriend.

How it could have been better:

1) We were repeatedly told how impressive the holowhore was. She wasn't impressive at all. What if the Binars had created a *really* pretty girl for Riker, not that bimbo with the big chin, and showed her *credibly* seducing him? And what if the computer had created a second holowhore to seduce Picard, and show us how she also seduced him?

2) When Picard and Riker realize what is going on, they get phasers and get ready for the battle to retake the ship and... there is no battle. Only sleeping Binars. A total letdown. It would have been more interesting if there were a dozen Binars, all armed with phasers, and Picard and Riker had to shoot them all, using their knowledge of the Enterprise to give them an advantage to compensate for being outnumbered. Imagine Picard and Riker, hunting throughout the ship, engaging in battles with Binars as the countdown to self destruct proceeds. Now that's more compelling then beaming onto a bridge full of sleepy robot eunuchs!

Too Short a Season

The plot:

A very old admiral takes a drug to make him young to resolve a hostage crisis. The drug soon kills him.

What works:

Not much.

What doesn't work:

1) Mrs. Admiral says at one point she does not want to become young like Mr. Admiral. Ridiculous.

2) The "old" makeup for the Admiral with the fake hair looks ridiculous.

3) At the end when the Admiral beams down and is writhing in pain before his enemy, it looks pathetic.

How it could have been better:

The whole storyline was boring. How about making the admiral younger to start with, and his taking a drug that gives him some special power, like immunity to phasers. Then he solves the crisis but becomes so arrogant and out of control that Picard has to find a way to stop him. That's more interesting than this sad story.

When the Bough Breaks

The plot:

Sterile aliens kidnap Enterprise children, including Wesley, and Picard has to find a way to neutralize their technology to get them back.

What works:

1) When it briefly appears Wesley might be leaving the Enterprise permanently.

2) When one of the aliens asks Picard, "Why do you want them back so badly? You can always have more!"

What doesn't work:

1) Watching all the little Enterprise kids doing artistic things and behaving like annoying brats. Sorry, not interested.

2) When the hidden planet materializes, it just appears on the viewscreen--no sense of a giant, massive object appearing in space, more like a 2D photo.

3) Isn't Wesley a little old to be taken? Much older than all the other kids. Not that I'm complaining!

4) Theme of the episode: Technology evil! What's that Picard is flying around in, a canoe?

5) A very quickly everything-resolved ending. Crusher immediately diagnoses and cures the alien sex problems, even though the aliens are far more advanced technologically than the Enterprise.

How it could have been better:

1) What if Wesley sacrificed himself to save the other kids, agreeing to stay behind?

2) What if before they were rescued, the kids were brainwashed to want to be there?

3) What if the aliens were all black people, and what if the kid's DNA were changed to make them all black people, and this was a permanent change, and from now on Wesley would have to be black? You see, if an episode had consequences, if things changed because of the events of a single episode, instead of pressing the reset button, it would be more compelling.

4) What if the kids were returned but they find out only later that the aliens cloned them?

5) What if the aliens returned the kids but it turns out the kids they returned were android copies, and we only find this out 3 years later when Wesley starts malfunctioning?

Home Soil

The plot:

Federation terraformers accidently (or not accidently?) kill a crystal life form. Picard feels very bad about this, grabs his ankles and apologizes.

What works:

1) When Data fights the laser drill!

2) The sensitive half Chinese terraformer is hot, even though she's wearing a man's jumpsuit.

What doesn't work:

1) The characters are not compelling. There is the vaguely evil fat guy with the big nose, who doesn't seem really evil. There is the sobby half Chinese girl, and the Swedish guy with no personality.

2) Fat guys and tight jumpsuits do not go well together.

3) A lot of the episode consisted of technobabble about terraforming, which was boring.

4) From the way the episode aired, it appeared Data dodged AFTER the laser fired.

5) When she learns the crystal is intelligent, the half Chinese terraformer actually cries for crystal creature. Very dopey. But she looks good with her hair down.

6) Much of the episode consists of the crew being fascinated by a single flicker of light from the crystal. It's hard to get excited about that.

7) When the crystal talks, it sounds almost exactly like Data talking while holding his nose.

8) They defeat the crystal by turning off the lights. Boring and anti-climactic.

9) The crystal calls them ugly, arrogant, and primitive. Troi and Picard apologize. Annoying.

How it could have been better:

Have an evil protagonist, not a misunderstood one. Have the crystal want to kill the crew of the Enterprise, suppose it feasts on their blood. Say it can grow rapidly into giant rock monsters that roam the hallways of the ship, soaking up the crew's blood. Show the crew fighting back with phasers to destroy it.

And put the half Chinese girl in nicer clothes, not men's work clothes. And don't let her talk too much.

Coming of Age

The plot:

Wesley takes the Starfleet test, but fails. Admiral Quinn and Command Remmick come aboard. They harass everyone for no reason. The end.

What works:

Not much.

What doesn't work:

1) The repeated scenes of Remmick questioning the crew in a hostile matter (to create dramatic tension) is pointless, because at the end of the episode we learn it's all about nothing. We never even find out in this episode what Admiral Quinn's purpose is. I understand in retrospect that they were setting things up for the "mouth invader crabs" in the episode conspiracy, but this episode doesn't really contribute much. Instead it feels more like a filler episode, where they had to fill an episode but didn't have much money or idea what to write a story about.

2) At one point we casually find out that Picard is responsible for death of Crusher's husband. No details are given. Ever.

3) Wesley is in this weird competition to get into Starfleet--he has to compete against three other people on one planet. Aren't admission tested usually scored based on the entire group competing? Otherwise, couldn't Wesley have tried for admission on a less competitive planet?

4) Wesley's final test was very dumb. Rescue one guy but not the other. And after that, Wesley did not even get admitted to Starfleet! It makes you wonder if he rescued the wrong guy.

5) The scene where Wesley helped a competitor with his test was very dumb.

6) The blue alien seems to constantly be inhaling some kind of smoky substance. Crack cocaine?

8) Wesley wears a very weird baggy shirt on top that narrows down really tight to his waist. He looks like a cartoon character.

9) The matte painting they used for this base was taken from a Buck Rogers episode.

10) Perhaps the most ridiculous moment came after Remmick had finished alienating the entire crew, he told Picard he wanted to transfer to the Enterprise.

How it could have been better:

1) I suppose we are to assume that Admiral Quinn and Remmick did not yet have their mouth crabs. So there was no drama here. I think for there to be drama they would have had to introduce at least one guy with a mouth crab doing something subversive. Maybe they wouldn't find out about the mouth crab, but they'd have to deal with the mouth crab guy doing bad things.

2) There was one ridiculous scene where Wesley confronts a giant alien, threatening him with violence, because Wesley thinks the giant alien's culture requires he say that. But what if Wesley was wrong about that and the giant alien beat Wesley up? Then Wesley's Chinese supervisor could go to Wesley's bruised and bloody body and tell him how he confused two very similar looking species, the one who liked to be threatened and the one who didn't.

Heart of Glory

The plot:

Three Klingons come aboard. They're evil. Worf kills their leader, makes an "ummmmm" sound.

What works:

1) I liked how the evil Klingons taunted Worf about being in Starfleet
"Does it make you gentle? Does it fill your heart with peace?"

2) I like the idea of an episode where Worf confronts tough Klingons. Just not this episode.

What doesn't work:

1) We learn that when a Klingon dies, other Klingons make a "mmmmmmm" sound and then growl. It's ridiculous. It looks like a training exercise in acting school.

2) When asked what to do with a dead Klingon, Crusher is told, "It is only an empty shell now. Please treat it as such". So what does she do, throw it in the garbage?

3) We learn Worf's adoption story. He was found by humans. But why didn't they return him to the Klingons? Never explained.

4) When they speak to the Klingon ship captain on the viewscreen, he seems to be in a smoke filled room--do Klingons smoke a lot?

5) And why does the Klingon captain transmit the United Federation of Planet logo with his image?

6) When the evil Klingons use Lego parts to make a disrupter, it looks like they are using Lego parts to make a disrupter.

7) When evil Klingon #2 killed, evil Klingon #3 didn't make mmmmm sound.

8) When evil Klingon #3 was in engineering, why didn't they just beam him out of there? Never explained.

How it could have been better:

1) The battle was too brief. The most exciting part was when the Klingons escape and actually shoot some security guards. But that battle was way, way too brief. They should have showed the Klingons running around the ship engaging in pitched battles, not just with phasers but hand to hand. This would give us an opportunity to see how wild Klingon warriors really are!

2) Worf's battle with Klingon #3 was way too brief. He just walked up to him and shot him. Boring. They should have fought each other and wrestled, until finally Worf killed him. Worf is always said to be a great warrior but we have never seen it. Show us, for once. Show us Worf being a great warrior in a big, four minute battle with the evil Klingon.

But that was not to be. What we got was a short speech, one phaser shot, and a growl.

The Arsenal of Freedom

The plot:

Nearly all the senior staff beams down to a planet with automated killer robots. They fight the robots, and Picard eventually turns them off.

What works:

1) In one sense, it's really nice having an action episode where they fight killer robots. But the killer robots look like flying lamp fixtures. They simply aren't very intimidating.

2) When Riker meets the fake image of his friend Rice, he senses something is wrong so he tells Rice that the name of his ship is the Lollipop, and Rice responds:

"What's the armament on the Lollipop?"

3) To save Tasha from a laser beam, Data lifts her with one arm and casually throws her across the forest.

4) The solution to shutting down the robots was innovative--to tell the controlling computer that Picard agreed to buy them.

5) The solution to fighting the invisible ship was innovative--make it go into the atmosphere so atmospheric drag would make it visible.

6) I like how Data casually jumped down a 20 foot drop and everyone stared at him as he landed.

What doesn't work:

1) The theme of this episode is: Guns bad! Why doesn't Starfleet disarm itself, then??

2) We learned Riker gave up the chance to command his own ship to be first officer on the Enterprise. That's retarded.

3) When Riker is in trouble, Picard beams down with Crusher, but doesn't feel the need to bring any security guards to fight the killer robots.

4) Data fires a phaser at the force field holding Riker in an attempt to free him, but he aims at Riker's arm... wouldn't it be better to aim at an empty space between Riker's legs, so when he blasts through the force field he won't shoot a hole through Riker's arm?

5) Being attacked by an invisible ship saves money, but is not dramatic.

6) Suddenly in this episode, we hear from a new chief engineer named "Logan"? What? Who? We have never heard of this guy before. He is abruptly introduced as the evil white guy who tries to take command from Geordi. He has a lot of dark hair gel that makes his hair look like the chocolate pudding monster from Skin of Evil. Geordi banishes the evil white guy from the bridge leaving him, Worf, a Chinese lady, and a Spanish guys. No white people allowed on Geordi's bridge.

7) Ensign Zhu is sitting in a recliner chair at Ops and has sagging breasts which are very distracting. She needs either a push up bra or a bra with a stronger structural integrity field, because she has the breasts of an 80 year old woman.

9) The scene where Crusher lies injured and Jean Luc tends her is boring. Gates McFadden is a terribly wooden actress, and hearing her talk about roots and herbs is boring.

10) Geordi separates the saucer section. Once again the ship looks ridiculous, like a flying headless ship. Geordi also orders the saucer section to go to a Starbase. How can it go there without warp drive?

11) When Data jumped down into the cave, why didn't he simply shoot the master computer to stop the robots?

12) The invisible ship continued to fight the Enterprise even after Picard agreed to buy the weapons and ordered the "demonstration" ended. There is no explanation for this other than the need to make Geordi a hero.

How it could have been better:

1) Have the killer robots actually be sinister looking, and don't have them chirp like birds. Have them look more Terminators like and less like lamps from I Dream of Jeanie.

2) Cut out the Dr. Crusher suffer porn and show Picard spending more time and effort trying to outwit the computer. It would be much more entertaining showing Picard trying to understand how the Computer thinks and how to change its program directives than watching him tending to the bad acting Crusher.

3) Have Geordi investigate and find out why new Chief Engineers suddenly keep appearing at random. Have him discover a dimensional rift in Engineering which keeps sending new Chief Engineers from parallel universes.

Symbiosis

The plot:

The Enterprise gets involved with two planets, one full of drug dealers and one full of drug addicts. Crusher wants to help the drug addicts but Picard cites the Prime Directive.

What works:

1) They raided the minor actors from Star Trek II, the Wrath of Khan, having Judson Scott playing a drug dealer and Merritt Buttock playing a drug addict. Was Christie Alley unavailable, or had she gained too much weight by then? By the way, Merritt Buttock, who played the whining drug dealer, played Kirk's son in Star Trek III where he was killed by Klingons, but then the actor himself died a short time later, killed by AIDS.

2) I loved the wide eyed expression on Riker's face when Buttock zapped him with his electricity touch.

3) Judson Scott is dressed like futuristic pimp.

What doesn't work:

1) The drug addicts act like retards, they can't fix their own ship. It raises the question, how did they ever manage to build them in the first place? It makes the entire plot seem impossible. Worse, the drug addicts only have three ships. How is that enough to supply the entire needs for two planets in two way trade? Also very improbable.

2) One of the drug addicts is a guy wearing a dress. Not only a drug addict, but a transgendering drug addict.

3) The entire episode shows the drug addicts and drug dealers arguing over the drugs. Boring.

4) Crusher is not allowed to tell them they will be cured simply by non-use. A dumb prime directive drama.

5) The scene where Wesley asked what narcotics are, and why people use them, was very painful to watch. It is unbelievable that a teenager would be so ignorant, so it looks like Wesley is play acting. His pretending to be dumb is very stupid.

Wesley: "I guess I just don't understand!"

Tasha, with smile for a 5 year old: "Wesley, I hope you never do."

6) Dr. Crusher has huge amounts of red makeup on cheeks, looks like a circus clown.

7) Not one doctor on the drug addict planet realizes that they are addicted to drugs? Not one person missed a dose and realized they could survive without it? Unlikely.

How it could have been better:

If they're drug dealers, have them act like drug dealers, and addict the crew, maybe with an air spray. Have Picard and a few crew members not addicted have to fight a takeover effort from the drug dealers and members of the crew who are now addicted. That would be much more compelling than watching the two sides whine about drugs and the prime directive for 45 minutes.

Skin of Evil

The plot:

The chocolate pudding monster takes Troi hostage. Picard gives a speech, makes it sad, and Troi is released. Tasha is also killed senselessly.

What works:

1) The chocolate pudding monster (CPM) is a great antagonist--he actually wants to make the crew suffer, so there is a lot of dramatic tension.

2) Riker yelling, "Data, something's got me!" and being dragged into the CPM. A great touch--he instructs the others not to interfere. He's so ridiculously selfless! And then, later we see the CPM sticks Riker's head out, covered in chocolate pudding, his mouth open in a silent scream. Great drama!

3) The appearance of the CPM is innovative--not your typical head putty alien. But the voice, meant to be scary, sounds simply silly instead.

4) Some great lines:

Riker: "We believe everything in the universe has a right to exist."

CPM: "An interesting notion I do not share."

Data:"I would guess that death is no longer sufficient to alleviate its boredom"--funniest line!

What doesn't work:

1) We have yet another chief engineer, Leland T. Lynch. White guys don't last long down there. We know he is pompous because he keeps speaking of himself in the third person and accentuating his middle initial. He speaks to captain saying things like "Leland T. Lynch here Captain." So we won't forget his name, and that he's a pompous white guy.

2) Leland T sets the ratio of matter antimatter 25 to 1... but in Wesley's Starfleet academy test, we are told it is always one to one.

3) The dilithium crystals are very irregular shaped--doesn't they have to be symmetrical or smooth?

4) Tasha has a senseless death. Realistic but dull.

5) They can't beam Troi out because the CPM is covering her shuttle and blocking the beam. But when they beam down, the CPM is not covering shuttle.

6) The weak climax to this episode features Picard gives the alien a lecture until it lets Troi go. Very bad ending.

7) When they beam Tasha up, her legs stick out between transporter pads. Her legs should beam up in pieces.

8) CPM plays with Geordi's visor, has Data point his phaser around at the others, but they don't act remotely scared so these scenes are not compelling. At one point the creature asks Crusher to pick someone to die and Crusher picks herself. Real people do not act so fearlessly, so selflessly. It robs the entire story of drama; if the crew is not afraid of the CPM, why should we be?

9) Troi has a long psychobabble conversation with the CPM. Very boring, and it robs the CPM of some of his antagonism.

10) The crew's phasers look like hand vacuum cleaners or "dust busters".

11) When Crusher talks to Troi, she asks if Troi's all right, but never asks about Troi's minority shuttle driver; no concern for the spanish dude.

12) The CPM expels Riker. Riker: "It felt so much frustration it had to get rid of me." In other words, Riker was so sweet, so sensitive, that it repelled the CPM. Makes the CPM look weak.

13) Tasha made a death hologram--do all the crew do that? Tasha hologram says she died quickly on duty--how could she know that? Tasha hologram actually addresses every member of the crew at her funeral! How does she know who will be there? Does she update her death hologram every time there is a crew change?

14) An unintentionally funny line: Tasha: "I realized I could be feminine... without losing anything." Tasha had a butch haircut like a man and was almost completely flat chested like a boy.

15) In her goodbye message to Data she didn't thank him for the sex. And she missed a final opportunity to talk about the rape gangs, a subject she loved to mention over and over.

How it could have been better:

1) I understand the writers had to write out Tasha in a hurry since the actress who played her wanted to leave the show. But her senseless death was poorly written. They should have had her dying while accomplishing something. The way it was written was like, "Tasha's got to go. Ok, kill at the ten minute mark. Done."

2) If the CPM was a skin of evil, Picard should have synthesized a skin of good, made from the goodness of the ship's crew, vanilla in color, and mixed it in a swirl with the CPM to neutralize it. Or Picard should have found some other way to destroy the CPM more dramatic than simply giving a speech. That was the weakest part of the episode.

3) What if the CPM had animated Riker and made him evil, with black chocolate pudding eyes, and Picard and the others had to fight him? That would have been more dramatic.

We'll Always Have Paris

The plot:

There's some sort of problem with dimensions or time or something in a lab. Data goes down and fixes it.

What works:

Not much.

What doesn't work:

1) This is a very slow episode. Most of it focuses on Picard's former blonde girlfriend who he wish he had boned more.

2) At one point there are several Datas in the lab, and he asks which is the right one, and one responds, but we never know how which Data knows he is the right one.

How it could have been better:

1) There was a somewhat similar original series episode with a guy named Lazarus who travelled between dimensions and caused intergalactic problems. I can't say that was the best episode either, but at least Kirk got to wrestle with him a little on Vasquez Rocks. This didn't even have that.

2) If they want to do an episode about an interdimensional rift or a rift in time, show antagonists coming through and causing them problems. When the entire episode simply becomes shutting down a device in a lab, there isn't enough material to sustain it and you have to pad the episode with long scenes of Picard staring at blondie.

Conspiracy

The plot:

Alien mouth crabs have invaded the Federation. Picard shoots their momma, and they all die.

What works:

1) Data laughs at a joke, but what comes out is a very disturbing forced laugh that is also funny.

2) When Riker says he wants to call Data to see the alien mouth crab that Admiral Quinn has brought aboard, Quinn grabs Riker's wrist tightly and says, "It doesn't like your science officer! It does like you"! Then Quinn kicks Riker in face, laughing. That's so over the top--an old man kicking Riker in the face--that it's very funny.

3) When Remmick tells Picard that his food is getting cold--this is before Picard realizes he is having centipedes for dinner.

4) The episode was edited to give the appearance in sickbay that Riker had been taken over by an alien mouth crab, but then we found out it wasn't so. Great misdirection!

5) There's a subtle satire at the end when Remmick, his neck pulsing with an alien creature, tells Picard he wants peaceful coexistence. What he's doing here is parodying Picard, who always tells aliens he comes in peace right before they abuse the Enterprise. The look on Picard's face when he hears that, and then looks at Riker as if to say, "What do we do now?" is priceless.

6) I enjoyed the scene where the aliens ate live caterpillars, and the evil admiral says, "Eat up! Raise your hand if you want more!"

What doesn't work:

1) Why didn't Admiral Quinn put the mouth crab into Riker when he was unconscious? No explanation. Why did Admiral Quinn reveal himself by attacking Geordi and Worf? When Riker called for security, Worf showed up, but so did Geordi. Since when does Geordi work in security? Then Crusher shows up and phasers Quinn. Since when does Crusher carry a phaser? All this is out of character.

2) While the second half of this episode was great, the first part of the episode was very slow. Picard talked to some Starfleet captains about their vague feeling that something was wrong. Then we learn after the fact that one of their ships blows up (of course, we don't get to see it blow up, that would be too dramatic). This is all filler and not very interesting.

3) The solution to this episode, phasering one alien to kill all the others, seems too easy, too simple.

4) We are supposed to be shocked that the aliens eat live bugs, but Klingons eat live worms, so this is not so shocking.

5) We are briefly introduced to a black lady captain who is supposed to be brilliant theoretically because she was the youngest captain ever. Later we see she has been taken over by the mouth crabs, so maybe affirmative action based on race is not always a good thing.

6) Blowing Remmick's head apart and seeing the flesh of his brain explode was way overboard. Watching Picard zap the alien coming out of his headless body made it feel like Aliens, not an episode of Star Trek, though it was satisfying when it screamed as they disintegrated it.

How it could have been better:

Resolved way too quickly. First of all, cut the slow first half of the episode. Send them immediately to Starfleet command. Have Picard find out what is going on, and have Riker beam down with a dozen security guards to fight a bunch of mouth crab controlled people. Have them spend the entire episode clearing out Starfleet command and finding out who is controlled and who isn't. Then maybe have a second episode where they have to clear out some starbases or other starships that have also been infested. That would have been a lot more interesting.

The Neutral Zone

The plot:

The crew revives a weepy woman, a dumb redneck, and an evil capitalist from cryogenic suspension. They investigate some missing outposts at the Neutral Zone. Picard lets himself be insulted by Romulans. The end.

What works:

1) When the redneck says: "What do you guys do? You don't drink and ain't got no TV. It must be kind of boring."

2) When the redneck invites Data to get a pair of women they can both have sex with.

3) When the redneck pats Dr. Crusher's ass, and she says, "Much obliged!"

What doesn't work:

1) This is a very slow episode where nothing happens and there is a lot of filler--conversations with the defrosted people. The constantly crying defrosted woman is very unpleasant to watch. The redneck makes a few good jokes but is mostly there to show how stupid southerners are. The evil capitalist is so two dimensionally evil that he is a cartoon caricature of 20th century businessmen.

2) The southern fried redneck guy is an early version of Trip Tucker from Enterprise. He acts like a redneck retard. He also has an enormous wart on his nose, I wanted to phaser it.

3) When the Romulans show up and verbally abuse Picard, he merely says, "We have made some progress here. Let us not ruin it with unnecessary postering," acting very weak.

3) This episode, the last of season one, was clearly meant to be part one of a two part episode, to be resolved at the beginning of season 2. The mystery of the missing outposts was not solved. The evil capitalist, crying girl, and redneck were supposed to stay on the ship for a while. But when the next episode starts, the trio are gone, and the missing outposts are never mentioned again (though it is presumed to be done by the Borg). So a part I with no resolution makes for an empty episode.

4) Crusher says:"In the 20th century, people feared dying. It terrified them." And it doesn't terrify them in the 24th? Ridiculous.

5) Picard to evil capitalist: "A lot has changed in 300 years. People are no longer obsessed with the accumulation of things." Does he mean things like commanding a starship?

6) Picard seems actually annoyed that Data saved the lives of the frozen people, saying they were already dead. They weren't; they were just frozen, and they could all be saved. His annoyance at Data saving lives is puzzling.

7) The evil capitalist demands to talk to his bank, brags about his lawyer, and wants a copy of the Wall Street Journal. I know Star Trek is left wing and hates capitalism, but this is just too much of a two dimension parody character to take seriously.

8) When Picard sees the outposts are gone, he refuses to go to red alert, saying, "This is not the time for rash actions"--he won't even raise shields. What a pacifist dummy.

9) We see the Romulan ships for the first time. They look like turtles! Not very impressive.

How it could have been better:

1) Have the Romulans set some kind of trap for Picard. Have the evil capitalist help Picard realize that it's a trap and help him figure a way out of it.

2) Have Troi bitchslap the weeping woman, forcing her to stop acting like a crybaby.

3) Have the southern fried redneck have sex with a bunch of crew ladies and have this unrevealed until women start showing up in sickbay with mysterious bumps on their genitals.

The Child

The plot:

Counselor Troi gets boned by an alien energy source. She gives birth to a baby who rapidly ages, then retroactively aborts himself before saying anything noteworthy.

What works:

1) Riker has a beard! Very good. It distracts from his watery eyes.

2) There's a scene where Wesley follows Picard around inside a turbolift and Picard instinctively moves away from him. Brilliant.

3) Great line! "A life form of unknown origin and intent is breeding inside Counselor Troi."

4) Worf wants to give Troi an abortion. Precisely what phaser setting would he use?

5) Dr. Pulaski has one funny scene where she calls Data "Datta"

"My name is Data."

"What's the difference?"

"One is my name. The other is not."

What doesn't work:

1) The scene where the alien energy ball impregnates Troi is somewhat lacking. If she's having sex, even alien sex, she should moan and enjoy it more.

2) Worf is now a yellow shirt! Looked better in red. In fact, they all do.

3) Dr. Crusher has been replaced by an old lady with an irritating voice.

4) Geordi is chief engineer??? Where did that come from? Has he ever worked, say, in engineering?

5) Riker always sits in the chair opposite Picard's desk by putting his leg over it. He's a giant. But it's very disrespectful to Picard.

6) Wesley has a ridiculous child's Starfleet uniform! He should get a child's toy version of a phaser and tricorder as well.

7) Most of the episode is very boring. Watch the kid grow up. Watch the kid say nothing. Watch the kid abort himself.

8) If the kid was harming the ship's latest science project, why not put him and Troi in a shuttle? No one thought of that.

9) The ship's computer sometimes has a man's voice! Is Majel Barrett transgendering?

10) The guest star scientist has a very bushy moustache, it doesn't look Starfleet regulation.

How it could have been better:

The episode needs an antagonist. There is none. It would have made a great horror episode if the alien child had bad intent but pretended to be good. Let him pretend to be friendly to the crew but use telepathy or telekinesis to cause bad things to happen. And have him bite people and turn them into alien zombies. Have Picard & Worf fight the zombies, disintegrate the alien, and restore the crew--all except Dr. Pulaski.

Where Silence Has Lease

The plot:

Nagelum! The second half of this episode is one of the best ever. Nagelum pays the Enterprise a visit and threatens to exterminate half the crew, all in the name of science.

What works:

1) Wesley is in this episode, but mysteriously disappears from his post right before they meet Nagelum. A black man takes his place. I knew immediately he would die. Sure enough, Nagelum asks, "What is death?" and uses the black guy to experiment. It was not funny that a black guy died per se, but it **was** funny that they suddenly swapped out Wesley right before this, and then when we see the anonymous black guy, we know someone is about to die. The telegraphing of the writers' intention was what was funny.

2) The intro scene for this episode, which is usually something lame like a card game, was actually exciting, a scene where Worf and Riker fight skull holomonsters.

3) Another great scene where Nagelum simply says, "Data." And Data responds by simply saying, "Nagelum."

4) A great scene was where Troi is asked why she didn't sense Nagelum and she said he was, "Perhaps an intelligence so vast it eluded me."

5) Pulaski: "Forgive me, Mr. Data, I am not accustomed to working with non-living devices."

6) When Nagelum announces he wants to kill "1/3 of crew to study every kind of dying... maybe half" and then Worf says that "50% casualties are acceptable." Worf likes this, he's into it.

7) When Nagelum asks Pulaski to demonstrate sexual intercourse. "Please demonstrate how this is done."

8) When the phantom Romulan ship fires on the Enterprise, Picard says "Warn them we will return fire." Warn them????

What doesn't work:

1) When they explore the alternate Enterprise, Worf loses his mind when he keeps walking on and off the same bridge. "One bridge, one bridge! One Riker, one bridge!" It seems a minor thing to go crazy about.

2) When Picard says, "Starfleet can send a science vessel to investigate this further" What is the Enterprise, if not a science vessel?

3) There was a scene where Nagelum apparently pushed a twirling Dr. Pulaski into a bulkhead. Pulaski's bad acting as she whirls around is comical.

4) Nagelum claimed he learned a lot about death from the short speech Picard gave about it. Ridiculous.

5) Picard's decision to blow up the ship, killing everyone, so half the crew would not be killed by Nagelum was ridiculous. And then, once he sets the self destruct, he goes back to his quarters to listen to elevator music!

6) Suddenly, the Enterprise self destruct has flexible timing, a feature it didn't have in the Binars episode.

7) No one notices that while Nagelum threatened to kill half the crew, he never got started on it after he killed the black guy.

8) After killing the black guy, Nagelum lectures Picard, saying humans are too aggressive and too hostile!

How it could have been better:

Like many episodes, the first half was slow. They spent a lot of time conjecturing about empty space. They spent time wandering around the duplicate copy of the Enterprise. It was all filler. Instead of having Nagelum simply show up and threaten to slaughter half the crew, have him do other experiments first. Show him trying to use pain and pleasure stimulus to train the crew to do certain things, like scientists training mice in a science experiment. Nagelum also asks about sex. Have him use his powers to get Troi and Crusher to demonstrate. The strongest part of the episode was the Nagelum part, and until he showed up, it simply wasn't interesting.

Elementary, Dear Data

The plot:

Data pretends to be Sherlock Holmes. A holodeck malfunction creates a Dr. Moriarty who takes control of the ship. Moriarty gives up without a fight. The end.

What works:

1) The idea of Data solving a Sherlock Holmes mystery for an entire episode (which he never does).

2) It's funny watching Data beat up a mugger simply by pinching his fingers.

What doesn't work:

1) The beginning of the episode where Data solves "mysteries" very easily is slow and boring.

2) When Moriarty tells Pulaski "I shall fill you with crumpets"--it sounds like he is trying to make her constipated.

3) Data's Sherlock Holmes voice isn't amusing, sorry.

4) Data runs away in panic when Moriarty draws a picture of the Enterprise. Why is he so scared? Why can't he simply say, at that moment, "Suspend program", or at least try to?

5) Why can't Geordi cut power to the holodeck? This is never explained, and is a constant weakness with runaway holodeck stories.

6) Why didn't Data Bash Moriarty in the head and end this immediately?

7) Moriarty is not frightening, leaving us with zero dramatic tension.

"You're not frightened of me?"

Pulaski: "No,"

"Your every silence speaks volumes" Very dumb and unbelievable.

8) Pulaski isn't even tied up; she can apparently leave at any time.

9) Worf gets all dressed up to go on the holodeck, and then never goes.

10) Moriarty gives up after an anti-climactic talk with Picard. A big disappointment.

11) Pulaski tells Moriarty that the next time he sees her, she may be an old woman. Well, what is she now?

How it could have been better:

Here's a radical idea: if you're going to have an episode ostensibly about Data solving a Sherlock Holmes style mystery, why not have an episode showing Data solving a Sherlock Holmes style mystery? There's a brief time at the beginning of the episode where he solves one easily. Why not give him a real, challenging mystery that takes an entire episode to solve? The dramatic tension is already there, with Pulaski who bets that Data cannot solve it. Show Data matching wits with Moriarty, which we never get to see, and show Data eventually outthinking him. That would be an enjoyable story.

The Outrageous Okona

The plot:

A suspicious ship captain named Okona comes aboard. He is pursued by two other ships. It is all revealed to be a big misunderstanding. Okona bones two crew ladies, one of them Teri Hatcher with a case of bad frizzy hair.

What works:

Not much.

1) When Okona talks about "socializing" with members of the Enterprise crew, the camera mysteriously zooms to a close up of Counselor Troi, the sex symbol of the ship.

2) The best scene was the one where Data deleted the holocomedian, Joe Piscopo.

What doesn't work:

Most everything. This is another episode where nothing much happens.

1) The scenes where Data "learns" to tell jokes on the holodeck are painful to watch.

2) Why do Wesley's pants unzip in the back, and why are his pants actually open in the back? It's like an open invitation to anal rape.

3) Okona has weird hair over his forehead, maybe because he has a big dent in his forehead.

4) The actors who play the parents and children in the latter part of this episode are terrible actors, all of them.

5) At one point Okona reveals he has an expensive jewel, but it looks like a piece of cheap glass. How difficult would it have been to get a prop that sparkled?

How it could have been better:

This was trying to be a comedic episode. It wasn't. There wasn't much salvageable here. I would call this episode "The Outrageously Bad Okona".

Loud as a Whisper

The plot:

Riva, a deaf mute mediator, loses his translators, and must learn to cope without them.

What works:

1) Best scene: where mush face alien shoots all three of Riva's assistants, who obligingly stood very close together. When they got shot, you see how they get peeled down to their flesh and bones before disintegrating. Very dramatic!

2) In his sexy dinner with Troi, Riva tries to turn her on with this odd line: "The sound of the ship moves through my body like a great pulse."

3) I like how Picard grabs Riva's head and yells at him, as if Riva will hear better, even though Riva is completely deaf.

What doesn't work:

1) This was a very slow and boring episode. Most of it consisted of Riva being a pompous asshole and trying to bone Counselor Troi. Not very interesting.

2) Riva's solution to bring peace to two warring sides? Spend months teaching them sign language! The solution is so ridiculous that the entire episode becomes unbelievable.

3) There is an odd side view of Chief O'Brien where he actually looks pregnant.

4) Riva is supposed to be a great negotiator, and very empathic. But when Picard & Co. beams down the first thing Riva does is walk right up to them and stare at them coldly in silence. That's autism, not empathy. Riva also interrupts Picard midsentence, and puts his hand on Riker's chest the first time they meet. More autism. Riva is a fraud.

5) Is Riva a telepath, or his 3 assistants? If Riva is a telepath who can tell the others what to say, why does he need anyone else? Not explained. The whole rationale for the assistants makes no sense.

6) Riva asks if Geordi is unhappy being blind and having to wear a visor. Geordi says no, he really likes who he is. Right.

7) Riva says the specific dispute of this conflict has no relevance. Sure.

8) Riva's poorly written sign language date with Troi is painful to watch.

9) Pulaski says she can give Geordi his eyesight back. Geordi doesn't want it "I'd be giving up a lot." Come on!

10) Why is Troi wearing white makeup all over her face? Is she an android like Data?

How it could have been better:

A bad episode all around. Very slow. Riva was a pompous ass. But what if Riva, instead of being brilliant, was actually insane? What if in his insanity his "secret of success" was to deafen and blind the leaders of the warring factions to "create empathy"? What if Riva made the fighting worse and led a cult of people who deafened and blinded people and Picard had to stop them?

The Schizoid Man

The plot:

A dying man downloads himself into Data. Picard gives him a lecture, and he leaves Data's head.

What works:

1) Data with a beard--it's a parody of Commander Riker's!

What doesn't work:

Everything.

How it could have been better:

There's no antagonist in this episode. Dr. Graves takes over Data, but he is not evil, merely insanely jealous of his blonde assistant he wants to bone. He gives up when Picard gives him a speech. The worst he does is slap Geordi and Picard. Yawn.

What if a truly evil person downloaded himself into Data, and Data started actually torturing and killing people? That would be a lot more dramatic, a lot more suspenseful. Instead of lecturing Data, Picard would have to capture him, deactivate him, and find some way to restore his original programming.

Unnatural Selection

The plot:

Dr. Pulaski catches the disease that makes her old, even older than she already is. They use the transporter and press the reset button.

What works:

1) There is a brief moment at the end of the episode when Dr. Pulaski does not look old. It is right after she is restored from being very old and is restored to merely middle aged, she does not look so old by comparison. By the next episode, however, she looks old again.

2) At the beginning of the episode they encounter a Reliant-class ship which has been infected with the make-you-old disease. Picard takes control of the Reliant-class ship using the prefix code, just like in Star Trek II: The Wrath of Khan! And then at the end the Enterprise destroys the Reliant class ship with a photon torpedo, again like Wrath of Khan!

3) I liked the scene where Pulaski beams up a shrink wrapped boy.

What doesn't work:

1) This episode is not suited to specifically making Dr. Pulaski old, because she is already old. They should have done it to Wesley for more dramatic effect.

2) How can a boy be in "stasis" while shrink wrapped on a table without any electrical equipment?

3) These kids are genetically engineered. I thought genetic engineering outlawed after eugenic wars?

4) Solving the problem with the transporter has been done too many times and is lazy writing.

5) Pulaski wears a maternity version of her blue uniform because she is chunky. I miss Dr. Crusher. She was a terrible actress, but wore her jumpsuit well, especially during season four and later when she got pregnant and her boobs grew.

6) Data has no worries about catching the get-old disease, but then he beams back to the Enterprise--can the transporter reliably disinfect him? This is never discussed.

7) Why does Chief Obrien wear a lieutenant's uniform?

8) Why can't all the get-old people be put into stasis to buy time until they can find a cure? Never discussed.

9) The people on the space station were infected at the same time as the crew of the other Reliant ship. So why were the Reliant crew dead much faster than the space station crew? No explanation.

How it could have been better:

A disease that makes people old is boring. How about a disease that makes them younger? Make the crew younger and younger. Give Picard hair. Eventually replace them with younger actors, then finally have their teenage selves find a cure, but regrettably not in time to save Wesley.

A Matter of Honor

The plot:

Riker goes on an exchange program on a Klingon ship. Due to an unlikely misunderstanding, the Klingon ship prepares to attack the Enterprise.

What works:

1) The idea of Riker exploring the culture on a Klingon ship is interesting. It was just poorly done here.

2) I love it when Worf goes over to the Benzene guest star and intimidates him with, "Ensign Mendon--you may impress me!"

3) I like seeing the Enterprise's scan of the Klingon ship--it's very rare in Star Trek that we get to see any instrument panels or readouts, it makes it seem more real.

What doesn't work:

1) Picard very casually tells the visiting benzite that he should have been "indoctrinated". That's an odd choice of words. It sounds like brainwashing.

2) Why is eating live worms ok for Klingons but eating caterpillars horrifying in the episode with the mouth crabs?

3) Watching Riker eating Klingon food at the beginning is nauseating. One dish looks like an alien face hugger.

4) The Klingon captain is a little guy. Bad choice for the part.

5) The B story of the autistic benzite is not interesting. It looks like he's constantly smoking crack cocaine from his chest dispenser.

6) Chief O'Brien's double chin moves independently from the rest of his face, very disturbing.

7) Riker taking command of the Klingon ship is ridiculous. They'd never accept him.

8) The Klingon ship is two big dark rooms with dim red lighting. It looks very cheap.

9) The Klingon woman with pimples seducing Riker is disgusting.

10) The Klingon paranoia that the Federation is trying to attack them is not believable. When Riker says "It makes no sense [for them to attack] with me on board", he's right, and they should realize that.

11) If the Klingon captain really believed the Federation were attacking him, why would he not execute Riker on the spot? And yet he trusts Riker. It makes no sense.

12) The Klingons say that the virus eating at their ship can't be stopped. Why can't they simply cut off the affected sections of their hull?

13) Wesley walks around with his ass zipper wide open, a clear invitation to anal rape.

14) Picard finds a way to surrender in this episode, this time to Riker on the Klingon ship. In the early seasons Picard seems to be gleeful every time he can find a way to surrender to someone else. It makes him look weak.

15) It is ridiculous to hear Klingons speak of kilometers and minutes.

16) Riker lets himself be beaten up by the Klingon Captain to help him save face. Ridiculous.

17) Riker and Picard act like wimps in this episode.

How it could have been better:

The idea of this story, exploring Klingon personalities, was a good one. It just wasn't carried off well. We learn that the Klingon first officer is a big guy but secretly sensitive. A Klingon girl with pimples wants Riker for sex. That's about it.

How about making a Klingon character who is cynical? How about one who hates the Federation? How about one who is in competition with another Klingon for authority on the ship? You know, characters with distinct personalities. If they told a Klingon based story with interesting personalities, that might have worked.

The story they told, manipulating the Klingons to attack the Enterprise with Riker on board, was improbable; letting Riker take command, highly improbable. Why not forget the Enterprise and show the Klingons, with Riker on board, take on a mission against the Romulans?

Measure of a Man

The plot:

Data is put on trial to see if he has rights like a real person. He is found to have rights, including the right to refuse to be taken apart for experimentation.

What works:

What doesn't work:

1) In general trial episodes are very boring, especially when we can easily guess the results in advance, as here. It's slow moving, there's not much action, and while the parties try to create drama, it comes off rather uninteresting.

2) The whole idea of Data being on trial for his rights is ridiculous. Once he was ruled capable of joining Starfleet as a person, his rights were established then. The whole episode makes no sense.

3) The trial judge is a lady with lesbian hair and a man's voice who calls Picard "sexy".

4) It is not explained why Data keeps a hologram of Tasha. True, she had sex with him, but she also rejected him immediately afterwards. Was the sex so good for Data that the little matter of Tasha's rejection meant nothing to him?

How it could have been better:

1) Does a robot have rights? Personally, I don't really care. When I see a robot on a science fiction TV show or movie I want to see the robot do interesting things. I want to see the robot do fast calculations, I want to see the robot solve problems the others can't, I want to see the robot acting logical and smarter than everyone else. I don't want to see him on trial talking about his philosophical rights. It's the most boring use of a robot character.

The Dauphin

The plot:

Wesley tries to bone an alien princess, only she turns out to be a shape changing monster.

What works:

Nothing.

What doesn't work:

1) The entire episode consists of Wesley chasing after the space princess. It's not enough to sustain an episode, and it's really boring. Meanwhile he's still walking around with his pants open in the back, seemingly inviting anal rape. They tried to spice the story up by having the princess's bodyguard turn into a monster from time to time, but it didn't really help.

How it could have been better:

If the Princess can change into different monsters then she's like Maya from Space 1999. Instead of giving her an aborted romance with Wesley, have her go on a mission with the Enterprise crew and use her shape changing abilities to fight enemies, and go into places that the others can't get to.

Contagion

The plot:

Picard discovers a machine that creates instant gateways to other planets. He has to blow it up before the Romulans get their hands on it.

What works:

1) This episode works well. There are very high stakes--the Enterprise might blow up, Data ceases to function, the Romulans might get their hands on advanced technology.

2) The Iconian probe that shoots lightning bolts is very menacing!

3) The idea of an instant gateway to other planets is very interesting!

4) Watching Picard and Data figure out how to use the control panel, even with Data being blinded, was very dramatic!

5) I like how Picard finds another way off the planet, using the gateway.

6) It's a great idea to sabotage the facility by having the space probes blow themselves up.

What doesn't work:

1) The minute I saw a black captain on the Yamato I knew the ship was about to blow up.

2) The solution to saving the ship--reboot the computer! Too simple.

How it could have been better:

While the second half of this episode was great, the first half was kind of slow. We saw the Enterprise suffering malfunctions caused by the Iconian probe. But the malfunctions aren't life threatening and so are just a nuisance, and so the first half of the episode is the standard, "Geordi, fix the ship!" kind of story. To make it better, they should have accelerated to the second half of the story more quickly. Show the Romulans coming down to the planet. Have them fight the Federation for the technology. Show a Romulan being tossed by Data through a doorway to another planet. Maybe have other aliens come through one of the doorways on the other side. There are a lot of possibilities.

The Royale

The plot:

Riker, Data and Worf get trapped in the equivalent of a holographic hotel on an alien planet, made to be the home of a now dead astronaut. They have to figure out how to get out by reading the book on which the hotel is based on.

What works:

Not much.

What doesn't work:

1) This is a clichéd story about a casino and we're supposed to find all the cliché characters funny. They're not. They just look and sound very dumb and cringe worthy.

How it could have been better:

If Riker & Co. have to be trapped in a holodeck (again!), make it a better story. Make it a story where they are trapped on a space station, or they are in the middle of a war, or they have to solve a murder mystery. Deep Space Nine redid this very episode a number of years later (rescuing Vic Fontaine by buying a nightclub), and neither version was very entertaining.

Time Squared

The plot:

A Picard from a few hours in the future comes to them to reveal that the Enterprise will be destroyed in a few hours. They have to figure out how prevent the ship from being destroyed, again.

What works:

1) It's interesting watching the Enterprise fall into a "space waterfalls".

2) Picard murdered his future self! Why wasn't he put on trial for that?

3) The idea of a future self coming back to the present is interesting, but very poorly done here.

What doesn't work:

1) This entire episode is a cock tease. Future-Picard spends most of the time making wide eyed expressions in sickbay and saying nothing until the last five minutes of the episode. It's boring and it's slow.

2) Most of the episode is spent uselessly hypothesizing about the future event which will destroy the Enterprise.

3) How is it that the Enterprise goes into the space waterfalls at full speed and rams the power source at the center, and doesn't get destroyed? Why does the alien intelligence controlling the space waterfalls destroy the Enterprise every time it escapes? None of this is ever explained; at the end the Enterprise simply escaped, no explanation.

How it could have been better:

1) The idea of the episode was sound. It just needed to be executed better. Instead of having Future-Picard incoherent, have him talkative from the start. Have Future-Picard and Present-Picard work together to get the Enterprise out of the crisis. Make the crisis more complex than one decision at one moment. Have Future-Picard help the crew through several steps. Show F-P working with his present self and the crew and interacting with them. That would have made for a great episode--same concept, totally different execution.

The Icarus Factor

The plot:

Riker is offered another command. He turns it down because he wants to be first officer for life. His Dad show up, and they play blind ice hockey and blow off some steam.

What works:

1) Wesley thoughtfully arranges a pain stick birthday party for Worf.

What doesn't work:

1) Watching Riker and his dad blindfolded and hitting each other with sticks is bizarre, like parody.

2) Most of the episode shows Riker arguing with his Dad, complaining about his childhood. Not scifi. Boring.

3) Worf tells people that he wants to be alone. They ask him that because he is sitting in Ten Forward surrounded by many people. Why he is in Ten Forward if he wants to be alone?

How it could have been better:

1) Riker bitches that his Dad neglected him as a child. Boring. It would be a lot more dramatic if Riker's Dad sexually molested him as a child, and Riker tried to kill him. Or if his dad was an alien or a robot and Riker found out he was adopted. Something, you know, with science fiction. Or drama. Or both.

2) And stop offering Riker his own command. If he takes it he leaves the show, and so continually getting and turning down such opportunities is unrealistic.

Pen Pals

The plot:

Data corresponds with orange monster mask girl, then beams down for a visit. Dr. Crusher thoughtfully erases her brain afterwards.

What works:

Nothing.

What doesn't work:

1) Nothing really happens in this episode. There is a lot of padding and filler. We are supposed to be riveted by Data talking to a little girl on the space radio?

2) The B plot features Wesley in charge of some crewmen for some kind of survey, and Wesley coping with their disgust with being bossed around by a 16 year old. Also boring.

3) The Prime Directive says, don't interfere, but Picard has no problem erasing brains left and right.

How it could have been better:

1) Have the apparently harmless little girl actually be a monster who eats androids.

Q Who

The plot:

Q introduces Picard to the Borg.

What works:

1) As a brand new, original adversary, the Borg are a very creative addition to the show! And I really like how the first one has a whirring power tool for a hand!

2) I like how Q played handball in the shuttle while waiting to wear Picard down.

3) The second half of the episode was great, but the first half, before they encountered the Borg, was too slow.

4) A GREAT ending where the Enterprise is about to be destroyed and Picard tells Q that he needs his help, very dramatically, with feeling, very well done!

Picard: "We're frightened! We're inadequate!"

5) Picard actually thanks Q at the end of the episode for shaking him out of his pacifism, even after 18 of his crewmen died!

6) I like how the Borg cut out a piece of Enterprise, we see the decks being cut out like slicing a layer cake!

7) There's a great scene near the end of Q lying on the floor, looking amused, during the desperate chase scene where the Enterprise is being pursued by the Borg.

What doesn't work:

1) Last time we saw Q he promised not to bother humanity again. So he shows up in a distant shuttle and brings Picard there. Isn't he bothering Picard in the shuttle, and isn't Picard part of humanity? I think they tried to write Q out a little too quickly at the end of "Hide and Q" and regretted it.

2) Q and Whoopi/Guinan do some kind of hand action. Does Guinan have hand powers?

3) After the Enterprise temporarily damages the Borg, Picard decides there is leisurely time for talk in the briefing room.

3) Picard raises hands in surrender to Borg and says, "We mean you no harm". Ridiculous.

4) When the Borg tries to take over, Picard says mildly to the Borg "I cannot allow you to do that." I cannot allow you to do that? How passive aggressive is that? What about "Stop what you are doing or we will blow your ugly head off?", as being a more realistic response.

5) Q tells Picard the Borg are only interested in technology, not people. Totally untrue.

6) The visit to the Borg ship is not very interesting. Love the view from the balcony, but the big discovery was a box of Borg babies. Not a dramatic find.

7) The ship's phasers didn't work the first time they fired on the Borg ship, but they did work the second time. No explanation. Then in the battle at the end, the Enterprise kept using photons, which didn't work, never again trying phasers, which did work. No explanation.

How it could have been better:

1) Speed up the encounter with the Borg to earlier in the episode. Fill more of the episode with dialog with a Borg drone, you know, an opposing personality. Have them fight more drones on the ship. Have Guinan get assimilated by the Borg, and return to harass them in later episodes.

Samaritan Snare

The plot:

Geordi gets kidnapped by a race of dumb fatties with bushy eyebrows. Picard has heart surgery but first has a boring conversation with Wesley on a shuttle.

What works:

1) The Pakleds are kind of funny, especially when they say, "We are smart." I also like how they say, "We need things to make us go." It sounds like they are constipated.

2) I like when Geordi gets phasered. When most people get phasered, they fall down. When it happens to Geordi, he jumps into a bulkhead.

3) There's a funny scene where the retarded Pakleds tell each other "We are strong!" and give each other big retarded grins.

What doesn't work:

1) The Pakleds claim they are smart, but we quickly see they are very dumb, allowing Geordi to easily fool them, and they talk like retards, saying things like:

"We are smart. We need their computer things."

2) Wesley and Picard talk about their feelings in the shuttle. Very boring.

3) Only Worf questions the wisdom of sending Geordi over to an alien spaceship alone. When the crew acts stupidly, the entire episode loses its drama. Even when Troi warns Riker of the danger, Riker still does nothing.

4) When Geordi is taken captive, Riker is too afraid to use the ship's phasers to knock down their shields and rescue him.

5) Riker can't even insult the Pakleds after they phaser Geordi:

"You think we are not smart."

Riker: "I think you need to continue to develop."

Who talks like this? On a show full of wooden characters, Riker is woodenest (except perhaps for Dr. Crusher).

How it could have been better:

1) The Pakled story was not very compelling because they were retards. Instead of retards pretending not to be retards, make the Pakleds brilliant, super-geniuses, who after capturing Geordi suddenly start talking brilliantly. Make them more of an intelligent adversary.

2) The story of Picard and Wesley in the shuttle made me sleepy. Why not talk about something that concerned them both, like Picard's role in the death of Wesley's father. Did Picard really causes his death? Explaining that to Wesley could be very compelling!

Up the Long Ladder

The plot:

The Enterprise finds some backwards Irish colonists, one of whom Riker sticks his penis into. Then they find a race of clones, who try to clone Riker and Dr. Pulaski. In retaliation, Picard forces the clones to have sex with the backwards Irish people.

What works:

1) The title of this episode sounds like a porn video.

2) After the clone people illegally cloned Riker and Pulaski, Picard forced the clone people to have sex with the backwards Irish people. I thought that that was an appropriate punishment.

3) When the leader of the clone people says he doesn't like sex, he purposefully looks at Riker when he says it! Riker has just finished having sex with the Irish whore. How did he know? Did Riker still have her smell on him?

4) I very much liked the long needle that went into Riker and Dr. Pulaski.

What doesn't work:

1) The Irish whore has sex with Riker about 1.4 minutes after beaming aboard the ship. How realistic is that?

2) Irish people are portrayed as being drunks, lying with farm animals, supposedly an amusing stereotype--would it have been half as amusing if they had done that with blacks or hispanics?

3) When O'Brien beams up the backwards Irish people, he also beams up a sheep and even straw. Why does he do that? How does he do that?

4) When Riker gets shot with a phaser, he doesn't remember being shot later. How can he not remember being phasered?

5) When Riker zapped his clone, he was killing a living life form! There were no consequences. Was it considered ok because it was kind of like an abortion?

6) Why did the clone people take DNA from Riker and Pulaski to clone, but not from Geordi? Was it a black thing? Or did they just not want any blind clones?

How it could have been better:

The backward Irish people plotline was the "B" plot even though it came first. It was supposed to be amusing but it wasn't. The clone story had a little more potential. What if the clones took DNA samples of every member of the crew, made clones, and then used the clones to try to capture the Enterprise? Imagine Picard and Riker fighting copies of themselves! Now that would be exciting!

Manhunt

The plot:

Mrs. Troi tries to seduce Captain Picard. She fails.

What works:

1) When Wesley gives Worf a back-handed insult: "Worf, you look handsome... for a Klingon"

2) When Mrs. Troi speaks to the ship's computer, which also is her voice.

What doesn't work:

1) This episode is part of the Mrs. Roddenberry welfare program that we all must be forced to watch.

2) Mrs. Troi wears a dress with a plunging neckline so we can admire her 70 year old breasts.

3) What are they drinking in the holodeck bar? Will it disappear from their stomachs when they leave the holodeck?

4) Picard spends a long time in his Dixon Hill mystery, but somehow fails to solve anything.

How it could have been better:

This episode would be better if it had a plot. There was none. Picard sitting around a holodeck simulation is not a plot. Neither is Mrs. Troi lusting after Picard.

How about an episode, just one episode, where Picard actually has to solve a Dixon Hill mystery? For all the times he's been in the Dixon Hill simulation, he's never actually done that!

The Emissary

The plot:

Worf's Klingon girlfriend pays a visit. He wants marriage. She wants sex. They settle for sex.

What works:

1) The ostensible plot is about intercepting a Klingon ship which was in cryofreeze for many years that has just thawed. But that was like the last five minutes of the episode. It was handled well, but the real story was about Worf and his Klingon sex partner.

2) It is great watching them fight monsters on the holodeck and then having rough Klingon sex, though that last is only intimated.

What doesn't work:

1) Worf's Klingon girlfriend has a very annoying sounding voice. It gets worse when they argue.

2) The whole basis of this story is that a Klingon crew went into suspended animation for decades during the previous war with the Federation, then thawed to complete a vital mission. Why would they be frozen so long? It is never explained and makes no sense.

How it could have been better:

1) For a change, why not have the man (Worf) seduce the woman for sex instead of the other way around? I know all the teenage boys who watch prefer it this way, but I prefer realism.

2) Or, have Klar (that's her name), seduce Worf, bed him, but then proceed to bed other members of the crew. Show her doing Riker, Geordi, Troi, anything that moves. Then show Worf beating Klar up for being unfaithful to him, and then see how the crew juggles feminism with moral relevance when it comes to respecting other cultures. That's a lot more exciting than the sleepy romance we were treated to, and it even comes with a moral dilemma!

Peak Performance

The plot:

Picard participates in war games against Riker, who is given an old ship. A tactical expert named Kolrami comes aboard who is arrogant and abuses the crew, especially Riker.

What works:

1) I like it when Picard admits he was initially against the idea of war games, but admits the Borg shook him out of his pacifism.

2) I like it when Riker plays Strategema against Kolrami, and considers it an honor to last about five seconds. And then later, when Data beats Kolrami, that is funny too. You see, friction between characters, it works. Here's a great line where Kolrami agrees to play against Riker:

"An opponent of limited dimensions can often be quite diverting."

What doesn't work:

1) The whole war games concept makes no sense because the Enterprise tremendously overmatches the Hathaway, and thus the whole storyline makes no sense.

2) The twist at the end where the Ferengi attack is resolved in a very undramatic way. The writers labor to create ways in which the Enterprise will not use its weapons in actual battle.

3) A lot of the story features Riker's crew getting the Hathaway ready for battle. That's very boring.

4) For an episode about war games, we don't see more than a few seconds of war games.

How it could have been better:

1) How about having an episode about war games that actually has war games? Feature the Enterprise fighting against several smaller Federation ships, and show Riker and Picard, working together, trying to figure out tactics to beat the superior force. Even if only a game, the rivalry between Picard and the other Captains could be very entertaining, if they introduce the other captains and give them some personality.

Shades of Grey

The plot:

Riker gets infected by a killer plant, and has to think bad thoughts to purge it from his system.

What works:

1) This is a clips episode, but it is a GREAT clips episode, basically a "Best of" scenes from the past two seasons. At first, they show boring clips of Riker meeting Data, and Troi crying, but it quickly gets better, when Riker remembers the planet of blonde people having constant sex, the holowhore he once met, acting as a gigolo to the ruler of Angel One, having sex with the backwards Irish whore, watching Tasha getting zapped by chocolate pudding monster, getting kicked in the head by Admiral Quinn, blowing up Commander Remmick's skull, getting zapped by Mettrick Buttock in Symbiosis, being dragged into the chocolate pudding monster, and watching pompous Riva's assistants getting zapped by the gun that turns people into skeletons. All great scenes!

2) The plot, that Riker must think upsetting thoughts to make himself better, makes no sense, but that is ok.

What doesn't work:

1) This episode features the most unrealistic and dopiest Riker attitude yet. He's not mad at the plant that's trying to kill him, he says it's just trying to make a living. By killing him. Not upset at all. Totally unrealistic. It's hard to relate to characters who don't act like normal human beings.

2) When Geordi beams down with Data to the killer plant zone, why doesn't Geordi wear protective gear so he doesn't get stung as well?

How it could have been better:

1) Have Riker die at the end and be replaced with a character who acts like a normal human being, who feels anger and resentment when a normal human being would.

Evolution

The plot:

Nanites, microscopic robots, threaten the ship. A scientist shoots some of them, and is forced to apologize. The end.

What works:

1) Dr. Crusher returns, and says about Wesley, "I missed about two inches of him." Was she talking about his penis?

2) They have new uniforms with collars! Very good, I don't have to see as much of Picard's wrinkled neck. But now zippers are in the back so Beverly can't unzip the front of her shirt for Jean Luc like she did in the Naked Now. Perhaps they moved the zippers to the back of the shirts when they found out Beverly was returning to the Enterprise. Practically speaking, though, how does anyone zip up their own shirts? It's not possible. They must get dressed every morning and run into the hallway to find someone to zip them up.

3) Beverly sees Wesley going out with a girl, and says it pleases her not only as a mother but also as a doctor--she thinks Wesley has a medical need for sex?

What doesn't work:

1) We constantly see red and blue jars in sickbay. They become very overused, and very dumb props.

2) Crusher is back. But she has frizzy hair--was her hair caught in a rainstorm in space?

3) Most of this episode, like many episodes, focuses on the very slow investigation of malfunctions on the Enterprise, leading to the very slow discovery of the nanites. There is also a lot of time spent on the annoying scientist trying to launch his science box into space. None of this is interesting.

3) Data and Picard express concern for civil rights of nanites. Ridiculous.

4) At the end of the episode Data surrenders control of himself to the nanites. Ridiculous.

How it could have been better:

Instead of making the nanites the virtuous ones, make them into an enemy. Have them take over the ship's computer, and Data, and try to destroy the crew, and have the crew fight back.

The Ensigns of Command

The plot:

Data lands on a colony and has to convince them to evacuate because an aggressive alien race called the Shelliac are coming. He scores some lip action from a girl with cute bangs.

What works:

1) The cute girl with bangs who comes on to Data and tries to get him to bone her. She makes out with Data because he "appears to need it".

1) For the first time in a very long time Picard gets the better of an alien species instead of apologizing to it. After enduring verbal abuse from the Shelliac, Picard finds a treaty provision that will prevent the Shelliac from taking immediate possession of the human colony. After all their rudeness, Picard takes the opportunity to be rude to them. When they call the Enterprise Picard makes them wait, idly walking around the bridge and admiring the plaque on the wall. A great scene that shows personality! It's a shame there are so few of them.

3) The idea of Data having to carry out a mission on his own is a great one. Just poorly executed.

What doesn't work:

1) This episode is called "The Ensigns of Command" but Data is a Lieutenant Commander. Really it should more properly be called "The Lieutenant Commander of Command" but that is a dumb title as well.

2) The Shelliac have the voice of Tasha's chocolate pudding monster! The Shelliac even have the same body shape!

3) It makes no sense that the colony leader would rather die than relocate.

How it could have been better:

The main idea of this story was watching Data beat the stubborn colony leader who didn't want to relocate. It would have been better if Data had outsmarted the colony leader, as Picard did with the Shelliac. Show Data's brilliant brain out-thinking the colony leader. Show the colony leader setting traps to kill Data, and show Data evading these traps. Show Data convincing different constituency interests in the colony to evacuate, each time using arguments tailored to their needs and interests. That would be a lot more interesting than watching Data stun three guards and fire a phaser into a water pipe.

The Survivors

The plot:

Aliens destroy a colony leaving only two survivors, a man and a woman. Picard tries to figure out how they survived when everything around them was destroyed.

What works:

1) Counselor Troi has a new asymmetrical cleavage dress, that shows more cleavage from her right breast than her left. I approve!

2) This is a great mystery story that was not easy to figure out from the beginning. But I like how Picard started to figure it out, understanding that the alien ship that attacked them wasn't using its full power. When Picard returned to the planet, he sarcastically apologized for interrupting their celebration dance--they thought the Enterprise had left.

3) When the old man reveals that he destroyed not just the alien ship, but the entire alien species, that was a game changer. We had never seen anything like that happen before! It was an unexpected development.

What doesn't work:

1) Picard never explains how he realizes that the man is real but the woman is fake.

2) If the man is real and the woman is an illusion, and he controls her, why does he permit her to disagree with him?

3) Why didn't the man save his wife with his super powers? Or why didn't he just fling the enemy ship a million light years away? Was his only ability to commit mass genocide, and nothing else? This is a big plot hole that makes no sense.

4) Another plot hole occurs when Picard refuses to put the alien on trial for wiping out an entire race.

Picard: "We're not qualified to be your judges. We have no law to fit your crime." Sure you do. It's called genocide. I think Picard is just afraid to mess with this alien who can eliminate an entire species with a single thought.

5) The alien blocks Troi's telepathic abilities with music box music, which tortures Troi. Couldn't he have blocked her telepathic abilities without torturing her with repeating music?

How it could have been better:

Troi should have gone mad, embracing the repeated music and dance and sing to it, twirling around the bridge and going "La, lalalala."

Otherwise it was a pretty good episode with a very unexpected twist--meeting the alien who could wipe out an entire species with a single thought!

Who Watches the Watchers

The plot:

Primitive aliens discover the Enterprise crew watching them, and believe Picard is a god. Picard volunteers to get shot with an arrow to prove he isn't a god.

What works:

1) It's very funny when the primitives erroneously worship Picard. They call him "The Picard".

"I believe I have seen our overseer. He is called... The Picard."

"The Picard will be pleased!"

What doesn't work:

1) Picard volunteers to get shot with an arrow to convince the primitives he is not a god. Somehow Picard and Riker always seem to be the first to volunteer to surrender or be shot or lower their defenses. Their self-sacrificing nature does not make them seem human; it makes them seem like unrealistic cartoon characters, and robs the story of drama.

How it could have been better:

This entire episode is about convincing the primitives that Picard is not a god. Ok, it's an original story. But not very exciting.

But what if Picard were taken over by a virus, and in his sickness, decided that he was a god? What if he acted like a god to the primitives and set himself up as their king? Then Riker & Co. would be in the even more challenging position of deposing Picard without hurting anyone and Riker would have to match wits against Picard. Now that would be drama, and that would be entertaining!

The Bonding

The plot:

A little boy loses his momma to a boobytrap. Aliens feel sorry for him, and send one of their own to pretend to be his momma.

What works:

Nothing.

What doesn't work:

1) The little boy has really greasy, slick backed hair with a lot of hair gel. It doesn't work on little boys. It makes him look like he was dressed up by a pedophile to be a sex toy.

2) Little boy has some very vomit inducing scenes with Wesley where they talk about their feelings. Please no.

How it could have been better:

Star Trek is not about little boys. We need protagonists who we can identify with.

Booby Trap

The plot:

The Enterprise is stuck in an energy draining, radiation shooting trap. Geordi has to figure a way out so he works on the holodeck and creates a holowhore so he can score while saving the ship.

What works:

1) Geordi gets rejected by a white girl on a date! I love it because it's realistic! I mean, what normal girl (of any race) would want to date a guy with a banana hair clip on his face?

2) Guinan says she's attracted to bald men. Picard!

3) I like how Geordi gets visibly aroused by the holowhore.

Holowhore flirting: "You must know me inside and out. I'm with you every day Geordi, every time you look at it you're looking at me, every time you touch it, you're touching me."

What doesn't work:

1) How can this trap suck energy from the Enterprise while simultaneously emitting radiation? Wouldn't the energy sucking part also absorb the radiation?

2) At one point Riker & Co. beam aboard a nearby shipwreck. How can they do this while the nearby rocks are beaming out radiation at them?

3) This episode features a LOT Of technobabble. A little is ok. A lot is filler and is not entertaining. That's the main problem with this episode.

4) We learn that if the Enterprise crew is exposed to radiation for 26 minutes, they will all die. But 25 minutes, and they are fine. Ridiculous.

How it could have been better:

1) The Enterprise is stuck in a trap. It might as well have been a natural phenomena because there was no antagonist in this story. How about a living alien being in charge of this trap and Picard has to outwit him? That would, you know, create drama between an antagonist and a protagonist. It's hard to get excited when the enemy is a bunch of rocks and the solution involves 30 minutes of technobabble.

2) It would have been good if in later episodes Geordi returned to the holodeck to consummate his love with the holowhore. Then when a cleaning crew found sperm in the holodeck and Dr. Crusher analyzed the DNA and traced it to Geordi, he could be disciplined by Captain Picard.

3) The holowhore isn't very pretty. Given the technology of the holodeck, Geordi definitely can do better.

The Enemy

The plot:

Geordi is trapped on a stormy planet with a Romulan. They have to work together to escape. Meanwhile Picard has a confrontation with a Romulan ship, but quickly grabs his ankles and surrenders his Romulan prisoner.

What works:

1) Dr Crusher has long hair again. This new wig is much better than her previous frizzy hair wig.

2) A lot of the story concerns Worf's refusal to give a blood transfusion to a wounded Romulan prisoner. Romulans killed his family.

"If you had seen them kill your parents, you would understand it is always time for those feelings."

In other words, Worf is acting rationally. How refreshing. It's ironic he acts more human than Riker or Picard.

What doesn't work:

1) For plot reasons, we are supposed to believe that Klingon and Romulan blood types are compatible. Makes no sense, completely different species.

2) Picard ends the crisis by releasing the Romulan prisoner, even though he was spying in Federation space. More pacifism.

3) Geordi forms a friendship with the Romulan in the Star Trek cave. We have seen this "Enemy Mine" plot, where two enemies become friends on an inhospitable planet, too many times, over and over.

How it could have been better:

Have Geordi stranded on the planet being hunted by a bunch of Romulans, maybe six of them. Introduce us to them, show us a little about each one's personality. Have Geordi elude them, knock one or two out, get captured, interact, escape, and so on. Don't have him become friends with them. Create drama between antagonists and a protagonist.

Have the Romulan prisoner on the Enterprise escape, take hostages, and have Worf kill him by cracking his spine. Now that's dramatic.

The Price

The plot:

The Federation negotiates for access to a wormhole. But one of the negotiators, a Pretty Boy, negotiates access to Counselor Troi's wormhole at the same time. Geordi and Data travel down the wormhole to make sure it works. Pretty Boy does the same with Counselor Troi's.

What works:

1) There's a tremendous scene where Troi and Beverly are doing yoga in the middle of a hallway (don't ask) next to a giant mirror. They are wearing yoga outfits so tight that you can see that it really digs into their ass cracks and vaginas. As Troi and Beverly spread their legs and twist back and forth, it's oddly even more erotic than even Troi's love scene with Pretty Boy.

2) Once again, I have to say I like Troi's new asymmetrical cleavage outfit. She shows a big chunk of her right breast. She's a great ambassador to alien races.

What doesn't work:

1) The sex scene between Troi and Pretty Boy is kind of empty. They are in bed together wearing clothes. He rubs her foot with oil. They talk like they are drugged.

2) When I saw the tall alien with the giant walnut on his head, I thought, It's Gumby! The other alien with the elaborate teeth braces was just as ridiculous. Why can't aliens be aliens without ridiculous makeup and elaborate face putty?

3) There's a very, very weird scene where Pretty Boy tries to taunt Riker, flaunting the fact he is boning Troi, who is Riker's former girlfriend. Riker merely smiles and says how happy he is that Pretty Boy is making Troi happy. This is totally ridiculous. No human male would act this way. It makes Riker unrelateable, and is symbolic how in many ways all the characters in this show are unrelateable.

How it could have been better:

This episode focuses on Troi's romance, Data and Geordi in the shuttle, Pretty Boy winning access to the wormhole but then losing as well after the wormhole is discovered to be useless. None of this is compelling. Once we find out the wormhole is useless, the entire episode loses its drama.

What if the wormhole really was valuable? And what if Riker had to find a way to out think Pretty Boy? Ironically, Riker is appointed negotiator, but we never get to see him negotiate. If you're going to have an episode about high stakes negotiation, then show the characters engaging in high stakes negotiating. To raise the stakes even further, have one of the bidders secretly be an assassin and pair that as the action story with the negotiating story. That would make it all more compelling.

The Vengeance Factor

The plot:

The Enterprise tries to help a planet make peace with a band of pimple pirates, but a young girl named Yuta tries to ruin things by assassinating the pimple pirates.

What works:

1) Even though it was illogical, I love the scene where Riker disintegrates Yuta. I mean, when have you ever seen Riker shoot anyone, much less kill them? It gave the show some rare drama.

2) I like how Troi knows when to leave so Riker can be alone with Yuta. Troi knows that Yuta is Riker's next conquest.

3) I like how Yuta's fat lady boss sends her over to Riker's quarters to whore for Riker.

4) I like Yuta's submissiveness:

Yuta: "Tell me what you want William. I will do anything that you wish. Don't you want me to give you pleasure?"

What doesn't work:

1) When Riker is trying to flirt with Yuta, he calls one of her dishes "Parthos ala Yuta!", trying to sound Italian, but he says it in such a strained way, so unnaturally, that it just comes out weird. Very bad acting.

2) Yuta tries to whore herself out to Riker, but Riker rejects her because he likes "equals, not subordinates." Come on, a pretty girl wants to have sex with Riker, and he pushes her away? Again, he's not acting like a human being.

3) Yuta's boss is a fat lady with a white stripe in her hair that makes her look like a skunk. She has a very deep voice and looks like a guy in a dress. Fat skunk boss wants to take the pimple pirates back to her planet, but they are disruptive criminals. Her desire to reimport these criminal elements makes no sense.

4) This is a slow episode with a lot of filler. You know an episode has filler when one of the pimple pirates sits with Wesley in 10 Forward and asks if Wesley likes him.

5) Riker keeps upping the phaser power, but can't stop Yuta until he disintegrates her. It makes no sense that he couldn't burn a hole through her leg first.

6) Picard thinks nothing of beaming aboard a pirate ship that's just attacked the Enterprise. He could be taken hostage. It makes no sense.

7) Yuta says she was altered to become ageless. Without further explanation, it makes no sense.

How it could have been better:

Have Riker bone Yuta before he kills her. That would make the killing of Yuta more dramatic. Also, try to put a little more plot on the bones of this story. Have several different factions who want to kill each other, not just Yuta vs. the pimple pirates. Maybe strand them on a planet with Riker and force them to work together, but one of them slowly kills the others, and Riker has to figure out who the killer is. That would add some drama to a generally sleepy episode.

The Defector

The plot:

A Romulan defector tells Picard that the Romulans have established a secret base in the Neutral Zone to launch an attack from. Picard debates whether to go into the Neutral Zone to check it out.

What works:

1) To a certain degree, I like the back and forth--is the defector genuine or isn't he? To a certain point, it's a good story line.

2) I like Picard's countermeasures, having cloaked Klingon ships accompany them but only reveal it at the end. That was a great twist to the story that I hadn't anticipated.

3) I thought the scene where the defector realized he had been tricked, he had been used by the Romulans, and his surprised, depressed reaction, was a great, dramatic scene. You don't often get dramatic scenes like that in Star Trek, and this one came from a guest star.

What doesn't work:

1) Riker tries to insult the defector by calling him a "Varoule" (whatever that is!), but the way words come out of Riker's mouth, it sounded polite rather than an insult. Bad acting and/or writing.

2) When the Enterprise encounters the defector on a scout ship, Picard tells Geordi to extend the shields five miles to cover the scout ship. Why not simply move 5 miles closer to it? Or why not simply beam the occupant aboard immediately?

3) When the pursuing Romulan ship left immediately without argument shouldn't that have been a big clue that something was not valid about the defector?

4) In the middle of the story they figure out that the Romulan ship hadn't pursued the scout ship as vigorously as it could have. That should have ended the investigation right there. But the "is he or isn't he a real defector" story kept dragging on a while further, unnecessarily.

5) Picard was told that if he destroyed the Neutral Zone base the threat would be over. Why? Why couldn't Romulan ships launch attacks without a base in the Neutral Zone? In fact, by attacking a Romulan base, wouldn't that actually start a war with the Romulans? Never explained.

6) Why not just send a single cloaked Klingon ship to check the base out, with zero risk? Not explained.

7) Picard only brought 3 Klingon ships with him. What if the Romulans had shown up with an entire fleet?

8) There are no other Federation ships on the border of the Neutral Zone other than the Enterprise? It is unbelievable they don't have any patrols.

9) Why would the Romulans let an admiral defect, even with false information about a secret base, when the Romulan admiral certainly knew a lot about Romulan technology and tactics that could aid the Federation?

How it could have been better:

The story was pretty good, but the "is he or isn't he" dragged on a little too long and wasn't enough to sustain the plot. They could have made it faster paced by adding another character, like Captain Tomalock, who could have reassured Picard in his oily way that the Romulans had no warlike intentions, and then Picard would have to figure out who is lying.

The Hunted

The plot:

A soldier who has been genetically modified to be aggressive is captured by the Enterprise. He leads everyone on a chase, twice, and then returns to his home planet and demands better treatment.

What works:

1) There is a GREAT battle scene at the beginning where the soldier mops the floor with two security guards, Chief O'Brien, and Commander Riker! Only Worf was barely able to overtake him. A security guard screams as the soldier starts to twist his arm off! You don't see such intimated combat in Star Trek! Very dramatic, as are O'Brien's frantic calls, "Need security, more security!".

2) I laughed when I saw Worf momentarily hiding in the elevator when the soldier was beating up Enterprise security guards.

3) The "space chase" scene, where Data had to stop the soldier from escaping in a spaceship, was also a great scene, especially when Data starts to anticipates the soldier's actions.

What doesn't work:

1) The rest of the episode, after the soldier is captured, is a disappointment. Most of it consists of Counselor Troi getting in touch with his feelings. We quickly find out he's genetically modified and doesn't want to be violent but can't help it. We spend most of the rest of the episode wallowing in the ethical implications of that. Too slow. Too dull.

2) When the soldier was being beamed out of his cell, somehow he escaped--evading a transporter beam, and the force field. No explanation.

How it could have been better:

1) There should have been less psychoanalysis with Counselor Troi.

2) The final chase, where the soldier runs around the Enterprise, lacks drama. Except briefly at the end where he beats up Worf, he doesn't actually fight anyone, he just crawls around Jeffries tubes. It would have been more exciting if he had to beat up guards or crewmen at different points.

3) The ending is supposed to be dramatic but somehow lacks drama. The soldier and his buddies go to the planet and confront the President. The President is wearing a jumpsuit that makes his penis stick out. The soldier simply demands his rights. There is no violence. There is no drama. If the soldier had beaten up a bunch of the President's soldiers, and his side had taken casualties in the process, it would have been more dramatic. If the President, instead of being a wimpy muffin in spandex, had been outwardly antagonistic or cruel, it would have been more dramatic.

4) What if a number of these super soldiers tries to take over the Enterprise, and Picard and his crew had to stop them?

The High Ground

The plot:

Crusher gets kidnapped by terrorists. The terrorist leader gets an erection for Beverly. Then he dies.

What works:

1) I like the idea of the big haired terrorist having a crush on Beverly. But it never goes anywhere. He draws sketches of her. How... exciting....

2) When Counselor Troi comforts Wesley in a dress with enormous cleavage, it is GREAT!

3) The terrorist attack on Enterprise where they planted a bomb in engineering was great! So was Picard leaping forward and punching a terrorist in the face! For a moment, I had to ask myself if that was really Picard, if I was really watching TNG.

What doesn't work:

1) The debates about the ethics and efficacy of terrorism. There is a LOT of it, with (a) Riker, (b) the police lady with the huge breasts, (c) Data, and (d) Picard. It's the theme of the episode, I get it, but when more time is spent explaining the theme than actually having things happen, the balance is off.

2) The end battle in the standard Star Trek cave was brief and anti-climactic.

How it could have been better:

1) Have the big haired terrorist bone Beverly. Have him seduce her and brainwash her, Stockholm Syndrome style, and turn her against the Enterprise, maybe use her to capture Picard.

2) Have the terrorists plot to plant a bomb in a stadium, or a power plant, and have Riker and Worf beam down with a security team to fight them and disarm the bomb before it kills thousands. That's much more dramatic than a quick zap zap in a Star Trek cave.

Deja Q

The plot:

Q is stripped of his powers and sent to the Enterprise. He must learn how to cope as a human. Some aliens try to attack Q. Q tries to sacrifice himself, and in the process regains his powers.

What works:

1) Q appears, floating naked on the bridge. I've never seen that before! And it's funny when he drops to the floor, and smiles, saying "Red alert!"

2) Q has a lot more hair now. Each time we see him he seems to get more and more. It's very bushy up there now!

3) A lot of great lines, when Q calls Jean Luc his friend, and Picard stares at him, surprised.

Q: "What must I do to convince you people (I am human)?"

Worf: "Die."

Q: "Very clever, Worf. Eat any good books lately?"

Q to Worf: "I can't disappear, any more than you can win a beauty contest."

Q: "I'm not good with groups. It's difficult to work in groups when you're omnipotent."

4) The ending, where Q appears with a Spanish band and starts dancing, is hysterical. It gets even better when Q puts cigars in Picard and Riker's mouths, gives Riker some whores, and when Riker complains "I don't need your fantasy women!" Q responds, "You weren't so stolid before the beard!" and then Q gives the whores to Worf, who looks startled when they start caressing him! A tremendously funny scene!

5) Corbin Bernsen was great as the other Q too.

6) When Q gets his powers back, it's very dramatic, with feeling.

"I'm immortal again!! Omnipotent again!!!"

What doesn't work:

1) There's a subplot about the need to shift the orbit of a moon. Geordi says they could do it if they had 47% more power--why can't they find a second ship to help?

2) Why is Dr. Crusher caring for Data when he is damaged? He's a machine, not a person.

3) They gave Q a tight grey outfit with his penis sticking out! And he looks like he's wearing a tight girdle around his waist!

4) How did the Calamarain know that Q was mortal, and where to find him? Never explained.

5) The red and blue jars of liquid in Sickbay continue to look dumb.

6) The idea of Q becoming sensitive and sacrificing himself seems out of character, even given the situation. The idea that Q sacrificing himself would redeem himself to the other Q, who are not the self-sacrificing type, also seems unlikely. But who cares about minor plot holes in an otherwise amusing episode?

How it could have been better:

This was a great episode. The humor really worked, and the pacing was good.

A Matter of Perspective

The plot:

Riker is accused of killing a scientist. The holodeck is used to recreate the crime from several different perspectives.

What works:

1) I like how Picard stood up for Riker, and didn't agree to extradite him for trial even under heavy pressure from the local putty faces. For once Picard showed some backbone!

2) It was funny watching Riker's version of story, where the putty head girl tries to rape him and Riker gallantly refuses to have sex with her.

3) But I also liked the wife's version of story--We see Riker acting like a predator, locking the door and making the moves on putty faced girl, pulling off her clothes. It's funny because we know Riker would never have the balls to do that.

4) I love Deanna's new outfit. With her new dress with its enormous cleavage, every time Deanna exhales, it is quite an event.

What doesn't work:

1) Riker such a pacifist, that when the scientist punches him, he simply ducks out of the way.

2) Riker is accused of phasering the scientist during beamout. Couldn't they check Riker's phaser to see if it had been fired? When he returned to the Enterprise, his phaser wasn't even in his hand; if he had fired as he beamed out, wouldn't have been? These important plot holes are never addressed.

3) Wesley has so much hair spray that his hair stands straight up. Looks weird on a child.

4) Why can't Deanna tell that the wife is lying? Never explained.

How it could have been better:

1) The idea of the story is interesting--replaying the events from different perspective. But the story is a little too repetitious--four points of view. And it dragged in parts. It would have been more interesting if the POVS had differed even more. Maybe the wife's perspective could show Riker talking down to the scientist, making fun of him, things which would be funny because we

know Riker would never talk like that. Show more of Riker romancing the putty wife, from her POV, having him say corny love lines. They have a love and murder story, but it has no life because there are no interesting lines or funny conflict with the scientist or his wife, because Riker is so stiff.

Yesterday's Enterprise

The plot:

The Enterprise encounters another Enterprise from the past which shifts the timeline and puts the Federation in a losing war with the Klingons.

What works:

1) The idea of time travel affecting history.

2) Some great lines:

Guinan: "Tasha, you're not supposed to be here."

Tasha: "Where am I supposed to be?

Guinan: "Dead."

Picard: "Let's make sure history never forgets the name... Enterprise."

What doesn't work:

1) I was very confused with this episode when I first saw it. It involves not just time travel but changing the *current* timeline that affects our main characters. When I saw Picard and the Enterprise change, I thought they were not "our" Enterprise but an Enterprise from a different dimension. It was not explained clearly from the beginning. Usually in a time travel story one constant is that the characters experiencing time travel are unchanged, so you can figure out from that what has changed. When the main characters change without prior explanation, it is hard to figure out what is going on--for a while I thought it was a story about a parallel dimension.

2) Tasha returns! But she has an even more man-like haircut.

3) The Enterprise "C" had a girl captain! Now, that's hardly realistic, is it? (Ha, ha, just joking!)

4) Both the girl Captain of Enterprise C and Riker are killed by exploding rocks on the bridge. What are exploding rocks doing on the bridge?

5) They tried to militarize the Starfleet uniforms but were too cheap to make new ones, so all they did was accessorize and add belts and shoulder straps to the standard jumpsuits. The belts and shoulder straps seem to serve no purpose and so look silly.

6) In the new Enterprise, the bridge is dark, how can they see anything?

7) At first the crew of the Enterprise C doesn't want to go back to the past, because they were in a hopeless battle. Then, because the plot demanded it, later they do. Their sudden change of mind makes absolutely no sense.

8) Similarly, Tasha's wish to die on the Enterprise C makes no sense. It makes sense to try to give her a dramatic ending, but it must be in character. Senselessly volunteering to die on the Enterprise C makes no sense.

9) Tasha has a romance with the Spanish man, but it's not believable; she looks hardcore gay in this episode with her really extreme lesbian hairdo. She has so much gel in her short hair she looks like a serial rapist of other women.

10) The Spanish guy, Castillo, is played by a guy who looks completely white. What's up with that?

11) The main point of the story is that the Enterprise C goes back in time to fight the Romulans and impresses the Klingons. But if the Enterprise C loses the battle, how will the Klingons even know they fought for them? This is never explained.

12) The Klingon battle cruisers are actually birds of preys that move more slowly and have different sound effects for their weapons

13) I like how Picard jumps over the railing at the end.

How it could have been better:

Time travel and changing the timeline is always interesting, but it is just not done well here. The "C" has to go back in time to lose a battle, to get Klingon sympathy? It makes no sense. What if the "C" had to go back in time to WIN a battle, and prevent the Klingons or Romulans from winning a war 30 years ago? That would be more believable and make more sense. Then if Tasha left the ship to save the timeline and win the battle that would make more sense as well.

The Offspring

The plot:

Data makes an android named Lal. She tools around the ship for a while until the evil right wing admiral upsets her and she self destructs.

What works:

1) There's a great scene where Lal, who is still in basic robot form, has to choose her gender. She looks at a hologram of a woman with small breasts and says:

"Gender Female"

"That's right, just like me," said Troi, in her classic green dress showing her huge overflowing breasts.

Lal "I choose your sex and appearance." Hysterical! She loves Troi's breasts!

2) Another great quote from the evil right wing admiral: "She is capable of 60 trillion calculations a second, and you have her working as a cocktail waitress."

What doesn't work:

1) Why are there so many evil right wing admirals in Starfleet? I honestly think there are more villains inside Starfleet than outside.

2) Most of the episode is spent showing Data teaching Lal basic things, like she's a real child. Guess what? That's really boring to watch.

3) If Data had downloaded his brain into Lal, why did she start out so ignorant?

4) The evil right wing admiral wants to take Lal away, and keep Data away from her, for good measure. This is meant to create conflict, but there is no justifiable reason for keeping Data away and every reason to keep Data with her, so the evil right wing admiral's decision sounds contrived, and makes the plot not credible.

5) I still don't understand why Data can't use contractions.

How it could have been better:

Let Data create an offspring, but make her fully aware and functional from the start. Give her a different personality from Data. Have her go on a mission with Data and show the two of them working together on a mission, both androids, but with subtly different perspectives and abilities. That would be interesting. Watching a robot child grow up is boring. And don't give her short lesbian hair or choose an anorexic actress with no breasts. Make her sexy.

Sins of the Father

The plot:

Worf's brother Kurn pays the ship a visit. He verbally abuses Worf and the crew. Then they go to the Klingon planet so Worf can go on trial.

What works:

1) The first third of this episode is great. In Kurn we get a Klingon with a great personality--aggressive but with a great sense of humor! Some samples:

"I find the constraints on this ship difficult to conform to. Just a short while ago I had to stop myself from killing Commander Riker."

"This entire ship seems built on comfort, relaxation."

"How long has this bird been dead? It has been lying in the sun for some time. I shall try some of your burned replicated bird meat."

Kurn taunts Worf, standing next to him and staring him down and basically calling him a retard, causing Worf to yell "I am a Klingon! If you doubt it, a demonstration can be arranged!"

2) I liked how Worf unexpectedly smacked Durass in the face at the end.

What doesn't work:

1) The second part of this episode, the whole discommodation thing regarding Worf's dad, is boring. The Klingon sets are all dark and hard to see. The database analysis of the Khittomer massacre is boring.

2) Why would the Klingon High Council tolerate a traitor's family on the council, no matter how powerful they were?

3) An old Klingon lady saves Picard in knife fight. Pathetic.

4) Discommodation is a dumb word. Reminds me of commode.

How it could have been better:

Trials in general are not well done on Star Trek. Let's try something simpler: Worf learns that the Durass family killed his father. Kurn gets Worf to go back with him to get vengeance. They plow through the Durass family to kill Durass. That would be exciting.

Allegiance

The plot:

Picard gets transported to a jail cell with three other aliens, while an imposter takes his place. Picard realizes that they are being studied to see how they respond to authority.

What works:

1) There's a great scene where a monolith appears above Picard's bed and it makes a copy of him like he is in a copy machine.

2) The prison plot is great--Picard is transported to a cell for reasons unknown. For once, the characters are rich and diverse. There is the aggressive monster man, the cowardly powder face, and the kind of whiny fish girl. And there is great character conflict:

Powder face: "We are a race of thinkers!"

Monster face: "A race of cowards!"

3) Great dramatic tension is created when we learn that Monster face cannot eat the jello food provided to them, and that Monster man has a sharp knife he can use on the others.

4) I like at the end when Picard complains about being kidnapped, the aliens respond:

"This concept of morality is a very interesting human characteristic. We shall have to study it some time."

5) Another great scene at the end when Crusher, thinking Picard is attracted to her because of their date, comes onto the bridge and gives Picard a "I'm ready to be fucked" look, and Picard, recognizing the look but not the reason behind it, appears startled.

What doesn't work:

1) The Picard imposter is in command of the Enterprise, but he doesn't do very much. He sings. Boring. He has a date with Crusher, but just as things get interesting, boots her out of his quarters. Until the end, when he essentially orders the ship to destroy itself, he doesn't do very much at all. It doesn't feel like the writers had any idea what to do with this plotline.

2) Both Picard and Crusher wear very weird dating outfits. Picard's looks like a wimpy bathrobe. and Beverly wears a weird dress with hanging folds that hides her breasts. She actually looks much sexier in uniform.

How it could have been better:

1) The prison plotline was actually fine. It was the Enterprise imposter plotline that needed work. Have the imposter Picard give more questionable orders.

A) Have him order Wesley to scrub the warp nacelles with a toothbrush.

B) Order Data to take himself apart and put himself back together again.

C) Ask Geordi to work without a visor for a day just as an experiment.

D) Fuck Beverly's brains out, then toss her out naked into the corridor, then drag her back in and fuck her again.

E) Fuck Troi's brains out, then toss her out naked into the corridor, then drag her back in and fuck her again.

F) Order Worf to play one of his violent holoprograms and order him to purposely lose and let the monsters beat him.

That would be a lot more interesting then the very timid actions the imposter Picard took.

Captain's Holiday

The plot:

Picard goes to Risa for a vacation, but ends up going on a hunt for treasure with a girl named Vash, who he bones.

What works:

1) The minute Picard beams down to Risa, the first thing we are treated to is a scene of a woman walking by who is not wearing any pants.

2) I liked how Riker fooled Picard into buying a Horgon, a "I want sex now" symbol, and all these women come up to Picard thinking he wants sex.

3) I like how the time travel aliens have time travel buttons built into their heads. That's very convenient.

4) Vash wears a very revealing bathing suit, but covers it up with a shirt. That sort of works.

5) The idea of Risa, a sex planet, is very interesting, but needs more explanation--all the women offering sex to Picard, are they hotel employees, paid by the hour, or simply locals or visitors who can't get enough of it?

What doesn't work:

1) Time travelers from the future want the treasure, the tax u tat, which is some kind of weapon. When Picard finds it and destroys it they note that this is what history records. If so, why did they bother coming back for it? If they can travel to any point in time, why not travel to five minutes earlier and recover it themselves? None of this is ever explained.

2) Vash looks good in a bathing suit but is a terrible actress, she does way too much overacting. She has excessive facial expressions and acts like she's still auditioning for the role. She's also irritating.

3) The idea of the plot was good but the execution was boring. They go and dig for the tax u tat and find nothing. Everything is resolved in one minute at the end of the episode. There isn't much of a climax.

4) Vash hid the tax u tat in a horgon in the lobby? What if someone had taken the horgon with the tax u tat in it?

How it could have been better:

The idea of the story was good--a treasure hunt. Vash and Picard and Rom (yes, the Ferengi in this episode is Rom), should have gone off together to hunt for it, and had adventures. They should have gotten stuck in traps. They should have been captured by savages and had to escape. They should have had to argue with each other and fear that each one was holding things back and would try to steal from the others. In other words, they should have played off each other's personalities.

They did that, a little, in this episode, but it could have been much more. Imagine Picard ridiculing the Ferengi's greed, and Rom making fun of Picard's mock Federation nobleness. It could have been a really fun episode, instead we got a sterile romance between Picard and the unlikeable Vash.

Tin Man

The plot:

An oversensitive telepath feels a connection to a living spaceship that looks like a flying loaf of bread.

What works:

1) Not much.

What doesn't work:

1) Most of the episode features Sensitive Boy discussing his sensitive thoughts for the flying loaf of bread. It's boring.

2) When the Romulans fire on the Enterprise, the Enterprise does not fire back, as usual.

How it could have been better:

1) Instead of making the flying loaf of bread a harmless life form, make it another doomsday device. Force Picard to work with the Romulans to figure out how to destroy it. Have Sensitive Boy link to the flying loaf of bread to figure out its weakness and how to destroy it. Have the flying loaf of bread take control of Sensitive Boy and have him try to sabotage the ship. That would be much more dramatic than watching Sensitive Boy moan about the flying loaf of bread for 40 minutes.

Hollow Pursuits

The plot:

The nerd Barclay has holodeck fantasies involving other members of the crew.

What works:

1) The opening scene, where Barclay beats up Riker, and Troi becomes sexually attracted to him, is very amusing!

What doesn't work:

1) If this is a holodeck fantasy, why is Troi in a dress with no cleavage?

2) Barclay has a weird comb over; being bald he has a bunch of hair he has grown really long and combed forward. It looks very odd.

3) Barclay can't stand the demands of being a crewman on the Enterprise and yet Picard and Geordi coddle him. Not realistic.

4) Once again, Wesley's pants are open in the back..

How it could have been better:

This is supposed to be comedy, but except for the first scene where Barclay beats up Riker and seduces Troi, the rest is boring. Troi in a sheet calling herself the goddess of empathy, Wesley on a swing, Picard, Geordi, and Data as the three musketeers... it's just not that funny.

What would have been more funny is if the holodeck fantasy had taken place on the Enterprise, with the crew looking as they really are, and Barclay having to solve a "mission" (really, a holonovel), where he is in charge and the rest of the crew are bumbling idiots. That's why the first scene was so effective, it worked as parody because it was so close to reality. Imagine if there were a typical Star Trek episode where they had to stop the warp drive from exploding. Geordi could act retarded and Barclay could save the day. Or imagine if Barclay has to work with Troi to make contact with an alien race and Barclay casually seduces Troi. In the holodeck, these things are possible.

Then you could have someone like Geordi secretly enter his holonovel, and, pretending to be the holographic version of Geordi, observe what's happening. That would be entertaining.

The Most Toys

The plot:

Data gets captured by an art collector, Kevas Fajo, who wants to add him to his collection.

What works:

1) Kevas Fajo is a GREAT character--charming, witty, greedy--a fully developed personality, very rare in a Star Trek adversary. He has a lot of great lines.

"Data, you belong in Starfleet about as much as I belong in a verbal contract."

"You may not know it, but you are going to sit on the chair!" And he does! He trains Data like a dog.

2) The Veron T Disrupter, the slow killing phaser, is very exciting.

3) I like how Fajo burns off Data's uniform to give Data the "choice" of changing his clothes or being nude.

What doesn't work:

1) Why didn't Data destroy Fajo's artwork, knowing it would upset him greatly?

2) Why does Data keep a Tasha hologram? Does he masturbate to it?

3) Fajo purposely throws away his gun after he has killed his putty face assistant. He is so confident Data will not pick it up and use it. It is unrealistic to expect he would take that chance, or allow himself to be unarmed around his subordinates. It also strains credulity that he would store his weapons in the same room in which Data is kept, even with a combination lock. These are big problems with the storyline.

4) The scene showing the crew coping with Data's loss is boring. More interesting would be auditions to consider who could take Data's post.

5) At the end of the episode, Data lies about firing the weapon. Data cannot lie.

How it could have been better:

It was a great episode. A little less moaning about missing Data on the Enterprise and it would have been perfect.

Sarek

The plot:

Sarek comes aboard for some negotiations. But he has the "emotions disease". He has to transfer his shit emotions to Picard so he can be sane for a while.

What works:

1) Not much.

What doesn't work:

1) Most of the episode features the slow, slow discovery that Sarek has the emotions disease. It is obvious from the start but takes a long time to fully discover and confront Sarek with. Boring.

How it could have been better:

Here was an opportunity to have a tremendous guest star from the original series and what did they do? Turn him into a retard. I would have jettisoned this plotline entirely and show Sarek at his peak negotiating a complex deal with an alien race. You notice how in all these "negotiating" episodes they don't actually *show* negotiations? Why not for once do that? Show Sarek negotiating with a hostile, aggressive race and show Sarek using logic to put them in their place and getting concessions and forcing them to a just agreement. That would make a satisfying episode. Also, if he is going to replace his wife with a young woman, she should be 22 and wear a tight jumpsuit. That would be the most logical thing to do.

Menage a Troi

The plot:

Riker, Troi, and Mrs. Troi gets kidnapped by a Ferengi who wants to use Mrs. Troi's telepathic skills.

What works:

1) The scene where the Ferengi beam Troi out of her clothes.

What doesn't work:

1) Once again, the back of Wesley's pants are wide open to ass rape. But finally, finally Wesley gets a real Starfleet uniform, so this is the last episode to feature his ass rape outfit.

How it could have been better:

Most of this episode features Mrs. Troi trying to manipulate her Ferengi captor, whose IQ suddenly goes down 40 points after he captures Troi. It is a juvenile plot which is both boring and unconvincing. It is supposed to be humorous but it is not.

Why not have the story actually be about what it is ostensibly about? Show Mrs. Troi being forced to use her telepathy to help the Ferengi. Show the Fergeni becoming rich and powerful because of it. Troi escapes and tries to rescue her mother, but tragically a Nausican from a rival gang gets to her first, and at the end they have a touching holofuneral for Mrs. Troi, where the holorecording of Mrs. Troi says she is sure she died in the line of duty and knows the name of every person at her funeral, like Tasha did.

Transfigurations

The plot:

A friendly alien in a white leotard makes everyone feel good. Then he turns into a ball of energy.

What works:

1) There's a funny scene where Geordi lusts after a normal white girl who rejects him. Realistic! Why can't Geordi pursue handicapped women who might be less picky?

2) But later, white leotard man gives Geordi a sex drive, and he bones a white girl. Good work, Geordi!

What doesn't work:

1) Most of the story is about the white leotard guy's slow recovery and his a friendship with Dr. Crusher. Awwww. Boring. I think they were trying to go for a romance but the writers were afraid to go there.

2) His white leotard is so tight that his penis sticks out. There is one scene on the bridge where Crusher's breasts stick out and white jumpsuit guy's penis sticks out and you have to wonder if looking at one caused the other.

3) At the end, white leotard man turns into a glowing energy ball who wishes goodness on everyone. Awwww. Boring.

4) When they encounter the cardboard villain of the episode, he gives the Enterprise two hours to turn over white leotard guy to him. Two hours???

How it could have been better:

1) This episode acts like a G-rated show where they can't even intimate relationships which is why leotard's "Friend romance" with Crusher is so pathetic. Otherwise they could have had white leotard man bone Dr. Crusher and have, you know, a relationship with her. I think Beverly is frigid although in later seasons she does do it with a worm and a gas cloud so maybe she loosens up a little in time.

2) Why not have some of white leotard's man energy go into each member of the crew and affect them differently? Show Geordi working his way through all the girls in 10 Forward. Show Picard

growing hair. Show Worf becoming gentle and friendly. Gradually have the entire crew become sensitive, but also very weak and unable to perform their duties. Only have Data unaffected, and have him figure out a way to boot white leotard guy off the ship.

The Best of Both Worlds Part I

The plot:

The Borg return. A blonde with big boobs wants Riker's job. Picard gets captured by the Borg and is fitted with a number of custom appliances, including a red flashlight.

What works:

1) The battle scene with the Borg was good.

2) It was a very, very interesting twist to see Picard captured and turned into a Borg appliance. I especially liked his red flashlight. And then he changed his voice and talked like a robot. Very effective!

"I am Locutus of Borg. Resistance is futile. You will service us."

When he talks about servicing, you can see the horrified look in Crusher's eyes. I think she picks up something sexual about it.

3) Even the slow first half of this episode sort of works. Shelby (the blonde babe with the big boobs) is a bitchy social climber, but her tension with Riker, who she is trying to get rid of, works, dramatically speaking.

4) The episode ends dramatically where the Enterprise tries to blow up the Borg ship.

What doesn't work:

1) Why did the Borg steal people from a colony but also their colony buildings? What would the Borg want with buildings?

2) Riker turns down yet another command, this time of a big starship. Simply not realistic.

Riker even says at one point, "What am I still doing here?" I don't know either.

3) With the shields down, why do the Borg cut into engineering when all they want is Picard?

4) At one point Geordi says he lost a lot of people in Engineering, and there is heavy damage. Later, we see no sign of *any* damage to the engineering set.

How it could have been better:

It was pretty good as it was.

The Best of Both Worlds Part II

The plot:

Riker rescues Picard from the Borg. Picard tells the Borg to go to sleep. We all do.

What works:

1) Some great lines:

"Your resistance is hopeless, Numba Won."

"Take your best shot, Locutus, because we are about to intervene."

2) The shuttles have transporters? Who knew! Very unexpected twist!

3) I like the rescue plan. It's complex, I didn't see it coming. Data and Worf take a shuttle inside the Borg shield and beam in.

What doesn't work:

1) After Picard is rescued and returned to the Enterprise, the Borg simply go away. Why does the Borg simply not destroy the Enterprise or at least try to recapture Locutus? This is a big plot hole.

2) The fact that we did not get to see any of the battle of Wolf 359 was a big disappointment.

3) Worf and Data stand under the shuttle transporter but they are both too big to fit under it! Does it transport everything but Data's left arm and Worf's right arm?

4) The ending was a big disappointment. Sleeeeeep. Then the Borg ship obligingly self destructs without a shot being fired. Press the reset button.

How it could have been better:

Rather than rescue Picard initially, the Enterprise should have beamed sabotage teams aboard the Borg ship to try to reach a central destination to plant a bomb to destroy it. Picard as Locutus should have tracked the progress of these teams and it should have been a contest of strategies between Locutus and Riker. Maybe have Riker get captured and have the two watch the progress of the sabotage teams. Make it seem like Locutus is winning but then have Riker pull a trick that enables one last sabotage team to get to their destination, blow up the ship, first giving Riker a chance to beam out with Locutus. Show more interaction between Locutus and Riker for drama. That would have been compelling.

Family

The plot:

Picard goes home for vacation and wrestles with his brother in the mud. Worf has a pointless encounter with his parents. Wesley gets a pointless holomessage from his dead dad.

What works:

It's great to have an episode which follows up on the events of a previous episode. Just not this one.

What doesn't work:

1) Picard wears very low class looking saggy peasant clothes. Picard's civilian clothing always features these shirts with plunging necklines showing his flat hairy chest. Very odd.

2) Picard's French family all have British accents. Did Britain conquer France after the eugenics wars?

3) The climax of this episode was Picard crying in the mud about how the Borg raped him. Sorry, that's not enough of a payoff.

How it could have been better:

Have more meaningful and more dramatic family interactions.

Have Beverly take Wesley to a family reunion where the other kids pick on Wesley because he is a know-it-all. Or have the holomessage from Wesley's Dad where he reveals he is not really Wesley's Dad but maybe Captain Picard is, and Wesley has to confront Picard about it.

Have Worf help an old friend out who is being attacked by bullies and have Worf beat them up.

Instead of making Picard's brother a dumb grape guy, have him be an intellectual snob, a professor who ridicules Picard's career in Starfleet, and have the two compete for intellectual superiority. That would have been more interesting than watching Picard's brother bully the helpless Picard for 40 minutes.

Brothers

The plot:

Data, under remote control, hijacks the Enterprise, then meets Dr. Soong, his creator, and Lore, his brother. Lore kills Dr. Soong. Press the reset button and all is as it was.

What works:

1) The first 15 minutes of this episode, where Data takes command of the ship, is great. It's exciting watching him imitate Picard's voice and enter this incredibly long password. It's great watching them duel for control of the ship with Data, and Data using the ship's technology to make an escape route for himself. Very innovative and exciting.

What doesn't work:

1) Once Data beams down to the planet, we are stuck in sleepyland. Data has a long, boring conversation with Dr. Soong about the nature of artists and parents and why they feel the need to create and why old things are important and why did Data join Starfleet? Boring.

2) The monster makeup they put on Dr. Soong to make him look old is ridiculous.

3) Why is a white man playing the part of a guy named Dr. Soong?

4) There is a very, very annoying "B" story about two bratty kids who whine and hate each other. It's quite unwatchable.

5) The scenes with Lore are equally boring--Lore whines that he doesn't feel love.

6) When Worf and Riker confront Data on the ship, they each give Data plenty of time to issue verbal commands to the ship's computer instead of shooting him.

7) Soong dies without consequence, Data doesn't get his emotions chip, Lore gets away again, and nothing changes. Press the reset button.

How it could have been better:

1) Get rid of the very annoying subplot with the little boys.

2) Get rid of the long, philosophical discussion with Dr. Soong.

3) Idea #1: Have Dr. Soong modify Data in a way to make him more human (like an emotion chip) but have it backfire and they have to figure out a way to reset him.

4) Idea #2: Have Soong announce that he wants to mass produce androids based on real people and makes Data help him kidnap the crew and make copies of them, only some of the android copies are sympathetic and help Picard & Co. escape.

It's ok for Data to have some philosophical talks with Dr. Soong. But when it becomes the entire episode, I fall asleep. It has to be pared with some kind of action or event.

Suddenly Human

The plot:

The Enterprise encounters a human boy kidnapped by aliens who raised him as one of their own, abusing him and beating him up. Picard naturally returns the boy to his abusive alien "father".

What works:

1) I like it when the boy stabbed Captain Picard and Picard didn't angry about it. What a wimp. I think Picard actually enjoys it.

What doesn't work:

This was a terrible, terrible episode. Returning a boy to aliens who killed his parents? Returning a boy to abusive parents who beat him? All in the name of respecting other cultures? I hated this episode.

How it could have been better:

If instead of returning the boy to the abusive aliens, Picard gave himself over instead, so he could endure a life of beatings in the boy's place.

Remember Me

The plot:

Dr. Crusher is trapped in an alternate reality where everyone starts to disappear and the universe gets smaller and smaller.

What works:

1) It's great how when someone disappears there is continuity in that everyone else immediately forgets about the disappeared person. Finally when the entire ship is empty except Crusher and Picard and she asks him if he really believes the Enterprise is only a two person ship, Picard shrugs and smiles and says, "Well, we've never needed anyone else!"

2) This story unfolded very well. At first I thought the people disappearing were being zapped into an alternate universe, or maybe it was Wesley's alternate reality and Crusher was just sharing it. It took time for me to realize that it was Crusher herself was in the alternate reality. Very well done!

3) I liked watching Dr. Crusher slowly get hysterics when everyone disappears. She's not a very good actress but here she does a reasonably good job.

4) I liked watching the universe disappear around Crusher when it started breaking up the Enterprise. Very imaginative!

What doesn't work:

Everything worked.

How it could have been better:

Great episode.

Legacy

The plot:
The Enterprise returns to Tasha Yar's planet to rescue some kidnapped crewmembers. They are helped by Tasha's sister Ishara who has her own agenda involving warfare between rival gangs.

What works:

Not much.

What doesn't work:

1) The big payoff of this episode is supposed to be that Data, who trusted Ishara because she was Tasha's sister, "felt" betrayed by Ishara's betrayal. But it didn't really have much of an emotional impact. Ishara hadn't built up a long history of trust with the Enterprise so it wasn't much of a surprise.

2) It is totally unbelievable that Ishara would not leave the planet with Tasha. Sorry, not credible.

3) Where are the rape gangs? Every 12 second Tasha would talk about the rape gangs. There wasn't one in sight the entire episode.

4) Data told Ishara, "Tasha and I spent much time together." Not true. They had sex once under the influence of a drug, Tasha disavowed it afterwards, and they were never in the same room together alone after that.

5) The idea of everyone letting the government put warning implants in their body is unbelievable.

How it could have been better:

1) If Ishara stayed on the planet because she was a *member* of one of the rape gangs--a lesbian rape gang. Then she enlists Counselor Troi on her mission to rescue the hostages and instead takes her hostage.

2) A better plot--Riker and Data go down to rescue the hostages, dressed in disguise like locals. Make an Escape from New York type story where they have to navigate different gang territories to find the hostages and get them to a safe beam out point.

Reunion

The plot:

Picard is given the power to choose the next Klingon leader. One of them, Durass, kills Worf's girlfriend so he kills Durass. Worf discovers he has a mini-me. The end.

What works:

1) I like that Worf takes matters into his own hands and kills Durass. It's compelling because it comes right after Durass killed his squeeze!

2) I like Gowron's big, rolling, eyes, they make him look crazy.

3) I liked the "painstick the dead leader to be sure he is dead" ritual. Innovative!

4) I like it when Worf ships his mini me off to the Russians.

What doesn't work:

1) This story totally does not work because there is no way a Klingon leader would choose a human to pick their next leader. There is also no way any Klingon would accept a human in this role. This plot is totally, 100%, unbelievable.

2) Worf discovers he has a mini-me. Klar was a real bitch for not telling Worf she birthed a bastard. I don't see any purpose in giving Worf a three year old child.

3) Durass killed Klar when he discovered she was trying to find out about his family's role in the Khittimer massacre. Since the real story is common knowledge on the high council, Durass had no compelling reason to kill Klar, and that part was very contrived.

4) One of Durass's men detonated a bomb in his arm. Why would Durass have arm bomb guy detonate next to him?

5) After Durass is killed, Durass's ship meekly leaves without saying a word or doing anything hostile.

6) Where is the Klingon High Council in all this? Oh, I forget, they are unnecessary because we have Captain Picard there to decide the fate of the Klingon Empire. Weak.

How it could have been better:

As I've said, the political story is totally unbelievable. If there is a fight for succession, let the Klingon factions fight among themselves, and let Picard try to influence the factions, perhaps with information about Durass's family. But don't let Picard be the one to pick the next Klingon leader, that's too ridiculous.

Have more than two contenders; have four. Show the politics and personalities of four distinct families and contenders. Make this a two part episode and show Picard getting involved with the politics of the situation and figuring out which House would be best for the Federation, making alliances and being betrayed. A politics story could be a great episode or two, if we are introduced the personalities involved.

But making this a two Klingon story--Durass and Gowron--and having them stand in front of Picard to decide things makes it feel like there are only two Klingons in the entire Empire.

Future Imperfect

The plot:

Riker gets trapped in a holodeck fantasy where he is Captain of the Enterprise.

What works:

1) This was great because I could not figure out in advance what was going on. A drama is effective if you can't predict the ending. For a while I did think it was a Romulan plot, but there was another level to the story beneath that. Well done!

2) Geordi has eyes and looks like a normal black man!

3) Data always looks better in a red uniform.

What doesn't work:

1) This holodeck fantasy is supposed to be based on a machine reading Riker's mind and giving him what he really desires. Does Riker want peace with the Romulans, who he doesn't seem to trust? That's a plot hole. Also, why would he want to live in a future where his wife is dead, when he can have a live one--like Counselor Troi? Another plot hole.

2) Riker's "son", "Jean Luc", has greased back hair which looks odd on a child, and he wears a tight jumpsuit which makes him look like a child gigolo.

3) Troi's breasts look a lot smaller in a Starfleet uniform--again, how can this be Riker's fantasy?

4) Riker's phony relationship with his phony son is boring.

5) The Romulan espionage story was a lot more interesting than the lonely ET story.

How it could have been better:

As I said, I enjoyed the fact that the story had two levels to it, the Romulan deception, then the alien boy deception. I just didn't like the alien lonely boy part, it felt like a disappointment. Once again we have a story with no true antagonist. Maybe if the alien boy had bad motives, maybe if he fed off of Riker's mental energy, and Riker had to realize this and find a way to escape, the ending could have been more dramatic.

Final Mission

The plot:

Wesley, Picard, and a very bald Alan Carter from Space 1999 crash land on a hot desert planet. The only water is guarded by a force field. Wesley has to use his tricorder in a certain way to get the water. The end.

What works:

1) Wesley leaves the series.

2) Dr. Crusher suddenly has much larger breasts (the actress is pregnant).

What doesn't work:

1) Picard says something so obvious it's stupid:

Picard: "Try breathing through your nose."

2) After the crash, they make an arrow showing rescuers which way they've gone, but then start walking in a different direction.

3) Wesley wears an arab head dress. Wesley of Arabia?

4) The Enterprise is delayed hauling space garbage and cannot rescue them. But why can't Riker send a shuttle to assist in the search?

5) Most of the story features Picard wounded in a Star Trek cave and Wesley worrying about him. That's boring. An emotional story can be interesting, but only if it changes characters or reveals things we didn't know. If Picard revealed he was Wesley's father, or that he had killed Wesley's father, and we could see Wesley's reaction, that would be something. But there were no dramatic revelations.

6) The B story involved the Enterprise towing a radioactive ship. The crew was being exposed to radiation. Riker forgets that the ship can separate into two sections and that most of the crew can be evacuated, instead choosing to expose everyone to radiation.

7) At one point the ship's computer says, "Lethal exposure in 10 seconds". But they beat their deadline by at least 5 seconds, so everyone is totally unharmed. Ridiculous.

How it could have been better:

If you want to make a Wesley/Picard story, make one where we find out something new about the characters that changes the storyline. As mentioned above, what if Picard had killed Wesley's father, or allowed him to die, or something that would change Wesley's view of him? Or what if Picard talks about his love for Beverly? Something of substance! Instead, we got nothing.

The Loss

The plot:

The Enterprise is being dragged into danger by two dimensional bugs. Counselor Troi loses her "I sense something" abilities.

What works:

1) I like how Picard tried to photon torpedo the 2d aliens! He had no respect for alien bugs! Very rare to see something like that from him.

What doesn't work:

1) The central point of this episode was to show how Troi coped without her "I sense something" abilities. The answer is: poorly. She acts like a real bitch. It's not pleasant to watch. (Excepts when she snaps at Beverly!)

2) In the end, they talk a lot of technobabble to solve another natural disaster episode. Boring.

How it could have been better:

Instead of losing an ability, what if Troi gained one, temporarily? What if "space bugs" somehow gave her the ability to be a full telepath, like her mother, and she gained this ability during a tense and dangerous negotiations at a multi-species peace conference? She could be invaluable to Picard. Her ability could come and go unreliably and she could make mistakes. It could be a great storyline.

Data's Day

The plot:

Chief O'Brien becomes Keiko's slave for life.

What works:

1) Data's dancing lesson.

2) When Data's cat refuses to eat and Data observes:

"Perhaps hunger will compel you to change your mind."

What doesn't work:

1) This episode is an example of very laaaazy writing. There's no real plot, just a bunch of stuff mishmashed together. It feels like the writer fell asleep and woke up right before his deadline and just wrote anything to hand in to the producers.

2) Keiko calls off her wedding to O'Brien--no explanation. Then she decides to put it back on-- no explanation. Why should we care if we don't know what is going on?

3) We have seen O'Brien many times before. We have never seen Keiko before. Why should we care about her?

4) Keiko has chopsticks in her hair--does she eat with them?

5) The dancing lesson with Crusher was nice, but they choose to use a blurry lens which ruined some of it.

6) Dr. Crusher has radical hair changes in this episode, using several different wigs.

7) As Data writes a letter about the day's events, there is a very annoying violin cue playing in the background that is supposed to be cute, but is very annoying.

How it could have been better:

How about having a real story? Is that too much to ask?

Make Keiko a suction cup monster disguised as a Japanese woman, who feeds on transporter chiefs. Have Data investigate and find out just in time to save Chief O'Brien.

The Wounded

The plot:

An evil right wing Federation Captain is attacking Cardassian ships, and Picard has to stop him.

What works:

Not much.

What doesn't work:

1) In their first outing, Cardassians have mushy wrinkley makeup and have weird bars over their faces.

2) At first O'Brien seems to hate Cardassians, but then we find out he hates himself. That's the theme of this episode--no matter how nasty the aliens are, your side is worse. I hate this theme.

3) Picard betrays the right wing captain, giving the command codes for his ship (the Phoenix) to the Cardassians. They order the right Phoenix to lower its shields, and then attack, causing deaths on his ship. Yet right wing captain never seems to connect the dots and realize Picard was responsible for this. Nor does Picard get blamed for all the deaths this must have caused on the Phoenix.

4) We observe the battle between the Phoenix and the Cardassian ships as dots on a screen. Boring.

5) A Cardassian calls Canar K-nar!

6) It was unpleasant watching O'Brien telling the Cardassians how guilty he feels about the war.

7) O'Brien went from being tactical officer on one ship... to being a transporter operator on the Enterprise. Why would he accept a demotion?

8) The climax of the episode features O'Brien singing an Irish song with the evil right wing captain before he surrenders. It's a dreadful ending.

9) At the end Picard realizes the right wing Captain was right, that the Cardassians were getting ready for war, but the right wing Captain is still being treated like a criminal. I hate the pacifism theme of this episode.

How it could have been better:

If for once the Federation wasn't so pacifist and willing to avoid war at any cost. What if Picard agreed to go into Cardassian space and see the situation firsthand, and then, realizing the Cardassians were getting ready for war, the Enterprise and the Phoenix, together, had to fight their way back to Federation space? Now that would be a compelling story!

Clues

The plot:

The entire crew is rendered unconscious, except Data, and they have to figure out what happened.

What works:

1) This is a great mystery episode. I could not figure it out in advance. Very well written.

2) There is great dramatic tension when we realize that Data is lying about what happened, but doing so because he is trying to protect the ship.

What doesn't work:

1) When the aliens pulled their amnesia trick on the crew, did they expect the time differential (they were told they were asleep for a few seconds, but a day passed) to go unnoticed forever? What would happen the first time they checked the time at a starbase? Why didn't Data simply tell them that they were unconscious for a full day, so the time would match? Never explained.

2) The aliens trusted Data to keep quiet? Not believable.

3) Dr. Crusher has a weird wig--big hair that stands up. Looks very fake, like a wig. Which it is.

4) When the aliens take Troi over, she speaks in a guy's voice. Very odd hearing a woman with big breasts speaking with a guy's voice.

How it could have been better:

It was pretty good as it was.

First Contact

The plot:

Riker gets captured on an alien planet the Federation is about to make first contact with. They realize he's an alien. The aliens get angry and demand the Federation leave.

What works:

1) The scene where the alien nurse demands Riker have sex with her.

Riker: "Now, will you help me?"

"If you make love to me."

"What?"

"I've always wanted to make love to an alien!"

Riker bones her.

What doesn't work:

1) The leader of the alien planet agrees to beam up to the Enterprise alone? Not very likely! That makes the entire episode unbelievable.

2) They use the Angel One matte painting for this planet.

3) There is a very contrived happy ending, where Picard talks about how happy he will be to visit this planet decades later, but his mission is a failure--they are being kicked off the planet and told not to return for a long time. It's very odd.

How it could have been better:

This is an episode about a first contact mission gone wrong. Fine. But it lacks drama, because there are no real antagonists, though they try to make the minister of defense an antagonist, kind of. What if the aliens were hostile, and they captured Riker and tortured him? And what if they lured an away team to the planet with a false Riker distress call and captured and tortured them too? Then Picard and Data would have to be really smart and figure out how to retrieve them. That would be more dramatic, than the "We're all well intentioned adults here. Sorry things didn't work out!" boring story as written.

Galaxy's Child

The plot:

Leah Brahams, the real version of Geordi's holowhore, comes aboard. The Enterprise has to repel a giant space snail, while Leah Brahams has to repel Geordi.

What works:

Not much.

What doesn't work:

1) The romance between Geordi and Leah is very awkward. At first she's a very cold bitch and unpleasant to watch. Then she learns about the holowhore Geordi made in her image, and she gets bitchy about that. Then, inexplicably, as time runs out on the episode, she changes in an instant and all of a sudden likes Geordi and doesn't even mind the holowhore. Her change of attitude is sudden and unconvincing.

2) The Enterprise should have phasered the space snail the minute it threatened the ship. Once again Picard puts the safety of his crew last.

3) We have to endure 30 minutes of technobabble as they try to find a gentle way to get rid of the space snail. Boring.

4) Leah has what looks like a herpes wart on her upper lip. She's not very attractive to begin with.

How it could have been better:

There is so little going for this story. There is no romance. There is no antagonist.

What if a woman came aboard, a real woman, who Geordi could have a real romance with? What if she were black? (Geordi doesn't do black women, as a rule.) What if she had a disability, maybe a banana hair clip over her ears instead of her eyes? That would be an interesting couple.

What if the giant space snail were intelligent and could talk, and tried to drain all the energy from the ship, and Picard had to negotiate with it, and trick it into leaving? What if Picard realized that there was a giant grasshopper that eats giant space snails and he was able to lure one to the Enterprise to get it to attack the giant space snail? That would be more interesting than 30 minutes of technobabble and watching Geordi not having sex with Leah Brahams.

Night Terrors

The plot:

People go crazy on a Federation ship and kill each other, probably because they had a woman captain (ha, ha!). No, they were trapped in space and an alien was not letting them sleep so they went crazy. The same thing is happening to the Enterprise and Troi has to figure it out.

What works:

1) So this is the episode where the crew starts to go crazy. Picard hears a doorbell when no one's there. Chief O'Brien accuses Keiko of sleeping around. Riker imagines there are snakes in his bed. Dr. Crusher sees dead people moving around.

What doesn't work:

1) Troi spends a lot of time talking to a comatose Betazoid, and not learning anything of value. She also spends a lot of time flying around in a green cloud in a cheap looking dream sequence with green screening. Boring.

How it could have been better:

Of course, the aliens robbing them of their sleep and making them crazy have the best of intentions. They always do, because there are no bad guys in Star Trek, except the ones who work at Starfleet.

But what if the aliens had bad intentions and were trying to drive the crew crazy on purpose? And what if the crew really went crazy, more than Picard simply hearing imaginary doorbell chimes. What if Worf became violent? What if Riker became paranoid? What if Geordi became a manic depressive? If everyone suddenly became mentally ill and had to solve this mystery with such handicaps, that would be more impressive. And they wouldn't solve it by having Counselor Troi fly around in a green cloud. They would solve it by locating the hidden alien ship and photon torpedoing it.

Identity Crisis

The plot:

Geordi and some lady start to turn into an invisible glow in the dark leotard monster.

What works:

Not much.

What doesn't work:

This episode is very, very boring. Most of it is spent trying to solve the mystery of the missing Starfleet personnel who are turning into invisible glow in the dark leotard monsters. Geordi watches the same planetary video over and over and over. It's very uninteresting.

How it could have been better:

Talk about invisible. What if an invisible monster was roaming the ship, biting people and turning them into invisible monsters? Data would have to find a way to counter their invisibility, and the remaining crew would have to hunt deck by deck to flush them out, capture them, and make them into visible non-monsters again.

The Nth Degree

The plot:

An alien probe makes Barclay a genius.

What works:

1) Barclay becoming a genius. Doing things no other person can. Solving complex problems requiring enormous computational power and creativity instantly. It's very enjoyable seeing such a capable character doing such amazing things. And I don't even like Barclay! It's rare we see a regular or even semi-regular character get new abilities. It's a great episode in that sense.

2) When Barclay tries to bone Counselor Troi.

What doesn't work:

1) The opening scene where pre-genius Barclay acts in a play. It's very boring. Even Data said it was boring.

2) A probe made Barclay a genius so he would invent a space warp to take the Enterprise to the probe's home planet. Why wasn't the probe engineered to simply do the same thing?

3) The navigator in this episode is a Chinese woman who has very short, gelled hair that gives her a hard look, makes her look like a lesbian dominatrix.

4) When the probe starts chasing the Enterprise, Picard gives up when the probe is still pursuing at Warp 2. Doesn't even try going to Warp 3.

5) Each time we see him Barclay keeps getting more and more hair.

6) After this episode, the Enterprise never again as the ability to instantly warp to other places in the galaxy. Press the reset button.

How it could have been better:

It was pretty good as it was. We could have seen an even better contrast if Barclay wasn't so mild mannered, if in his genius state he looked down on the others for being relatively dumb.

Qpid

The plot:

Q puts Picard and his crew into a Robin Hood fantasy to show Picard that his affection for Vash is not a good thing. Vash was Picard's temporary sperm receptacle from "Captain's Holiday". There is some humor and some fighting.

What works:

1) There's a funny scene where Vash sits in Picard's chair on the bridge, basically announcing to everyone in sight that she had sex with him.

2) Data dressed as bald Friar Tuck is hysterical.

3) Counselor Troi shoots Data in the chest accidently with a bow and arrow but he encourages her, saying her aim is improving. Very funny!

4) I like it when Worf bashes Geordi's guitar against a tree to stop him from playing, and then apologizes for doing so clearly when he isn't unapologetic at all about it.

What doesn't work:

1) Vash is oddly offended that Picard didn't tell his crew about her. They met and had sex once. Why does that make her worthy of mention to Picard's crew?

2) Vash seems to know all about Picard's crew, when she and Picard only spent one night together.

3) Q has even more hair than he did last time, it keeps growing.

4) Q feels he owes a debt to Picard from their last encounter. But Picard did not save Q at their last encounter, the second Q did. That makes Q's reason for being here, and the entire episode, invalid. Q's reasoning is even harder to follow. He tells Picard not to feel affection for Vash, and then puts him in a Robin Hood simulation for some reason that I can't understand. The Robin Hood story and costumes are very cute, but the entire story makes absolutely no sense.

5) When Q offers Picard any gift of his choice, Picard shows no interest in any gift from a super powerful being. It's simply not credible.

6) At the end, Troi and Crusher participate in the fight by breaking pieces of pottery over people's head. It looks weak, like they just wanted to show a scene where the girls were somehow fighting too.

7) Worf says he will not play the fool for Q's amusement, and literally five seconds later he rushes into a swordfight for Q's amusement.

How it could have been better:

It was cute seeing Picard & Co. dressed as Robin Hood and supporting characters. It's just that the plot made no sense. And Vash is an irritating harpy.

Make things simpler. Simple is good, sometimes.

Have Q put Picard & Co. in a Robin Hood story. Force them to rob from the rich and give to the poor, for Q's own amusement. Have the bad guys be played by Romulans or Cardassians. That would be funny enough.

The Drumhead

The plot:

An evil right wing admiral (Admiral Satee) sees conspiracies everywhere, and Picard has to shut her down.

What works:

Not much.

What doesn't work:

1) I am really, really tired of seeing Federation Admirals as the bad guys. That's been done to death. Why can't aliens ever be the bad guys? If so many Federation Admirals are evil, why is the Federation itself not evil?

2) Most of this episode featured a slow interrogation of some guy. Instead of the Drumhead, I call this episode the Dumbhead because of how slow it was.

3) Why is Admiral Satee wearing a nightgown and not a Starfleet uniform? Never explained.

4) The climactic scene showed Picard maneuvering Satee, getting her to yell at him. Once she yelled at him, she was instantly discredited, somehow. I'm not sure why. Not only was the climax anti-climactic, but it wasn't explained clearly.

How it could have been better:

Have Picard uncover an alien conspiracy meant to make Starfleet Admirals look bad. Show how the aliens use mind control to make Admirals do dumb and evil things--like prosecuting innocent people, separating Data from his child, making cloaking devices when they shouldn't be, etc. Have Picard expose the aliens, only to realize that the aliens are really another set of Starfleet Admirals in disguise.

Half a Life

The plot:

Mrs. Troi is attracted to the guy who played Major Winchester from MASH. But Major Winchester has these really ugly glowing veins painted on his head, and is he so old that he is ordered to commit suicide. He comes from a mandatory old age suicide society.

What works:

Nothing.

What doesn't work:

1) How many times must we watch an "alien culture dilemma--will Picard respect a different culture that has different values from his own?" episode. This one is worse than most others.

How it could have been better:

This episode could have been better if it had an unexpected twist, a malfunction causing a photon torpedo to accidently fire at Mrs. Troi, vaporizing her instantly. A subsequent investigation from Data reveals the malfunction was caused by an overwhelming surge of fan letters requesting this specific plot development.

The Host

The plot:

Dr. Crusher falls in love with a guy who has a worm in his belly. Then the worm moves into Riker and Crusher does him. But when the worm moves into a woman, Crusher draws the line there.

What works:

1) Crusher actually hugging and kissing someone! Never seen that before. Especially kinky because we know the actress was very pregnant when this was filmed. And then she does it with Riker! They should have had a scene in bed together, and then have Picard accidently walk in on them.

What doesn't work:

1) Dr. Crusher has been a pretty frigid character. How does she suddenly drop her guard and let a putty headed alien bone her? A last fling before menopause? Not explained.

2) Worm guy explains why he never told Crusher about his worm: it never occurred to him to do so! Yeah, right.

3) It's very creepy when worm boy's belly bulges!

4) When Riker volunteers to take the worm, it's totally unbelievable. No one would do that. It's disgusting when Riker has the parasite put in him.

5) At the end, when Crusher rejects the sexual advances of the lesbian, she declines but is apologetic about it, saying she hoped some day she could be a lesbian too.

6) We are told the worm can only survive an hour in stasis--then why is it called stasis if it only lasts an hour?

How it could have been better:

1) What if the worm had gotten into Wesley? Would Crusher have done him too? What if it had gotten into Troi? The possibilities are endless!

2) What if the worm were hostile like the mouth crabs from "Conspiracy" and started to multiply, take over the crew, passing from person to person during sex? That would make for a very dramatic and very creepy episode!

The Mind's Eye

The plot:

Romulans capture Geordi and brainwash him to kill a prominent Klingon, hoping to end the alliance between the Federation and the Klingon Empire.

What works:

1) When the Romulans are programming Geordi to kill, they make him kill Chief O'Brien, dump him out of his seat, then sit down with his friends and enjoy a drink while O'Brien's dead body is lying right next to him, staring vacantly into space. Great! And the dialogue too!

"How long has Chief O'Brien served with you?"
"Almost four years."
"I want you to kill him."
"Ok."

By the way, one of the Romulan brainwashers returns as the head of the Tal Shiar (Romulan Secret Police) in a DS9 episode, and another in the shadows is Tasha Yar's daughter!

2) The Romulans send another black guy with a visor to Risa who looks almost exactly like Geordi!!!

3) It's fun seeing the "Geordi visor view" with all its colors and indicators.

4) I love the "brainwash camera view" we get when the camera follows Geordi and sort of takes a weird, spherical view around him.

5) It's great that Geordi is simultaneously committing sabotage and in charge of investigating it. In conscious mode he seems unaware of what he did in brainwash mode and is eagerly trying to figure the mystery out.

6) It was great watching Data piece together the evidence and solve the mystery.

What doesn't work:

1) Data says that either the Klingon Ambassador or Picard is hiding a transmission device used to trigger Geordi and both need to be searched. Seeing as Picard is wearing a skin tight outfit, where would he be hiding it, in his ass?

2) The Klingon governor goes from believing the Federation wants to kill him to believing his own ambassador is a Romulan spy... in just under two minutes. It is the only part of the story which is totally not credible, but unfortunately it is an important part.

How it could have been better:

The episode was a little slow in parts (like when Geordi first gets back to the Enterprise), but otherwise was pretty good.

In Theory

The plot:

Data gets a blonde girlfriend (Blondie).

What works:

1) Keiko plays the clarinet at the beginning. That's the nicest thing I've ever heard come out of her mouth

2) Data makes a comment to Blondie which, if said after they had become intimate, would have been a lot more effective.

Data: "Your rhythmic control has improved remarkably."

3) It was funny when one of Geordi's lady engineers with a man's hairdo got stuck between two floors and we just saw her top half stuck there.

What doesn't work:

1) Blondie's uniform unzips in the front, not in the back, like everyone else's. Was that to give Data easier access?

2) It's a slow episode. In the first part Blondie whines about her ex-boyfriend. Then Data seeks everyone's advice on dating. When they finally get to it, all we see is a kiss. We never see any tenderness between the two. Immediately after the kiss Data goes into comic routines of what he thinks it means to have a girlfriend, but there is no real intimacy.

3) When Data finally kisses her, it looks incredibly awkward.

How it could have been better:

I'm not sure if this episode was going for comedy or drama. If comedy, it wasn't funny. If drama, it didn't work because Data didn't show emotions. In fact we have seen Data show subtle emotions many, many times, but what is remarkable here is that the way he is written he shows absolutely none to the Blondie, treating her like a joke or a problem to be solved.

It would have been better if they could have shown Data actually expressing some subtle, intimidate feelings for Blondie, even if it just meant putting an arm around her (we never even saw that much.)

But more interesting, I think, would be if Data had gotten a robot girlfriend. What if an alien robot had manipulated one of Data's lower subroutines and got him attracted to her? That would be interesting! And then, when Data was in "love" with the other robot, the robot would use him to try to take over the ship. That would be a great story!

Actually, I think the Borg Queen actually tried that once. Though it wasn't done very well.

Redemption Part I

The plot:

The family of Durass starts a Klingon civil war with Gowron, the ruler of the Klingons. Picard stays neutral, Worf joins Gowron.

What works:

1) The idea of a Klingon civil war is interesting.

2) There's a funny scene where Picard stares at Lurcer's large Klingon breasts and then hastily looks away when she sees him looking at it.

3) Gowron, to his enemies: "Then go! Your blood will paint the way to the future!"

4) Crusher's enormous pregnant belly is cleverly hidden by camera angles and her blue bathrobe. She was like 41 years old when she got pregnant so probably she didn't use protection because she didn't think it could happen.

5) The big reveal is that Tasha is an evil Romulan! Or, someone who looks like Tasha. Great cliffhanger.

What doesn't work:

1) Gowron, the ruler of the Klingon empire, comes aboard the Enterprise without an escort. Instead of seeming to be the presumptive heir of the Klingon Empire, he seems to be one guy in a costume.

2) Durass's son is played by Nog. Please, no.

3) Most of episode features political maneuvering between Lurcer, Gowron, and Worf. Somehow, it's just not that interesting.

4) Worf destroys a Klingon bird of prey from Gowron's command ship! The trouble is we can see Worf at a cheap looking console that looks like a video arcade game machine, where the only thing on the screen is the Klingon logo. How can Worf target and fire weapons when the screen shows no targeting information, only the Klingon logo? Cheap!

5) Picard doesn't want to get involved in the Klingon civil war. It makes no sense because the Durass are allied with the Romulans and he knows that.

How it could have been better:

Lurcer was kind of interesting but Gowron and Worf were too simplistic to carry this story. Gowron is two dimensional, only interested in fighting, and Worf is not the most emotive of characters either. Perhaps this story could have benefitted from having additional Klingon characters added who had distinct personalities. I felt like I was watching a story without real characters, so I didn't really care what happened. The only Klingon I felt had a real character was Kurn, Worf's brother.

Redemption Part II

The plot:
The Federation sets up a detection grid to deter the Romulans from supplying the Durass family. Without those supplies, the Durass quickly lose.

What works:

1) There's a scene at the beginning with Kurn in charge. I like it when Kurn is in command. He has an aggressive Klingon personality, unlike all the other sensitive or moody types the Enterprise usually encounters.

2) The admiral in this episode is a black lady with the exact same accent as Lutan from Code of Honor. Could it be Lutan's Mom? There was a white admiral with her, but he wasn't allowed to speak.

3) So "Tasha" is a Romulan rape baby! Wow.

8) I like how Data uses his superior robot intellect to figure out how the Romulans are breaking the Taycon beam and how to counter that.

What doesn't work:

1) How does the Federation get access to the border between the Klingons and the Romulans? Shouldn't they have to enter Klingon or Romulan space to go there?

2) How can 23 Federation ships cast a detection net over many light years?

3) Why do the Romulans care if their ships are detected? Will people really stop supporting Durass's family if they know the Romulans are helping?

4) The "B" story is how Data faces racial or android discrimination from an evil white man. It's very dumb.

5) Chief O'Brien, the transporter operator, is Picard's first officer. No ensigns or lieutenants left on the Enterprise?

6) Shouldn't 23 Federation starships be commanded by an admiral, rather than Picard?

7) It seems anyone can challenge Gowron to a knife fight for leadership of the Empire. Why can't the Durass family keep sending knife fighters to kill him until one succeeds?

8) I rolled my eyes in disgust as Data asked Picard to spank him at the end of the episode for saving the day while disobeying orders.

9) Worf spares Durass's son, very stupid, and indeed Worf has to kill him later in a DS9 episode.

10) Worf returns to Starfleet duty after resigning his commission. Can people just resign and unresign from Starfleet at will?

11) Kurn flies into a sun, and knows exactly when to pull out so a solar flare will hit the ships behind him but not his ship. Very implausible.

12) The ending was too quick, too pat. The Durass are winning on every front. Then the minute their reinforcements from the Romulans are cut, they lose the war... happens within a minute or two of episode time. Totally unrealistic.

How it could have been better:

1) Cut the dumb "Data is discriminated against" subplot. Replace it by showing more of his brilliance in running a starship at peak efficiency.

2) Have the Federation actually fight a battle against the Romulans to prevent them from resupplying the Durass family. The story as written is: "Naughty, naughty! We detect your ships, so run along home now!" which is a very weak plotline.

Darmok

The plot:

Picard has to learn how to communicate with a race of aliens who speak in obscure metaphors.

What works:

Nothing.

What doesn't work:

1) I understand the basic idea of this episode. Communication with putty head alien species is always easy in Star Trek and they wanted to show a more "realistic" episode where it was hard. I get it. It just was done really poorly here.

2) A technologically advanced society could not function without a language that could talk with precision. If you needed to heat a bottle to 54 degrees for two hours, how do you say that when your communication is limited to "Darmok and Jelad at Tenagra" and a few other catch phrases? The answer is that you can't and the whole episode is ridiculous.

3) Darmok and Jelad at Tenagra. Darmok and Jelad at Tenagra. Darmok and Jelad at Tenagra. Darmok and Jelad at Tenagra. I got annoyed hearing that over and over.

4) The bad episode only gets worse when Picard starts telling the putty alien campfire stories.

5) When Picard makes his "breakthrough" at communicating, left open is the question of how the Federation will conduct further communication with a race with which it's basically impossible to have substantive conversations with.

6) Picard gets a red jacket! But now he's wearing a grey uniform. What?

How it could have been better:

Instead of making a "how do we communicate" episode, have an episode about "miscommunication". There was a great Twilight Zone or Outer Limits episode called "To Serve Man". People thought it was a book about serving mankind, but it was actually a cookbook. That sort of thing was cleverly done. Why can't the Enterprise meet an alien race that seems ostensibly friendly, but then the crew finds out that their initial friendliness means something else entirely?

That would have the cultural misunderstanding component and yet be much more interesting than this boring and very annoying episode.

Ensign Ro

The plot:

An evil right wing admiral tries to manipulate Ensign Ro and Picard into liquidating some Bajoran terrorists.

What works:

1) The idea of adding a new crewmember is good--just not Ensign Ro. Ever since Wesley left they've been filling his seat with bland white guys, black guys, women with hard lesbian 'dos, but no one seems to stick.

What doesn't work:

1) The addition of Ensign Ro. An unpleasant bitchy character. And she has a giant wart on her chin! Sometimes they smother her wart with white makeup, but that just makes it looked like a snowcapped mountain.

2) Ro's "early Bajoran" nose is not the crinkly type that comes later, her first Bajoran nosepiece is a crucifix. Ro has a crucifix on her nose!

3) We are supposed to hate Ro because of something unspecified she did in the past. Because it is unspecified, it is hard to hate her on those grounds.

4) Once again, the bad guys are not aliens, but another Starfleet admiral. Tiresome.

How it could have been better:

1) Add an attractive woman to the crew, who doesn't have any giant face warts.

2) Set the Enterprise on a straightforward mission to find and liquidate terrorists. Simple plots are not necessarily bad plots, as long as they have drama and tension.

Silicon Avatar

The plot:

A guest star grandma kills the Crystalline Entity, and Picard is angry with her for it.

What works:

The first three minutes of this episode were great.

1) A great scene of Riker flirting with soon to be deceased sex partner. Her name is Carmen, she's very cute, but, oddly enough, she doesn't look the least bit spanishy.

2) A great scene of Riker's sex partner gets snacked on by the Crystalline Entity (CE)! Now he has to find someone else to have sex with.

3) A great scene of devastation after CE attacks--Trees and grass becomes desert. Very dramatic!

What doesn't work:

1) The whole story is about Data's relationship with "Grandma". At first Grandma hates Data, then she loves Data and insists he call her Grandma. Watching Data having a relationship with a Grandma is not interesting. Some might even call it very boring. Grandma is not a compelling character.

2) Picard actually compares the CE to a sperm whale, saying it has the right to eat too, even though it has eaten a lot of people.

3) I thought it totally bizarre that when Grandma kills the CE, instead of being treated like a hero, she is treated like a criminal and Picard mourns for the mass murdering CE.

How it could have been better:

1) Have Picard find a way to communicate with the CE. Get it to agree to snack on uninhabited planets. Have the CE lie, hack into the Enterprise's database, and start snacking on some of the most densely inhabited planets on its way to Earth. Have the entire Starfleet mobilized to fight it in a massive space battle, and when that doesn't work, use an anti-matter bomb to destroy it. A little more compelling than a Grandma story, is it not?

Disaster

The plot:

The ship comes to a dead stop, is damaged, and everyone is stuck in different parts of the ship. Counselor Troi, wearing a leotard showing off her ample boobs, is the senior officer on the bridge and is in charge. Ensign Ro is also there but both she and her boobs are lower ranking and so is not in command.

What works:

1) I love it how an episode where Counselor Troi is in command is entitled, "Disaster"!

2) The subplot where Crusher and Geordi are stuck in a cargo bay and have to put out a fire by depressurizing the cargo bay is dramatic. The only problem is Crusher's bad acting.

3) The main plot, having to stop warp drive from blowing up, is compelling. Chief O'Brien has to play a game of Tetris to prevent the Warp Drive from exploding.

4) Data has his head taken off, just like the robot in the movie Alien! And he's totally ok with it, and Riker is the one who is totally uncomfortable with the idea! Great irony, great drama.

5) Doctor Crusher's new wig is very cute. She no longer has the clumpy hair look and has long wavy red hair.

What doesn't work:

1) Picard is trapped with whiny, crying kids in a turbolift. Really, really, really bad.

2) Also, the kiddies wear immodest skin tight outfits. They are children, not hookers.

3) Keiko gives birth and screams like a bitch. If possible, she's even more unpleasant than usual. Worf should have gagged her.

How it could have been better:

1) Cut out the Picard trapped with kids and Keiko subplots.

2) Have Picard get in a spacesuit and go outside on the hull to make a repair with Data (no spacesuit required). That would be exciting!

The Game

The plot:

Riker's latest sex partner, a woman with a head shaped like a buttock, seduces him into trying a game that brainwashes him. Then he returns to the Enterprise and gives the game to others to be brainwashed as well. All except Wesley and Data and Ashley Judd. Data saves the day with a flashlight. No, I am not kidding.

What works:

1) Riker has another sexual conquest!

2) The crew is brainwashed by evil aliens! It feels like a long time since we've had a real antagonist.

3) The scene where Wesley is being forced to play the game, watched by his brainwashed Mom and Captain Picard, is dramatic. They all cluster around him and watch him have game orgasms. There's something creepy and voyeuristic about it.

4) Equally creepy was the scene where Wesley comes to his quarters and finds Beverly there having game orgasms, and then having her pester him to play the game. There's something a little incestuous about this scene.

5) It was clever of Wesley to make a non-functioning version of the game headsets to fool the others.

6) I like how Crusher deactivates Data and lasers his brain to get him out of the way!

What doesn't work:

1) There is a reference to another Federation ship named the Zhukov--named after one of Stalin's evil communist generals. Star Trek loves communism, the more brutal, the better.

2) How does Geordi play the game when he can't see?

3) Wesley's know-it-all girlfriend (Ashley Judd) is like a female version of Wesley, and equally annoying. The long scenes of flirting between the two are cringe worthy.

4) Data saves everyone by using a "palm beacon"--in other words, a flashlight. That is such a weak ending. A flashlight to deprogram people? It makes absolutely zero sense.

5) The first half of the episode was slow.

How it could have been better:

1) Speed up the first half, and show Wesley and Data retaking the ship, flooding decks with gas, and getting other members of the crew not yet under mind control to assist them in fighting the mind controlled crew members.

Unification Part I

The plot:

Picard has to find Mr. Spock, who has gone to Romulus for peace talks.

What works:

1) Picard threatens to stir up trouble with the Klingons unless Gowron lends him a cloaked ship. For once, Picard is tough and canny!

What doesn't work:

1) As with most two parters, the first part of this story is slow.

2) Picard goes to talk to Sarek who is dying of emotionalism. It's sad and it's suffering porn.

3) There's a very boring B story about investigating a missing Vulcan ship at a junkyard. The only interesting part is that when they need the cooperation from a mush face alien, he refuses, until he sees Counselor Troi's large breasts.

4) Picard and Data have a long slow trip to Romulus on a Klingon ship where nothing happens.

5) They eat Romulan soup, then find Spock in a Star Trek cave in the last ten seconds of the episode, which is a real cock tease.

How it could have been better:

Get to Romulus almost immediately. Show Picard and Data constantly risking discovery. Show the Tal Shiar hot on their trail to create dramatic tension. Show them following clues leading to Spock. Have a local spy help them investigate. Have them find Spock while barely evading the Tal Shiar.

Unification Part II

The plot:

Picard and Spock have to foil a Romulan attempt to take over the planet Vulcan.

What works:

1) When they meet evil Tasha, and evil Tasha tells them she wishes she could do more writing in her job, Data says, "Perhaps you would be happier in another job." Her glare is priceless!

2) When Data gives evil Tasha the Vulcan neck pinch and Spock says, "Not bad!"

3) I liked how when Data make a hologram of Commander Riker, he didn't quite get the hair right, and Picard noticed and commented on it!

4) When Spock met the Romulan leader, he totally fools Spock, being very friendly and outgoing, even saying "live long and prosper"... and then once Spock leaves, evil Tasha comes out smirking. Now that's a clever antagonist!

What doesn't work:

1) Spock acts like a dummy, tells Picard peace can begin with a flower.

2) There is a Romulan Senator who is working for the Tal Shiar named Pardek. He knows about the Star Trek caves the dissidents hide in, and he knows many dissidents on sight. Yet at the end of the episode, the dissidents assure Picard that they have moved to different Star Trek caves and that the Tal Shiar will never locate them. Press the reset button.

3) The Romulans have sent three ships full of troops to take over Vulcan. That's totally ridiculous, which, being the lynchpin of this episode, makes this entire episode ridiculous.

4) If the Romulans wanted to send three ships full of troops, why didn't they simply save time and effort and send cloaked ships?

5) Data and Spock have their classic "You are not emotional, I am not emotional" talk. It's very predictable and boring.

How it could have been better:

The whole storyline can't really be salvaged because at the heart of it is a plan to invade Vulcan with three ships. It's totally ridiculous. A little more credible might be a story where Spock/Picard go to Romulus to secretly meet with a Romulan Senator who wants peace, then the Tal Shiar close in, and Spock/Picard have to escape. That would make it a more dramatic, and more straightforward, escape story. If one of them were captured and interrogated and resisted interrogation until rescue, that would add to the drama. But definitely not enough for a two part episode.

A Matter of Time

The plot:

A bald guy from the future claims he has come to the Enterprise to watch a dramatic historical event. In reality he is from the past and is stealing Enterprise technology.

What works:

1) A great line from Data: "I assume your handprint will open this door whether you are conscious or not."

2) The bald guy tries to bone Dr. Crusher. Her new wig makes her look more attractive.

What doesn't work:

1) Would a historian from the future really announce himself? No. That should be obvious to the crew.

2) This entire episode is a cock tease. Annoying bald guy teases the crew that he knows things they don't, but tells them nothing. It's irritating. And that's the entire episode!

3) Once again, the "B" story is about a natural disaster. That's all the Enterprise does, cope with natural disasters, and no true antagonists.

4) Picard claims the ship's computer deactivated all objects belonging to the Enterprise once the time machine's door opened. Really? How does the computer do this?

5) Why isn't Picard concerned that by *preventing* the bald guy from going back to his own timeline that he might not be *changing* the timeline? Maybe this guy had kids that were important to history.

How it could have been better:

1) A visitor from the future is only interesting when he can possibly influence the present. And yet the structure of this episode is a visitor from the past who does nothing to change the present, hence the boring nature of this episode.

2) It would have been more interesting if a real visitor from the future had come back to guide the crew, and not on the mundane subject of combating a natural disaster. What if, for example, the Federation is on the verge of making peace with the Romulans, but future Riker comes back

to the past to warn them not to do it? And then, if that isn't dramatic enough, future Picard comes back from the past telling them to do it! (And then Future Picard can be revealed to be a disguised Romulan spy.) Now that's drama using time travel!

New Ground

The plot:

Worf is having trouble toilet training Alexander.

What works:

Not much.

What doesn't work:

Star Trek is a science fiction show. It is not interesting watching an episode about child rearing. Once again there is a B plot about a natural disaster, but it is not any more compelling than any of the other B plots about natural disasters.

How it could have been better:

If Alexander, messing around with the transporter, accidently beamed his top half into space.

Hero Worship

The plot:
Data gets a "mini me", a little boy who dresses and acts like him.

What works:

Not much. We are supposed to think it is cute watching a boy imitate Data. It is cute, for about a minute.

What doesn't work:

Star Trek is a science fiction show for young adults and adults. It is not interesting watching an episode with a child protagonist.

How it could have been better:

Have an episode with adult protagonists.

Violations

The plot:

Troi, Riker, and Crusher get mind raped. Riker actually likes it and asks for more.

(Kidding!)

What works:

1) Something bad actually happens to the crew! Amazing. Troi's rape is dramatically shocking. Riker's mind rape, about something happening in engineering, is very boring. And Beverly's mind rape shows us a very rare scene--Picard with hair! Amazing.

What doesn't work:

1) The investigation is a little slow paced.

How it could have been better:

There are three suspects--three mushy headed aliens. Instead of being nice and polite to them, Picard should have had them severely interrogated, creating more tension in finding out who the mind raper really was.

The Masterpiece Society

The plot:

A genetically engineered society falls to pieces at the first sight of the Enterprise crew.

What works:

1) Counselor Troi gets boned by their leader.

2) Geordi realizes if he had been conceived on that planet he would have been an abortion.

What doesn't work:

1) This is supposed to be a nearly perfect genetically engineered society. And yet this society falls completely to pieces at the first contact with the Enterprise crew? The whole storyline does not seem credible at all.

2) Troi confesses to Picard that genetically engineered leader boned her. Why does she do that? I think the crew likes confessing being bad. Troi says she had a "relationship" with him. No she didn't. She had sex.

How it could have been better:

In the old Star Trek "genetically engineered" meant Wrath of Khan. In TNG it meant a sensitive guy playing a piano before he boned Counselor Troi. For this episode to be less sleepy and more dramatic, the genetically engineered guys have to be more like the former and less like the latter.

Conundrum

The plot:

The crew is given amnesia and manipulated by Reptile Man to fight a war against an alien race.

What works:

1) Finally, an antagonist! (Reptile Man). We notice this strange white guy has replaced Riker as first officer and wonder what's going on. In fact, the entire episode is "What's going on?" and it's good, not predictable.

What doesn't work:

1) Troi beats Data at 3d chess? Not likely!

2) It is not believable that the entire crew could all have their memory erased in a split second, and erased in such a way that they retained their skills but not their memories. Aren't skills connected to memories? This kind of brain amnesia is impossible to achieve in practice. So because achieving the precise kind of amnesia is pretty much impossible, the story doesn't hold together.

3) If Reptile Man could erase everyone's memories, why not make himself Captain instead of first officer? In fact, why not knock everyone out and take over the ship?

4) For the first time we learn the Enterprise has 10 phaser banks and 250 photon torpedoes. In 7 years we have never seen more than one phaser bank used.

5) While under amnesia, Ro gets Riker to bone her. She breaks into Riker's quarters and practically rapes him. I guess this is the only action Ro is going to get on Star Trek.

6) How does Reptile Man adjust everyone's memories precisely, as well as the ship's computer and Data's memory in seconds?

How it could have been better:

This episode had a lot of plot holes but if you close your eyes and ignore them it was a dramatic story. It was interesting seeing the crew trying to figure out who they were and what had happened to them. It was dramatic watching Reptile Man trying to manipulate them and watching Worf phaser Reptile Man at the end.

Power Play

The plot:

Data, O'Brien Troi get taken over by aliens. Really mean ones!

What works:

1) This is the only episode in any Star Trek series where Chief O'Brien bosses Keiko around! O'Brien suddenly has balls. You never see that again, not here and not in DS9.

2) Data is a hothead sadist who wants to shoot Worf!

3) Troi is an evil plotter--and what's more, she plays the part convincingly!

4) I like when O'Brien points to his baby, "I know what this is!" He tries to kiss Keiko and threatens to phaser the baby! Now that's drama!

5) In general this is a great episode because it has antagonists. These antagonists have personality, they have an agenda, they take action.

What doesn't work:

1) Picard agrees to make himself a hostage in return for releasing wounded? Would never happen in reality.

How it could have been better:

Excellent episode, no improvement needed.

Ethics

The plot:

Worf is crippled, wants to die. An unethical doctor takes risk to cure him. Worf is healed, press the reset button.

What works:

Not much.

What doesn't work:

1) Worf wants Riker to kill him, and we have the old culture versus ethics morality play again. It's boring.

2) A big container falls on Worf. That's the way he gets crippled. Weak.

How it could have been better:

What if instead of Worf being crippled, he takes an experimental drug that turns him temporarily into a super-Klingon with super muscles and super reflexes? No, better to have him lying in bed moaning to Riker, right?

The Outcast

The plot:

Riker does it with a flat chested boy/girl on the planet of the no-gender people.

What works:

1) When the he/she gets reprogrammed to be unattracted to Riker.

What doesn't work:

1) One of the flat chested boy/girls says to Crusher

"You are female?"
Crusher: "Yes."
"What is it like?"
"I've never thought about what it's like."

Come on. Please. Crusher has never thought about what it's like being a woman? She's never looked at her boobs in the mirror? Never had a thought about wiping off her period blood? Come on, human beings don't think like this.

2) Crusher has weird makeup--one cheek very red, one not.

3) So Riker does it with a creature that's both a he and a she. Excuse me while I throw up.

How it could have been better:

While Riker is mating with the he/she, an internal mouth inside the he/she's vagina clamps down and cuts off Riker's genital before it is digested internally. While Riker is being fitted with a prosthesis, Dr. Crusher warns him about the dangers of interspecies sex with an alien race we know very little about.

Cause and Effect

The plot:

A time loop shows us the last few hours of the Enterprise as it is destroyed over and over.

What works:

1) The idea of figuring a way out of a time loop.

What doesn't work:

1) The way this episode was written. We see the same events over and over. I was ready to turn it off by the third time I saw the card game. This sort of time loop has been done much better on shows like Stargate: SG-1 because they put some humor in it. Here there was absolutely none.

They play cards a million times. Crusher goes to bed and breaks a glass a zillion times. Geordi has double vision a zillion times. Each time the crew learns a little more, but it is painful for us, the viewer, to watch so many iterations of the same events.

2) Ensign Ro has a very odd lesbo haircut. After she scored with Riker did she figure that she wasn't going to get any action with the male population of the ship?

3) Crusher has ridiculous wig with a huge amount of hair all over the place

4) There was never any explanation how the destruction of the Enterprise sends them back in time over and over.

How it could have been better:

It is possible to do a good time loop story. Have events change more rapidly from loop to loop, have the crew learn what is going on more quickly, and each time have them try something different to evade their destruction. The idea of the story is sound, but they tinker so little from loop to loop that it is simply too slow going. One time they should try changing course; another, using ship's weapons; another, boosting engine output; another, hooking a randomizer into the navigation system; and so on.

The First Duty

The plot:

Kids at Starfleet Academy did something naughty that resulted in someone's death. Wesley has to speak up and take responsibility so a bald Dad can get justice.

What works:

Nothing.

What docsn't work:

If we're not interested in Wesley stories, we're certainly not interested in a Starfleet Academy full of Wesley-like cadets, even if one of them is Tom Paris.

How it could have been better:

Have Crusher find out that Wesley is really an android and for the past five years he has been kidnapped by the Traveler and held prisoner in a cage in a null dimension.

Cost of Living

The plot:

Mrs. Troi and Alexander misbehave and take mud baths on the holodeck.

What works:

Nothing.

What doesn't work:

Everything.

How it could have been better:

If Gene Roddenberry had never slept with Majel Barrett, we would have been spared all these awful Mrs. Troi episodes. Star Trek is not a situation comedy, but episodes like this one treat it as if it were. It's almost like there's Star Trek, and then there are episodes like this one, which have the same series name, but nothing else in common.

The Perfect Mate

The plot:

A space whore meant for a planetary leader begs Picard to bone her. He predictably refuses.

What works:

Nothing.

What doesn't work:

We are supposed to think that Picard is gallant for refusing to sleep with the space whore. Frankly, the "woman chases after shy/reluctant man" plot is so terribly, terribly overused in science fiction. I realize it's a lot of teenage boy fantasies, but it's simply been done too often. And it's so unrealistic. In our society, men chase after the women, not the other way around, and men don't turn down sex. Ever.

How it could have been better:

Have Picard publically refuse to sleep with the space whore, but then secretly sleep with her, and then show up in sickbay the next day with fungus growing on his private parts. Have it spread all over his body until he becomes a fungus monster. Have Beverly try one cure after another not to have it work, and then realize the only way he can be cured is by having sex with a normal female in his fungus form. Featuring special guest star Vash.

Imaginary Friend

The plot:

A little girl has an imaginary friend who is an alien.

What works:

Nothing.

What doesn't work:

Once again, Star Trek is not about little boys or little girls.

How it could have been better:

If the writers of this show realized that the median viewing age is over 10 years of age.

I Borg

The plot:

Picard captures a Borg and wants to infect it with a computer virus to destroy the Borg, but then gets cold feet when the captured Borg becomes sensitive.

What works:

1) Hugh is lonely! He calls Geordi his friend! Aw....

What doesn't work:

1) The Borg are the most terrifying of enemies, or should I say were. They've now been humanized and are no longer so terrifying. It's a disservice to a formerly great antagonist and future storylines involving the Borg.

2) Geordi's idea is to show the Bog an impossible geometric shape, and because it's impossible to understand, the Borg will blow themselves up. Totally unbelievable. Every intelligent being analyzes things it can't fully understand. It doesn't keep analyzing forever, it stops at a certain point. The assumptions about this method to destroy the Borg simply make no sense.

3) Almost as dumb is the idea that if the Borg reabsorb Hugh with his individuality, that will make the Borg more individualistic. But the Borg are always absorbing individuals, they have done it millions of times. Hugh would be no different but Picard pretends it would be different. It makes no sense.

How it could have been better:

What if Hugh stayed with the crew and became the new helmsman, sitting next to Data? He could be Data's new semi-robot friend. He wouldn't have giant breasts like 7 of 9, but his robotic perspective on things could be refreshing.

Or what if Picard sent Hugh back to the Borg and the Borg actually self destructed, and Picard got a medal for destroying one of the greatest threats Earth had ever faced. In other words, don't press the reset button, actually change things!

The Next Phase

The plot:

Geordi and Ensign Ro materialize on the ship out of phase, where no one can see them and they can walk through walls.

What works:

1) It's an interesting idea that's never been done before!

2) It's great how when we are still figuring out what happened to see Picard casually walk by Ensign Ro's body in the corridor.

3) There's a great chase scene with a Romulan who is also out of phase, they run through walls, then Geordi pushes him through a bulkhead into out into space! Meanwhile Data is having a conversation in the same room and is totally unaware of the struggle right next to him because it is out of phase. It's also great that they actually have an antagonist in this episode!

3) Geordi to Ro: "My uniform. My visor. Are you saying I'm some sort of blind ghost with clothes?"

4) It's great how Geordi tries to get Data's attention, plunging his hands into objects, setting off a disrupter which is out of phase. It was great seeing Ro shoot Riker in the head with the out of phase disrupter and Riker not even noticing! And then they set it to explode in a room full of people, but again no one even noticed! And then when Geordi and Ro reappeared for a moment, screaming for help, and Picard said, "What did we just see?" that was a great dramatic reward.

What doesn't work:

1) The transporter chief is an old lady! What happened to O'Brien?

2) Ensign Ro's wear a red hair band; was she on the way to yoga class when she beamed back from the Romulan ship?

3) If they can pass through walls, why not floors?

How it could have been better:

It was a great episode. Why can't all TNG episodes be action based episodes with great scifi angles?

The Inner Light

The plot:

Picard is given a lifetime of memories living on a hot planet where he plays the flute for 50 years.

What works:

Nothing.

What doesn't work:

1) Why would a dying alien race put important memories in just *one* guy's brain who will die someday? Why not record it in a memory file that many people can experience?

2) Picard looks ridiculous with bushy old man's hair. He already is an old man, so it is hard to make him look older without making him ridiculous.

3) Watching Picard live the boring flute life is boring.

How it could have been better:

Many people say this was the very best episode of TNG. Many people are retarded. Nothing happens in this episode. There is no antagonist. There is no dramatic conflict.

Time's Arrow Part I

The plot:

Aliens are going into Earth's Wild West past to snack on homeless people. Data goes after them but at some point his head comes off.

What works:

1) Gul Dukat plays a gambler! Great voice.

2) Aliens have a homeless zapper, like a bug zapper!

3) When aliens eat all these homeless people, the timeline does not change because homeless people have no impact on the future. Makes sense!

What doesn't work:

1) They find Data's head in a cave. Why can't they connect it immediately and find out what happened?

2) Data looks forward to death because it makes him more human. Ridiculous.

3) The character of Mark Twain is extremely annoying, especially his voice.

4) Most of the episode is spent wandering around a Star Trek cave and taking sensor readings. Boring.

How it could have been better:

Get to the Wild West part more quickly.

Time's Arrow Part II

The plot:

Picard & Co. stop the aliens who are snacking on homeless people in America's Wild West period. They reattach Data's head.

What works:

1) The Wild West costumes and hair styles the crew wore were kind of cute. I guess. I'm really stretching here because I want to try to find at least one thing that worked.

What doesn't work:

1) So finally, finally, finally we find out the mystery of the origins of the relationship between Picard and Guinan, which has been hinted to for years but not revealed until now. So here it is: Guinan was moderately injured in a cave. Picard sat with her until the ambulance arrived. The end. After I watched it for the first time, I didn't realize at first that I had seen the entire origin story. I thought there must be some other part I had missed, so underwhelmed was I.

2) Most of the episode featured the crew running around the Wild West set and Picard sitting in the cave with Guinan, until they figure out the best way to photon torpedo the cave. Boring.

3) More very annoying Mark Twain. That voice.

How it could have been better:

1) Have a more compelling origin story for Picard and Guinan. Have him actually save her life, rescue her from some bad guys.

2) The idea of fighting aliens who are travelling to our past is a compelling one, it was just done very poorly. Instead of figuring out the right frequency for the photon torpedoes (technobabble), how about fighting the aliens in the past by *fighting the aliens in the past*? Yes, going and hunting them down in Wild West San Francisco, shooting and killing them with phasers, tracking them down to their hideout and wiping them out? It's straightforward, but it's full of action and drama.

Realm of Fear

The plot:

Barclay sees monsters in the transporter.

What works:

Not much.

What doesn't work:

1) Barclay, except the time he becomes a genius, is a very unpleasant character to watch--the fearful white guy. Most of episode focuses on his fear of the transporter. That's boring.

2) How could Barclay see anything in the transporter when he was dematerialized?

3) Why did the other people in the transporter look like worms? Never explained.

4) Once again, the episode has no antagonist.

How it could have been better:

Have a real monster in the transporter episode. A monster who snacks on people while they are materializing and dematerializing. Find out a way to exist for some period of time and move around in the "dematerialized dimension" and send guys with phasers to kill this beast.

Man of the People

The plot:

An alien gives Counselor Troi all his garbage emotions, turning Troi into a sex machine.

What works:

1) When the old lady says to Counselor Troi: "Have you mated with him yet? That's what you want, isn't it? I can always tell! The ones with the certain look in their eyes!"

2) Troi has a counseling session with "Ensign Janeway"!

3) Troi fondles her karate outfit, gives a sexy look to an ensign, and then when Riker comes over, she's wearing a dress with her nipples sticking out. Later, she wears a dress with nearly all her breasts falling out.

4) Riker comes in to Troi's quarters just as Troi finishes having sex with an ensign, and then she proceeds to taunt Riker about it. Great scene!

5) A counseling session with whining woman. "How do you think it feels to sit and listen to someone whine about themselves all the time? You're not going to be coddled. If you can't take it here you might think about a transfer to a transport ship. If you aren't up to it, then you don't deserve to be here. So you better take a hold of yourself, or be prepared for transfer." WOW! Imagine if Troi were like that all the time!

6) Troi goes crazy and stabs Picard. Wow!

7) This was a GREAT episode because a main character underwent a fundamental change, even if it was temporary.

What doesn't work:

1) I don't understand how Troi getting the guy's bad emotions makes her sexy. I don't see the connection.

2) Why does the guy have to get rid of his bad emotions to be a peace negotiator? Makes no sense.

3) When Troi is rid of the garbage emotions, her old body immediately turns young again. It makes no sense.

How it could have been better:

It was a very good episode, both because of a major change in a main character, and Troi got to act sexy and crazy. It's a pity other characters can't act sexy or crazy without some intervening cause.

Relics

The plot:

They find Scotty suspended in a transporter buffer. Scotty feels alienated in what is to him a future time. He helps the Enterprise escape from a Dyson's sphere.

What works:

Scotty's idea to save himself on his damaged ship by storing himself in a transporter beam is great! High tech, innovative!

What doesn't work:

1) Scotty is huge. He looks about 250 pounds, which may be why he isn't wearing a Starfleet jacket, he's too obese!

2) Picard gives Scotty a shuttle at the end of the episode. Picard can just give those away?

3) Most of episode focuses on Scotty's feeling outdated/useless. That's valid, if not done to excess. Here it was done to excess and it was boring.

4) Scotty's visit to a holodeck version of the old Enterprise was supposed to be nostalgic, but somehow seeing him stand on a vacant bridge was just kind of sad and empty.

How it could have been better:

1) The drama here involved keeping the door to a Dyson Sphere open so the Enterprise could escape. That was mildly interesting, but could have been much more. What if, instead of spending most of the episode feeling sorry for himself, Scotty helped the Enterprise explore the Dyson's Sphere (perhaps a two parter, the sphere is huge) and eventually meeting the race who created it? With very alien technology, Scotty could help Geordi analyze their technology and provide helpful insights that could help Picard deal with the sphere builders if they turn out to be hostile.

Schisms

The plot:

Aliens who make clickity sounds do medical experiments on the crew.

What works:

1) It is dramatic when Riker and the others realize they have been experimented on in their sleep, and scary when they use the holodeck to recreate the torture table.

2) We find out Riker's arm has been severed and reattached!

3) I like the clicking sounds the clicking aliens make.

4) This episode features real antagonists, even though we never see their POV.

What doesn't work:

1) A long poetry reading with Data supposed to be funny, but was actually very boring filler.

2) When they got a report of an explosion in a cargo bay, we see Worf and Beverly walking *very slowly* to the cargo bay.

3) Riker pretends to be unconscious on the alien operating table. What if they started to cut his arm off while he was lying there?

4) On the alien operating table, Riker just sits for a long time and watches. He's armed and could take immediate action. When he does act, he rescues a crewgirl but doesn't shoot the aliens.

How it could have been better:

A good episode, but there is no payback against the aliens for doing this to them. Riker should have phasered them or taken one of them prisoner. We also don't get any alien POV which would have added to the drama.

True Q

The plot:

A blonde girl demonstrates Q powers and Q has to decide what to do with her.

What works:

1) Crusher has new, straight hair--much better than previous wig with mounds and mounds of hair going in every direction.

2) Q, to blonde girl. "You're attracted to Riker. How do you stand that hair all over his face?"

3) Blonde girl turns Riker into a mindless zombie, dresses him like a butler, and starts to make out with him.

4) A great scene where Q turns Beverly into a barking dog.

What doesn't work:

1) When Q gets thrown across the room, you can clearly see it's a stunt double.

2) Most of the episode features the blonde girl talking about her mixed feelings about having Q powers and being undecided what she wants to do. Sorry, but I'm not interested in the emotional angst of a guest star character I have never seen before, nor long discussion of her feelings with Dr. Crusher.

3) Blonde girl has a giant wart on her cheek. Couldn't they find guest stars with fewer facial warts? Does Ensign Ro do the casting for the show?

4) Q offers blondie the choice of voluntarily not using her powers or going to the continuum with him. But why can't Q just strip her of her powers? It was done to him. This was not offered as a choice. No explanation.

How it could have been better:

This whole episode focuses on the emotions of a young girl getting Q powers. Boring.

How about an episode focusing on a person getting Q powers, and instead of feeling guilty/anxious, actually uses those powers and enjoys it! Show him travelling the galaxy in the blink of an eye, changing the color of a moon, blowing up a star in a vacant solar system, whatever he wants, until Q teaches him responsibility. That would make a great episode.

Rascals

The plot:

Picard, Ro, and Guinan are turned into children, and have to retake the ship after the Ferengi capture it.

What works:

1) It's funny watching baby Keiko holding her baby!

2) It's very funny watching kid Picard call Riker "Number One."

3) The kid Picard has the posture and the intonation of real Picard down perfectly.

4) The kid version of Keiko is a lot nicer than the real Keiko.

5) When kid Keiko tries to snuggle, O'Brien worries about pedophilia!

6) Shrill Little Ensign Ro: "Our bodies have been violated!" I don't know anyone who would want to violate Ensign Ro's body.

7) When Picard is restored, the first thing he does is feel that his head is bald again.

What doesn't work:

1) Ensign Ro is wearing a weird exercise headband again.

2) Easy fix--transporter reset button. Used for most problems. Overused.

3) The Ferengi take over the Enterprise way too easily. How do a handful of Ferengi take over a ship with over a thousand people on it?

4) Worf fires at a Ferengi, misses, and the Ferengi fires at Worf, hits. How unlikely is that?

5) Kids retake the ship (groan).

How it could have been better:

The whole "cute kids retake the ship from the Ferengi" is a dumb plot idea. Additionally, aside from Picard they picked the least interesting characters to make young--Ro, Keiko, and Guinan. I think it would have been much more interesting to see a young Troi, a young Worf, and a young Riker. Then put them on a planet and have them on a mission. Say they have to negotiate with a new alien species. The species treats them like children but is surprised when they act very grownup. That would be interesting.

A Fistful of Datas

The plot:

A holodeck malfunction deactivates the holodeck safeties (again), and Worf has to fight holocharacters who all look like Data.

What works:

1) Data, to Spot the cat: "Perhaps hunger will compel you to eat your food."

What doesn't work:

1) How many times can we be forced to watch another "holodeck safeties are off" episode?

2) Counselor Troi has a terrible accent. Counselor Troi tries to be a tough cowboy. Well guess what? (A) There were no girl cowboys in the old west. and (B) Troi is the worst choice to play a cowboy of anyone on the ship. Her attempts to be a tough gunfighter are laughable.

3) Alexander is an annoying, whining character. Send him back to Russia.

4) Most of the episode is spent watching Worf interacting with Troi and Alexander, but since both are bad in these roles, it makes for a bad episode.

5) When the "father Data" comes to visit the "son Data" in jail, why does Worf not imprison them both?

How it could have been better:

1) Don't make this a comedy. It doesn't work as a comedy.

2) Have more compelling characters. Replace Troi and Alexander with Picard and Riker. If you want to have a Western shootout with the holodeck safeties off, fine, have it. Show Picard, Riker, and Worf beating up a bunch of bandits. That would be compelling.

Quality of Life

The plot:

Data fights for the civil rights of remote controlled machines.

What works:

Nothing.

What doesn't work:

1) Civil rights for remote controlled machines? Please.

2) When Data jeopardizes Picard and Geordi's life so his floating toaster friends can survive, Picard is pleased with his decision. Come on, they are machines. This plot is ridiculous.

How it could have been better:

Exocomps float through the hallways of the Enterprise, yelling, "EX-TERMINATE! EX-TER-MIN-ATE!" and the crew must be armed to defeat them. Behind it all is the Supreme Exocomp, who Data must take down in hand to hand combat.

Chain of Command Part I

The plot:

Picard prepares for a secret mission while Captain Jellico takes command of the Enterprise. Jellico yells at Cardassians and Riker.

What works:

1) Captain Jellico! He's a great captain! He's arrogant, but he gets results, and he's aggressive, something we have not seen in a TNG captain before.

2) He sets Riker in his place, not taking no for an answer.

3) He makes Riker work hard! He makes Geordi work hard!

4) Jellico purposefully insults the Cardassians. He makes them wait for a meeting with him.

5) He gets angry at the Cardassians and walks out on them! Picard would never insult aliens like that!

What doesn't work:

1) Jellico makes Deanna cover up her breasts!

2) We are forced to watch Beverly seduce a Ferengi. It is her absolute worst acting I have ever seen, and since she's a terrible actress, that's saying something. Watching Crusher as she masturbates a Ferengi's ear and tells him how "grateful" she can be is awkward and painful to watch because she is so unconvincing.

3) Troi has much smaller breasts in a standard uniform. I wonder why?

4) Picard & Co spend a **lot** of time wandering around a Star Trek cave lit in blue lights. Very boring.

How it could have been better:

Jellico's role with the ship and with the Cardassians is very interesting, but Picard's story doesn't get cooking until he gets captured at the end of the episode. Cut out the filler where he is wandering around the Star Trek caves. Either have him get captured earlier, or fill out the rest of the episode with Jellico having more friction with the crew and/or the Cardassians.

Chain of Command Part II

The plot:

Picard is tortured by a Cardassian who is trying to break him, while Jellico works out a plan to stop a Cardassian attack.

What works:

1) Riker wants Jellico to admit Picard was caught spying on a mission for the Federation so the Cardassians will respect Picard's civil rights. Jellico refuses. He is thinking of the bigger picture and doesn't want to show weakness to the Cardassians.

2) Picard gets naked and is hung from the ceiling! Never seen that before.

3) Data gets promoted! Data always looks good in red!

4) There are four lights... great! Especially the ending, the way Picard says it. It's a very dramatic contest of wills between Picard and his Cardassian interrogator.

5) For all the criticism of Jellico, he is the one who actually orders the Cardassians to release Picard at the end of the episode! Jellico is the hero of this episode!

6) We get to watch a hungry Picard swallow a baby egg octopus!

What doesn't work:

1) It is never explained why the Cardassians are trying to break Picard. Obviously not for secrets, as was revealed in the episode. Just for fun?

2) One shuttle is used to plant bombs on the entire Cardassian fleet. One shuttle has enough bombs for an entire fleet? The Cardassians would not detect the shuttle planting the bombs? The ending seems too quick, too easy.

3) The remote control which tortured Picard didn't make a sound or flash a beam at him. It would have been more dramatic if it did.

4) Picard is fooled too easily by the Cardassians into thinking Beverly is also a prisoner. He never even asks to see her.

How it could have been better:

1) The Picard torture story is very dramatic! But the Jellico-Riker conflict is boring.

2) Can you imagine if Beverly had been captured by the Cardassian and if she were hanging nude besides Picard? They could do it with the right camera angles and show them being interrogated together. The Cardassians could use Picard's love for Beverly against him.

3) Instead of having a shuttle plant a hundred bombs, which is unrealistic, show an actual space battle between a Federation fleet and a Cardassian fleet where the Federation fleet, under the command of Jellico, beats them.

Ship in a Bottle

The plot:

Dr. Moriarty traps Picard inside the holodeck and threatens bad things unless he is somehow freed from the holodeck.

What works:

1) It's a great idea for an episode, even if it is highly implausible that Moriarty could create a holoprogram for the entire ship in only moments.

2) When I first saw Moriarty walk off the holodeck, I wondered--how did he do that? And then the solution--he never did! Very well done!

3) Picard's solution, to trick Moriarty using the holodeck in the holodeck, was also a great solution. The only problem is, I never saw Moriarty entering the holodeck in the holodeck for this to work.

4) Picard, in trying to regain control with his command codes while not realizing he was still on the holodeck, actually revealed them to Dr. Moriarty. Clever!

5) It's a great scene where Picard, realizing Geordi isn't real, tells him to go away, and holoGeordi docilely obeys.

6) Another great scene is at the end, when Picard leaves the holodeck twice--first the holodeck in the holodeck, and then the real holodeck!

What doesn't work:

1) The idea and setup and resolution of this episode is great. The problem is the middle part of the episode, which is very boring, focusing on Moriarty's stereotype girlfriend who is totally uninteresting. You get the impression she was just added for filler.

1) Why didn't Moriarty ever ask about Dr. Pulaski?

1) Why is transporting Moriarty off the holodeck such a problem? If the transporter can turn energy into matter, why cannot it not turn holodeck energy into matter? This is never explained.

2) After Moriarty blackmails Riker into giving him a shuttle, Riker, always the polite one, gives Moriarty travel advice. It makes Riker look weak.

3) Once again, why can't Riker cut power to holodeck or beam Picard off it? Never explained.

How it could have been better:

Take out or minimize Moriarty's girlfriend. Use the extra time to show us how exactly Picard creates a holoprogram that simulates the ship and crew and how he sets up the details. That's something we've never really seen--how a holoprogram is set up. Have him and Data work out the details creatively in a way they think will fool Moriarty.

Aquiel

The plot:

Geordi bonds with a "sista", while they try to locate a shape shifting killer potato.

What works:

1) Geordi has some kind of crystal sex with the sista.

What doesn't work:

1) So there's this killer potato that mimics other people or animals. In this episode it was the dog who spent a lot of alone time with Geordi. If the killer potato was a dog, why didn't the killer potato eat Geordi or the visiting Klingon? It had many opportunities to do both.

2) Most of this episode was either listening to the boring log entries of the sista, or talking firsthand to the sista, which was also boring.

3) The sista was a black lady who had putty on her forehead that looked like little black breasts!

4) When Geordi was attacked by the killer potato, he fell on ground right next to giant killer potato and it still did not kill him. It waited patiently for him to get his phaser.

How it could have been better:

1) This is like a very, very tame remake of "The Thing". To be improved, it needs more crewmembers than just the sista--maybe five or six. Have Geordi be stranded on the station with them while the Enterprise solves some natural disaster somewhere. Have one of them be the killer potato, and have Geordi figure out who the killer potato is as it kills the station personnel one by one and have all of them be paranoid and suspicious of each other. In other words, have a drama, not a boring relationship with a black girl with vaguely breast-like putty on her forehead.

Face of the Enemy

The plot:

Troi is surgically altered to be a Romulan, then assumes the identity of a member of the Tal Shiar, and orders a bunch of Romulans around.

What works:

1) Great acting by Troi! She really can play tough parts, sometimes, though she was totally unconvincing in "Fistful of Datas", but here she was very convincing.

2) This is an incredibly great drama because of the believable, well written tension between Troi and the Romulan commander. The Romulan commander hates the Tal Shair and Troi has to pretend to be tough or she will be discovered.

3) A great scene when Troi's coconspirator destroys a freighter, and tells everyone Troi ordered it! And Troi, horrified, has to pretend it was her idea! A great scenes with several levels of emotion.

4) The (presumably British) actress who plays the Romulan captain is great, both in her delivery and in her mocking tone and mannerisms. She also had a major role in the episode "First Contact" but didn't shine there like she did here.

5) A great Troi line to Romulan commander: "If you do not wish to undergo another personal *experience* with the Tal Shiar, I suggest you not question me again."

6) Other great Troi lines: When asked if she liked the food, she says she smelled better food on prison ships. She calls the Romulan commander's father a traitor. She threatens to toss her out an airlock, and have her Romulan buddy executed. Wow!

What doesn't work:

1) This episode was so ridiculous, so unbelievable, in so many ways.

2) How does Troi know how to speak Romulan perfectly without an accent?

3) We are told Troi has special codes to get through the Federation sensor nets. I will bet good money that Troi knows nothing about this.

4) Troi is surgically altered to look like a Romulan? Really? How long did that take to accomplish?

5) After the Romulan defectors are transferred to the Enterprise at great risk, we never hear anything about them again.

6) The fat defector who reports to Picard wears a tight jumpsuit. Fat guys should not wear tight jumpsuits.

How it could have been better:

The dramatic execution of this story was great. But it was totally implausible. I think the only way this could work if it did not feature Troi but rather an undercover member of Federation intelligence, trained in Romulan language and customs, who played the same role.

Tapestry

The plot:

Picard dies, but Q gives him another chance, sending him back to his Starfleet Academy days.

What works:

1) Picard laughing when he is impaled.

2) Q falsely claims to be a god, and Picard's reaction:

"If I'm really dead, my only regret is dying and finding you here."

3) Picard bones the Greek girl at Starfleet Academy.

4) When Picard changes the past, he finds himself a junior grade Lieutenant doing menial tasks for Geordi. He meets with Riker and Troi who tell him essentially how worthless he is. Great stuff!

What doesn't work:

1) Most of the story involves Picard's relationship with his Starfleet Academy friends. It simply isn't interesting.

2) It's hard to believe that not fighting the Nausicans changed Picard's nature so much.

3) Why did Picard laugh the last time he got stabbed? At that point he believed he was going to die, why would he laugh?

4) And why did Q save him after he got stabbed? I mean, I think we know why, because he is fond of Picard, but it is never stated.

How it could have been better:

The idea of going back and changing your past is interesting, it was just done in a boring way here. What if Picard could go back in time and save Tasha or Jack Crusher, and see the unintended consequences from that? Maybe saving Tasha would have resulted in Worf's death at some point. Maybe saving Jack would have led to Wesley's death. That would have been more interesting to explore.

Birthright, Part I

The plot:

Data has boring dreams about his Dad, Dr. Soong, while Worf locates a prison where his father may still be alive... but isn't.

What works:

Not much.

What doesn't work:

1) Why is Dr. Bashir trying to evaluate a piece of equipment in sickbay? Shouldn't he be in engineering for that?

2) A rat faced guy sells Worf information about Worf's Dad being held in a prison camp. But if as we learn, Worf's dad was never there, how did rat guy even know to approach Worf with this story? Never explained.

3) We are told that Klingons must kill themselves rather than be captured, that it is dishonorable to stay alive, but when General Martok is captured in DS9 they make an exception, and Worf is captured all the time but we never see him killing himself.

4) Data has a dream where he sees a young version of Dr. Soong who tells Data he is a bird. Yes, I know the symbolism. But it is boring.

How it could have been better:

1) If a Data had dreams, why not make them more imaginative than walking around the ship and seeing Dr. Soong make a bird. Why not make really crazy stuff, like Picard in a bird suit or Riker with a beard down to his knees? But really, there is a much, much better version of Data dreaming in Season 7's "Phantasms" episode.

2) Most of Worf's story at this point is filler. If they wanted to make it more interesting, they should accelerate his arrival at the Klingon prison camp.

3) Dr. Bashir is wasted on this episode, I guess they are just doing a tie-in with DS9.

Birthright, Part II

The plot:

Worf tries to bone a young half Klingon half Romulan girl at the Klingon prison camp. He makes the Klingons angry enough to want to leave.

What works:

Not much.

What doesn't work:

1) Worf tries to awaken the heritage of young Klingons. Yawn. I get it, but it's really boring.

How it could have been better:

Instead of making the Klingons contented prisoners, make them real prisoner prisoners. Why can't Worf have a straightforward mission to rescue Klingons who are still prisoners? Was Rambo Part II such a bad movie? No, it was an excellent movie, and if it was redone with Worf in the main role, it could be almost as good. Have Worf go to the camp with several Klingons. Have them fight to take out the guards one by one and have them chase each other in the jungle and set up ambushes. Make a jungle warfare rescue episode. That would be great.

What we got instead, with Klingons coping with their feelings for Romulans, and what it means to be Klingon through the singing of songs, was just mush.

Starship Mine

The plot:

Terrorists try to steal bomb making materials from the Enterprise, which has been emptied of crew for spring cleaning, and only Picard is on board to stop them.

What works:

1) It's great how Picard gave Tuvok the Vulcan neck pinch! But how did he learn to do that? We never saw Spock teaching him.,

2) This is a great, high stakes episode with a lot of tension, as Picard and the pirates have to run away from the killer force field.

3) It's funny when Picard pretends to be a barber.

4) It's great when Picard shoots a mush face alien with a bow and arrow!

5) The action packed ending features Picard arranging for a bomb to detonate on the pirate ship, and Picard nearly being killed by the green force field! Very well done!

What doesn't work:

1) Why did Tuvok (who guest starred as a human hijacker) attack Captain Picard when Picard asked Tuvok a few questions? No explanation.

2) The head pirate is a bossy woman. Her assistant is a meek white man with his balls cut off. Welcome to the 23th century.

How it could have been better:

Have the head pirate be a bossy man, and his assistant be a meek woman.

Lessons

The plot:

Picard bones a Beverly Crusher look alike. He goes into her fallopian tube in a Jeffries tube.

What works:

1) Picard scores with a Beverly Crusher lookalike, who has enormous Starfleet boobs even larger than Beverly's that sticks out at him every time she faces him.

2) Riker acts like a human being for once, showing irritating that Picard's GF sticks her big boobs in his face and demands special treatment because she's the captain's girlfriend

3) When Picard's GF beams up from the hot planet, she materializes with another ladies face in her breasts. What's that all about?

What doesn't work:

1) Picard has breakfast with Crusher. Very boring. They have zero chemistry together.

2) When Picard's GF flaunts her relationship with Crusher, she shows zero reaction, like a robot. Wooden writing, wooden actress.

3) Troi gives Picard permission to bone a subordinate.

4) Picard and GF break up at the end, promise to keep in touch, never do.

How it could have been better:

What if Beverly had acted like a normal human being, showed jealousy, and competed with the GF for Picard? Then, when Picard dumped the GF for her, and the GF was safely off the ship, Beverly could dump Picard again and go back to being a cock tease.

The Chase

The plot:

Picard goes on a treasure hunt to solve a puzzle with galactic implications which is really quite boring.

What works:

1) Watching Picard have an orgasm when he sees an old artifact.

2) Watching Troi bounce up and down as she walks like a cocker spaniel.

What doesn't work:

1) The long, slow first part featuring the boring professor who expects Picard to give up his command to go artifact hunting is long, slow, and boring.

2) The long, boring second part where Picard goes on the galactic scavenger hunt is also long, slow, and boring.

3) The ending payoff is simply a holographic message from a Founder telling them "Good work! Goodbye!" What a disappointment!

4) Most of the episode featured long boring technobabble about solving the galactic scavenger hunt.

How it could have been better:

How about a galactic scavenger hunt for something that mattered, like a weapon, or new power source, or new source of energy? How about access to another network of Iconian gates allowing instantaneous travel across the galaxy? Then something would have been at stake. Show armed conflict with the Romulans, Ferengi, and renegade Klingons as the Enterprise fights to get the prize. That's called drama. What this episode actually featured, however, is called mush.

Frame of Mind

The plot:

Riker finds himself in a mental hospital. And sometimes he finds himself in a play where he pretends to be in a mental hospital.

What works:

I liked the mental hospital guard with the big belly.

What doesn't work:

1) Why is it entertaining to watch a play of Riker pretending to be crazy? Answer: it's not.

2) It's very boring watching Riker being crazy in mental hospital, and then flipping back to the Enterprise to be crazy there as well. Back and forth and back and forth. The big climax of the story is that he is actually in neither location, but is being scanned or something on a table, and once he wakes up he leaves immediately, a very quick and disappointing ending, dramatically speaking.

3) The mystery of where Riker really was dragged on way too long.

4) If Riker's communicator was nearby, why didn't the Enterprise find him immediately?

How it could have been better:

Have the entire crew appear to Riker as inmates in the mental hospital. Have Picard pretend to be a king and demand obedience from his subjects. Have Worf be a laughing fool. Have Geordi have huge, yellow eyes that stare at people. Have Troi be obsessed with sex. Have Data refuse to talk other than making "beep beep" and other stereotypical machine sounds. Now that would be entertaining! Classic Star Trek had an episode called "Whom Gods Destroy" which made a much, much more entertaining mental hospital episode than this one.

Suspicions

The plot:
A Ferengi scientist is killed and Dr. Crusher has to solve a murder mystery.

What works:

1) For the first time ever we see Dr, Crusher in a dress with black pantyhose! It's an ugly brown dress, but still.

2) There is a great scene at the end when she shoots as big hole in an alien and he keeps coming so she has to disintegrate him!

What doesn't work:

1) Crusher invites a Ferengi scientist over to prove that his sun shield works. Why does Beverly care about a subject that has nothing to do with medicine?

2) There is one of every kind of scientist--Vulcan, human, Klingon, Ferengi, and a Green man. But they all have one thing in common: they are very, very boring.

How it could have been better:

1) Put everyone on a planet so Beverly is at risk.

2) Give each character a personality. Have the Vulcan scientist and her husband be a bickering pair who attack each other for being too emotional or too logical. Have the Klingon be a cynical character who ridicules the others. Have the Green man be a creepy guy who stands very close to Beverly when he talks and stares intensely into her eyes. Add one or two more scientists with distinctive personalities, then start killing them one by one, and have Crusher figure out who's doing it. See how simple that is?

3) And when I mean put them on a planet, I don't mean a Star Trek cave.

4) And since this is the last appearance of Guinan in the series, make her the killer's first victim.

Rightful Heir

The plot:

Kahless, the #1 Klingon, returns from the dead. Worf has to decide whether this is the real Kahless and deal with the implications of this.

What works:

1) Worf gets angry and shows emotion at one point! "You are using the name of Kahless for some twisted game! For that you should die! And if you do not tell me what you have done, I will kill you right here!" Why can't he always be like this, instead of acting like a drugged Klingon?

What doesn't work:

1) The first part of the episode, where Worf, in the Star Trek cave, has to decide whether or not he believes Kahless is real, is slow.

2) The second part of the episode, showing the conflict between Gowron and Kahless, is also slow. More conference room talking.

3) How could the Kahless clone tell Worf that he appeared in a vision to Worf when Worf was just a child? How could he know that? Never explained.

How it could have been better:

1) Make it a two parter. Have Kahless return to the Klingon planet and gather followers, fanatics who will die at his command. Reveal that he is a megalomaniac, and Worf has to take a team of Klingons to penetrate his defenses and eliminate him.

Or the episode could merely show Worf, Gowron, and Kahless talking in a conference room. Which is more interesting to you?

Second Chances

The plot:

Riker, on an away mission, discovers another Riker (Riker2) who was stranded on a planet and has led a different life from his own.

What works:

1) Riker2 bones Deanna.

What doesn't work:

1) The tension be between Riker and Riker2 feels manufactured and phony. Riker is such a perfect, sensitive gentleman that I would expect he would get along perfectly with his own copy.

How it could have been better:

1) The episode needs an antagonist, as do most episodes of this series, but does not have one. The only solution is to make Riker2 evil and replace Riker. They could try to do it more creatively than "Datalore", where Data's evil brother tries to do the same thing. What if Riker2 opened up a dimension where there were evil copies of all the crew, and one by one tries to replace the Enterprise crew with them? It worked in a Lost in Space episode!

Timescape

The plot:

The Enterprise is frozen in time, caught in an apparent battle with the Romulans, and Picard & Co. who have been conveniently somewhere else, have to unfreeze the ship.

What works:

1) The idea of having pockets of time where time passes in different speeds, some fast, some slow, and some not moving at all, is very innovative. I like how Picard's fingernails got really long when he poked his hand into a fast time zone.

2) I liked how Picard laughed hysterically when he drew a smile on the smoke from a warp core breach.

3) The scene of the Enterprise frozen in battle with the Romulan ship was very impressive!

4) The image of Crusher frozen after having her guts vaporized by a disrupter was very impressive!

5) It was a very complex mystery.

What doesn't work:

1) At one point, everyone but Troi is frozen in the runabout. If the runabout is moving through an area where time is not passing, how could everyone right around her be frozen but not her? It makes no sense.

2) I don't like Troi's frizzy haired wig. She has straight hair in front, making the frizzy wig in back especially obvious.

How it could have been better:

1) Once again, no antagonists. Not the Romulans, not even the aliens in the warp core. It robs the story of some of its drama when everyone is well-intentioned.

Descent Part I

The plot:

The Borg are making new attacks and Picard has to investigate. Data has to cope with having bad feelings.

What works:

1) The very scary opening trailer works well. Data opens door and comes face to face with the Borg! Why can't every opening trailer start with a bang? Usually they start with a snore.

2) Admiral Nechayev slaps Picard down for not destroying the Borg when he had the chance: "Your priority is to safeguard the lives of Federation citizens, not wrestle with your conscience."

3) I love it when Picard says, "I don't want excuses Numba Won, I want aunsars!"

4) Data and Borg drone have this exchange:

"If you could feel emotions again, would you kill Geordi?"

Data: "Yes!"

What doesn't work:

1) This episode has one of the most unbelievable plot developments of any TNG episode ever. When Data disappears on the planet, and sensors can't find him, Picard decides to beam down nearly the entire crew of the Enterprise to search for Data on foot. What? Hundreds of people on foot? To search a planet? That makes absolutely no sense. One person in a shuttlecraft could cover more area in a few minutes than the entire crew could cover in days.

2) Compounding this is that Picard decides that he, Riker, and all senior officers will all beam down. He leaves his least experienced officer, Dr. Crusher, in charge. I understand the writers wanted to give Beverly her "turn" to command the Enterprise, but this plot development was so unbelievable that it just ruined the entire story.

3) Most of the episode is spent watching Data being upset about feeling negative emotions. Boring.

4) The alien planet looks like Los Angeles canyons with a yellow piece of plastic over the camera lens.

How it could have been better:

Show Data being corrupted. Don't just have him say he would kill Geordi. Show him seriously injuring Geordi and leaving him for dead. That's what drama is--doing, not saying. Show Data unsuccessfully trying to help the Borg take over the ship, and then fleeing to the planet.

Descent Part II

The plot:

Lore is making the Borg evil. More evil than they normally are. And he's making Data evil too.

What works:

1) A funny scene where Data, imitates Picard's voice, telling a blind Geordi "We're getting out of hear!"

2) The scene where Data puts straws in Geordi's head.

3) The funny scene where Lore smiles and tries on Geordi's visor.

What doesn't work:

1) So Picard grabs a random component from a Borg, and he can use this random component to reboot Data, and he can power it by pushing this component against the force field of his cell? Ridiculous.

2) Hugh refused to help Riker. Then he changed his mind immediately.

3) There is serious timing problems with this episode. We get to the scene where Lore is about to kill Data. Riker and Geordi are in the Star Trek cave with Hugh. Suddenly, Riker and Geordi are in the big room with Data and Lore. The battle starts, and suddenly Hugh and his Borg friends are also in the room with them. They must have used a transporter because they seem to get there instantly. The timing of these storylines is seriously off.

4) I found Hugh's whining irritating. The Enterprise freed him from the Borg, and all he does is complain that he didn't know how to handle being free?

5) I find it very unbelievable that the Borg simply collapsed when they absorbed Hugh's individualistic mind. Surely they have dealt with this millions of times before.

6) Why does Lore wear an outfit with a padded groin? Does he think the Borg will respect a leader with a larger android penis?

7) At the beginning of the episode Picard is surrounded by the Borg but Picard has his phaser aimed at Lore; however, Picard simply lets Lore take his phaser, as do the others.

8) The main theme of this episode is that Lore acts like a cult leader to the Borg. It doesn't work because cults only work when followers show emotion. The Borg don't have emotion so this

entire storyline is wasted on them. You might as well have Lore be the leader of a cult of exocomps, the flying toasters Data liberated in episode #224.

9) The Borg have lost their scariness and now are pathetic.

10) Meanwhile, on the Enterprise, the political correctness is so thick you could cut it with a phaser. Look, look, Beverly is in charge! And she is a woman! And she has a black woman assistant, and a spanish man on the transporter! But then an evil white man comes on the bridge. He is mean to Beverly's black woman assistant, until the black woman puts the evil white man in his place. Where do I go to throw up?

11) The scene where Data put straws in Geordi's brain is great; but realistically, that would give him brain damage immediately.

How it could have been better:

If you want to do a story where Lore is a cult leader, make him the leader of a cult of people *who can feel emotions*. Paring him with the Borg does not work. Give him human followers, who adore him and satisfy his very whim. That would be more entertaining. Show us this "cult of the robot" made up of nutty people who believe that robots are better than humans. Maybe Lore brainwashed them to be this way, and maybe he can brainwash Troi or Worf to be the same way. Maybe he plans to brainwash the entire crew until Picard escapes, gathers some security guards, has several intense phaser battles with the brainwashed people, and then blows Lore's head off.

This is more interesting than watching Lore counseling nervous Borg drones.

Liaisons

The plot:

The Enterprise encounters three aliens in yoga tights: an ambassador of arrogance, an ambassador of food, and an ambassador of transgendered sex. The ambassador of transgendered sex turns into a woman and tries to rape Picard.

What works:

1) When the pretend-girl tells Picard: "Tell me about your love or I will jump."
And Picard replies: "Go ahead, why don't you do it?"

Why can't Picard always be like that?

2) I kind of like the arrogant alien who treats Worf like a servant, giving commands like, "Bring me new food!" Although the arrogant alien is written very simplistically, he might as well be wearing a sign, "I am arrogant." Couldn't they have made his dialogue a little more subtle?

What doesn't work:

1) When the alien disguised as a woman tries to rape Picard. The "woman" is also very irritating, whining over and over "Love me! Love me! Love me!".

2) When the Food ambassador spends a lot of time fondling a black boy. I thought he's only interested in food.

How it could have been better:

The idea of aliens studying different human emotions and concepts that are unfamiliar to them is an interesting one. It was sort of well done with the ambassador of arrogance. It was poorly done with the food ambassador (boring) and with the transgendered sex ambassador.

There was once an episode where aliens kidnapped Picard and studied the concept of authority. That was interesting. The aliens here could have explored concepts like bravery, abstract intellectualism, and lack of reciprocity. Have one ambassador arrange to have Picard fight monsters with him on a planet, to study bravery. Have another pair up with Data to discuss the nature of reality as he sees it (which could be well done if written properly), and have a third be a "gimme gimme" alien who keeps asking the crew for more and more things until he reaches the point where they say no (say, asking for sex with Troi.)

Interface

The plot:

Geordi pilots a remote controlled droid on a stranded starship and sees his dead momma, who turns out to be an alien.

What works:

Nothing.

What doesn't work:

1) This episode confused me the first time I saw it. When I saw Geordi's momma I thought for a while that Geordi was a droid on the Momma's lost ship, but no, this was a *different* lost ship.

2) Most of the episode was boring. Geordi is basically a droid and he doesn't do much. His Momma turns out not to be his Momma, so goodbye.

3) Most of the episode shows Geordi whining about his Momma. Boring.

How it could have been better:

1) Wouldn't it be funny if Geordi's mother also wore a visor?

2) Instead of having Geordi control a droid, have Geordi control a drone. Have Geordi remote pilot a flying weapon on the other side of the galaxy. Have Geordi fight in some alien war we have never heard of, with him playing the part of the drone, and engage in fantastic battles he never would have been capable of as a mere person.

Gambit Part I

The plot:

Picard is believed to be dead, and Riker is in command. But it turns out Picard is still alive and has joined the space pirates. Riker joins them too.

What works:

1) After Troi yells at Riker that she was also upset over Picard's apparent death, it almost seemed like they were going to have makeup sex right there. But all they did was hug.

2) The Enterprise crew have a phaser fight with the bandits--in a real forest, not a Star Trek cave, not a set! That is a relatively new thing.

3) I like how the pirates wear patches on their neck that gives them pain.

What doesn't work:

1) Admiral Chakotay is a white guy! What's going on here? Does he know "Ensign Janeway?" who Counselor Troi once had an appointment with?

2) There is a patch of naked skin the middle of Riker's chin beard. It makes it look like a vagina.

3) Data in command--it could have been funny, like when Spock was in command, but instead they manufacture a phony conflict with Worf.

4) Try to follow this: Picard wants to show the pirate leader that he hates Riker so the pirate leader will trust Riker. This is a very tenuous line of thinking. So Picard advocates killing Riker when Riker is taken captive. What if the pirate leader had done as Picard asked? How would Picard have felt then?

The problem is there too much contrived conflict--Picard punches and kicks Riker, Riker punches Picard. It feels too phony, too forced, as if the writers said, "Let's make an episode where somehow Riker and Picard have to punch each other. How do we do it?" In one over the top scene, Picard kicks Riker in the ribs when he's on the ground. It's done for shock value, but it's too ridiculous.

5) Another ridiculous plot point: Riker is beamed aboard the pirate ship as a prisoner, but in moments the pirates quickly trust Riker and make him a pirate too. The whole "Picard and Riker pretend to be pirates" plotline is simply too ridiculous.

6) The Enterprise has an all too familiar drop-the-shields-in-the-face-of-the-enemy moment, the only difference being that it is Data that is doing it instead of Picard.

7) We are supposed to believe that the pirates beam people aboard their ship by vaporizing them with a phaser. None of it makes any sense.

How it could have been better:

Picard and Riker run away to join the pirates is about as believable as Picard and Riker run away to join the circus. The pirate leader is an easy dupe who believes everything presented to him. In general "pirate" storylines are weak ones, given a starship with the military abilities of the Enterprise.

Gambit Part II

The plot:

Picard and Riker, pretending to be space pirates, find an ancient Vulcan weapon.

What works:

1) There is a funny scene where Crusher acts intimidated around a giant 7 foot tall black Klingon.

What doesn't work:

1) The big, scary pirate leader is wearing a sweater. How can we take a bad guy seriously if he is wearing a sweater?

2) The scary weapon they find is an artifact that kills, but it only kills angry people. What kind of weapon is that? I think a phaser set on disintegrate held by an emotionless person is even scarier. This is what the entire episode is about. It's a big disappointment.

3) The actress who plays the evil one is Saavick #2 from Star Trek III: The Search for Spock. She's not a very good actress.

4) We are supposed to be shocked that Riker and Picard, pretending to be pirates, stage a raid on the Enterprise. It's ridiculous, like the rest of this episode.

How it could have been better:

How about uncovering a super weapon that justifies the drama, like a weapon that can blow up planets? That's a lot scarier than the "kill you but only if you're angry with me" weapon. How about having several groups searching for this weapon and showing the competition between them? But first replace all the pirate characters (yes, all of them). They are too weak, too boring, too trusting. Make scary pirate characters. What makes pirate characters scary? They kill people. These pirates never do.

Phantasms

The plot:

Space bugs are slowly killing the crew but only Data is aware of them, through bad dreams.

What works:

1) A black lady in engineering wants Geordi to bone her. But he isn't interested in the assignment because he only likes white women.

2) Data's dream scenes were VERY well imagined!

a) I loved the scene of Crusher sucking a straw coming out of Riker's head.

b) Data answering a phone inside his body.

c) Data eating a Counselor Troi cake.

3) The scene where Data stabs Counselor Troi is very tense and dramatic! Of course, she's ok, it's just a minor flesh wound. Press the reset button.

4) I liked when Picard watched Data's dream on the holodeck, and within Data's dream, they saw Data dreaming about himself, and the Data dreaming about himself said hello to Picard.

What doesn't work:

1) The idea of the whole episode is ridiculous because robots don't have a subconscious. (By the way, Data keeps saying "I am not a robot, I am an android." But never once in seven years does he explain the difference. So **he's a robot**.)

2) The scenes with Data and Sigmund Freud analyzing his dream were supposed to be cute. They were not. Freud's voice was very irritating.

3) Other-dimensional spider bugs are snacking on the crew. But if they are in another dimension, how are the spiders sucking on people in this dimension?

4) Crusher calls for a nurse, and a guy shows up! At least he's not wearing a miniskirt like in the first season.

5) If the other-dimensional spider bugs are so dangerous (on heads and necks of people), why are there no signs of illness among the crew? We are supposed to think this is a terrible danger, but no one has yet developed as much as a headache!

How it could have been better:

Take out the Freud parts. Add a few more innovative dream scenes. Remember when Data heard a ringing phone inside of himself? Hear crying from inside Counselor Troi and open her up to reveal a baby inside. Have Picard saying ridiculous things in an American accent while having a black afro. Have Wesley guest star as a talking piñata and have Data feel the irresistible urge to smack him open to look for presents.

Dark Page

The plot:

A big doggie chases Counselor Troi through Enterprise hallways. This all takes place inside Mrs. Troi's mind, where she is suddenly grieving for a dead child.

What works:

Nothing.

What doesn't work:

1) I suppose we can feel grateful that this is the last Mrs. Troi episode? This episode, like most Mrs. Troi episodes, have nothing to do with science fiction. Her character is an irritating one. People do not watch Star Trek to watch Mrs. Troi be unhappy about a lost daughter, or chasing after Picard for sex, or falling in love with an old bald man who has to kill himself.

How it could have been better:

If Gene Roddenberry had never slept with her and stayed monogamous with Uhura.

Attached

The plot:

Picard and Crusher can read each other's minds. Picard wants to bone her, but Crusher refuses to spread her legs for him, only for force fields (see below).

What works:

1) As Crusher works her tricorder by the alien force field, she inexplicably spreads her legs, pointing her feet outwards, and squats up and down, as if she is dancing with an invisible pole.

2) A great intimidated scene--we learn at the end that Picard had dreams of having sex with Beverly, and because of their connection Beverly was forced to listen to Picard's mind broadcasting pornography.

What doesn't work:

1) Picard and Crusher are captured by aliens. The aliens put devices in their minds to read their minds. Fine. But why would the devices enable Picard and Crusher to reach each other's minds? A big plot hole, and never explained.

2) Most of the episode has them run around a Star Trek cave, and then the canyons around Los Angeles. Can't they create a more imaginative indoor set or actual filming location?

3) Most of the episode features Picard alternatively bickering with Beverly and sharing feelings. Neither is very interesting.

4) Picard walks normally, but Crusher is not only a bad actress, she can't even walk like a normal person. She walks in an odd, exaggerated way, like she is trying to dance with every step, her feet pointed outwards, walking kind of like a penguin.

5) The biggest disappointment in this episode was when Picard confessed his love for Beverly, and she said nothing. He says they shouldn't be afraid to explore their feelings and she shuts him down, saying they should be.

So that's it? Really? After seven years of longing looks and cock teasing? This is the great resolution of the Beverly Crusher-Jean Luc Picard almost romance? How very, very, very disappointing. After watching this, I wondered what was the point of their whole seven year flirtation.

6) After saying no to sex with him, Beverly gives Picard a sympathy kiss and Picard looks pained! I felt pained too.

7) Crusher's tricorder is powerful enough to overpower a force field? No, not even if she is squatting up and down while using it.

8) Beverly's dinner with Picard was laughable. They put a horrible frizzy wig on Beverly, different from what she was wearing in other parts of the episode. They gave her the ugliest grey blouse possible, and a set of ridiculous looking puffy curtains for a skirt that didn't match her blouse at all. She looked horrible, like a woman getting ready for a costume contest at a science fiction convention.

How it could have been better:

1) After being rejected by Beverly, we should see Picard going to the holodeck to use one of Geordi's sex programs.

2) Obviously the episode would have been much more dramatic if it had had the opposite ending. What if their wild flight from the aliens had brought Beverly and Jean Luc together, and made them both realize they were really in love with each other? What if, instead of playing it safe and pressing the reset button at the end of the episode, Picard and Beverly actually began to explore a real relationship? It would have been a first, it would have been dramatic, but instead we got the disappointing ending the writers planned.

Force of Nature

The plot:

Picard finds out that the warp drive is polluting the environment. He puts out an extra recycling bin in main engineering to show his commitment to galactic ecology.

What works:

Nothing.

What doesn't work:

1) "The Warp Drive is polluting the environment" theme doesn't even appear until the last 20 minutes or so. Most of the episode is filler with Data and Geordi making small talk.

2) "The Warp Drive is polluting the environment" theme is so ridiculous. Now the Enterprise is a *big polluter*. They should shut down all starships and *live in huts*.

3) After this episode, aside from one brief mentioned, the fact that the Warp Drive pollutes the environment is never, ever mentioned again.

4) They set a warp drive speed limit to reduce pollution. The political correctness of this episode is ridiculous. Hey, why isn't anyone wearing seatbelts when they go to warp drive? Do they have airbags in their consoles in case of a collision?

How it could have been better:

Instead of a stupid, politically correct episode like this one, have them invent a new kind of warp drive that will make intergalactic travel possible. Have them test it out by exploring a nearby galaxy. That would be exciting, instead of what we were presented with here.

Inheritance

The plot:

Data's Momma comes aboard, only she's a robot like him.

What works:

1) While a boring episode, I applaud the way Data figured it out--he studied her blinking pattern, and saw it was the same as his. Also, he noticed how robotically precisely she played a musical instrument.

2) I like when Geordi opens her robot brain and starts poking inside her head with a probe.

3) I liked it when Data went to Counselor Troi's quarters and his robot momma thought Data was going to have sex with her. Given Troi's very public display of her Betazoid breasts, her confusion was understandable.

What doesn't work:

1) Data's robot momma is married to an alien with giant ears. Ridiculous.

2) Once again, we are told that Data's early memories were wiped, but are given no explanation as to why. It's lazy writing.

3) When Data met Dr. Soong, he never mentioned being married, nor did records show he was ever married. This is another example of lazy writing.

4) When Data sees Dr. Soong again in the holodeck, somehow it's anti-climatic.

5) When Dr. Soong's robot wife left him, why didn't he just create another? Or why didn't he reprogram the one he had?

6) All of a sudden, Data's quarters are larger and much more decorated. Suddenly he has red carpeting, and all kinds of sculptures and ornaments. And a pile of his painting. Lying on the floor. His quarters are as sloppy as the writing of this episode.

7) Data's robot momma is very weepy. Weepy about leaving Data behind. Weepy about leaving Soong. Weepy weepy weepy. And it doesn't matter in the end because we learn she's just a robot copy.

8) When Data and his momma do their musical performance, the crew looks like they are really bored.

9) They put putty on Dr. Soong's cheeks to make him look old, but he just looks like he has putty on his cheeks. And why does an obviously white man have a Chinese name like Soong?

10) The whole story is not compelling. Data's robot momma acts overbearing and intrusive. And then we find out she's not even his momma. Disappointing writing, disappointing ending.

How it could have been better:

Give us an antagonist. Make Data's momma really his momma. Make her evil and have her try to deliver the Enterprise to another Crystalline Entity. Have Data kill her to save the ship, and cope with the need to dispose of his momma. That would be real drama.

Parallels

The plot:

Worf is jumping into different alternate realities where things around him are constantly changing.

What works:

1) Worf's jumping into alternate realities is caused by his proximity to Geordi's visor, but it takes him a while to figure this out. Clever.

2) When Data's awful painting changes from one reality to the next, it is funny.

3) It is also funny how Worf's birthday cake changes from chocolate to vanilla, and Picard, who was not present, suddenly appears, eating cake.

4) Geordi gets burned to death! And no one seems to care!

5) Seeing Riker with a big bushy Borg beard is funny.

6) Seeing hundreds of Enterprises--looks like computer desktop wallpaper!

7) Troi of all people has a funny line for Worf: "You probably want to meditate on your birthday, or hit yourself with a pain stick or something."

What doesn't work:

1) Worf is married to Troi in the alternate reality. This is disappointing for two reasons. First, they do not have sex, so when things return to normal, we can hit the reset button because nothing has changed. The second problem is the timidity of the writers. Instead of showing Worf and Troi dating normally, they have them doing it in dream sequences or other dimensions. It is a cowardly way of writing a romance that doesn't even begin to take off until the last episode of the series.

2) Alexander's gift for Worf's birth is a cast of his forehead. Disgusting.

3) Troi is wearing a wig with highlights which makes her look old, but in all the different dimensions we get to see every kind of breast bearing outfit she owns.

4) Wesley is back in an alternate dimension where he has a very bad haircut.

How it could have been better:

It was a cute story. But it would have been better if it had resulted in some things changing. What if Worf had slept with alternate Troi, or killed alternate Picard, or did things which impacted him after the end of the episode so at least emotionally we didn't have a clean hit of the reset button?

The Pegasus

The plot:

Yet another evil right wing admiral forces Riker to help him recover a cloaking device.

What works:

1) The only good part of this episode was in the first 60 seconds, where Riker gives a GREAT imitation of Captain Picard's voice as he holds a little Captain Picard doll for Captain Picard day.

What doesn't work:

1) The Starfleet Admiral Picard talks to is one ugly old lady. Usually old lady admirals like Nechayev are more glamorous, with blonde hair. This one looks frumpy, like a school janitor.

2) The Enterprise is rendezvousing with a Federation ship called the Crazyhorse. Crazyhorse was an American Indian who killed white people. An odd choice for the name of a ship, you politically correct bastards.

3) And speaking of politically correct, a black Romulan? Looks bizarre.

4) This episode features yet another right wing white admiral. It is unbelievable that the Federation would sign a treaty that allowed the Romulans to have cloaking devices but not the Federation. If Kirk were around, would Picard throw him in jail too for stealing the Romulan cloaking device?

5) At the end, Picard basically surrenders to the Romulans, purposefully reveals that he has a cloaking device, when he could have just kept quiet and returned it to Starfleet. It's a ridiculous move--whose side he is on?

6) While Picard was so considerate of the Romulans, the Romulans had no qualms about sealing the Enterprise into an asteroid.

7) I like how Riker asked to be locked up at the end. All Federation members feel guilty, and nearly all villains work for the Federation. Riker should have stayed in jail and, for good measure, had an anal probe.

How it could have been better:

Well, it's obvious. Have the Federation develop a cloaking device in secret, and use it to take a daring scouting mission deep into Romulan space to see what they are up to. You probably would have to replace Picard as Captain of the Enterprise for this episode with someone like Captain Jellico, but Picard could have been sent on another mission to wander around a Star Trek cave lit with blue lights.

Homeward

The plot:

Worf's fat Russian brother forces Worf to help him transport some primitives with weird noses to a new home on another planet.

What works:

Nothing.

What doesn't work:

1) Worf's fat brother is boning Cassidy Yates, dressed up as an alien with a weird nose. He probably warmed her up for Sisko.

2) It's the Prime Directive in ridiculous excess--Picard feels he cannot intervene even to save these people from certain death.

3) Most of the story concerned keeping the primitives ignorant of the fact that they were on the holodeck while they were travelling to their new planet. Boring.

How it could have been better:

1) Have Worf's fat Russian brother lead the primitives in an attempt to take over the ship. Have him be a raving fanatical lunatic and have Picard, as his captive, find a way to out maneuver him. For maximum drama, have Worf kill him at the end.

Sub Rosa

The plot:

Since she's not sleeping with Picard, Crusher scores some sex with a gas cloud.

What works:

1) Beverly has some great orgasm scenes with the "gas cloud" (since she's alone, she's effectively masturbating for the camera). Her orgasms are almost as compelling as the ones she had in "The Game." Almost.

2) Beverly has great makeup and hair in this episode, cute bangs. I think it's her real hair at this point because I heard she stopped wearing wigs for the 7th season. But Troi is wearing her weird wig with frizzy hair in back that doesn't match her straight hair in front.

3) It's hysterical how Deanna accuses Crusher of "seeing someone". What she means is that Crusher is having sex, but while Star Trek can show nearly every inch of Deanna's breasts, it can't say the word sex, so the dialogue sounds like it's meant for 4th graders.

4) Beverly rubs her face against gas cloud guy's hand like she's a puppy dog.

5) It's great when Beverly's grandma rises from the dead and zaps Data and Geordi.

6) Beverly looks sad at the end when she phasers gas cloud man's candle (his penis symbol?) and realizes she will not have any more orgasms for the rest of the series.

What doesn't work:

1) Crusher didn't think it odd that her 100 year old grandma had a 34 year old lover

2) The colony is composed of mostly normal human people, but they are ruled by a guy with a pig face.

3) Beverly stays in her grandma's haunted house during storm and does a lot of bad acting "What's happening to me? Right now I feel so strange! I don't understaaaand!" in little girl's voice " Her acting is so bad... it feels like a parody of a horror movie.

How it could have been better:

1) If Gates McFadden were a better actress.

2) If, once again, there were an antagonist. All gas cloud man wants to do is bone Beverly. That doesn't really make him evil. He's got to have worse motives. Maybe he wants to bone all the women on the ship, and make them addicted to gas orgasms. Then when Picard gets involved we get a greater sense of urgency.

3) The plot took too long to get going, especially when it was all very obvious from the beginning. Have gas cloud man be more sexually active with more crewmembers sooner, and make him more of a threat for Picard to fight.

Lower Decks

The plot:

Very boring minor characters try to suck up to superiors like Riker and Worf for promotions.

What works:

Nothing.

What doesn't work:

1) The very minor characters are: a redshirt guy with greasy hair; Nurse Ogowa with a short, man's hairdo; a Bajoran girl with the ugly nose ridges; and a Vulcan guy who has no sense of humor, making him totally boring like the others.

2) The only drama in the story is manufactured. Picard "tests" the Bajoran girl by being mean to her. Then he reveals that he was being mean just to test her. Yes, that's the most dramatic moment in the story.

3) There is some kind of ridiculous plot involving a Cardassian and the shuttle, but that was not really the main story. The main story was the minor characters moaning about wanting to be promoted. It was very boring.

How it could have been better:

The idea of the story is interesting. You could show an episode from the perspective of minor characters. But why not do so using interesting characterizations. Have Geordi have an assistant who thinks he is smarter than Geordi and challenges him on some decisions. Have Nurse Ogawa start dating Captain Picard and make Beverly uncomfortable. Have a white guy who has hair like Riker and grows a beard like Riker and tries to imitate his mannerisms in the hopes of getting a promotion.

And have the ship doing something more interesting than launching a shuttlecraft. Have them encountering aliens, or negotiating an important treaty, or exploring a derelict spaceship.

Thine Own Self

The plot:

Data loses his memory and spreads some radioactive stuff around on a primitive planet; Counselor Troi takes the "commander test".

What works:

Not much.

What doesn't work:

1) I stopped understanding this episode at precisely the moment when Troi asked Crusher, "Why did you decide to become a commander?"

What? Being promoted to Commander is something anyone can do? All they have to do is take a test? Then why are there any Lieutenant Commanders, why don't they all take the test? This is ridiculous. Military outfits are not run this way. This undermines the entire episode.

2) During her Commander's test, Troi has to order a holographic version of Geordi to die. That's her test, if she will send a hologram to its death. Ridiculous.

3) You have to wonder, when Beverly took her Commander's test, did she have to order a holographic version of Wesley to go into a radioactive Jeffries tube?

4) The aliens in this episode have wicked spider tattoos on forehead, they're so ugly you don't really care that they get radiation poisoning.

5) Data knows how to read (he can read the word "radioactive"), but doesn't know the meaning of the words he reads? Doesn't know Radioactive? He knows the meanings of words well enough to speak them!

6) Data with amnesia is boring. It's more interesting if he has a different personality, or a more robotic or more human one.

7) Most of this episode is spent watching Data conduct experiments on the radioactive rocks. Which we already know are radioactive.

8) I love when it Deanna whines and demands a promotion, saying there is more to running ship than knowing how the ship works. How ridiculous is that statement?

9) I love how holoGeordi meekly goes to his death in Troi's test simulation, totally unrealistic.

10) I hated the feminist drivel when Troi gets promoted and tells Data to call her sir. And by the way, how do you call someone with big breasts sir?

How it could have been better:

1) Have Data accidently kill an entire village by spreading radioactivity, but when he recovers his memory, he doesn't have any memory of doing so, except a mysterious toy doll in his hand from one of his first victims.

2) Why not promote Troi to Commander for doing something *extraordinary*, like saving the ship? Have her sense that a peace delegate is actually a saboteur and about to plant a bomb to destroy the Enterprise, and Troi catches him in the act and saves the ship. And then she finds out there is a backup saboteur (who is also a Betazoid and can hide his feelings) and has to find and stop him as well. Then a promotion might be justified.

Masks

The plot:

Data, controlled by an alien force, takes on multiple personalities, while Picard puts on a mask and pretends to be someone the alien force will respond to.

What works:

Nothing.

What doesn't work:

1) Data wears an unwrapped condom on his forehead.

2) Most of the personalities Data assumes are very boring: A whiny person, an old man, and the nasal voice "Musaka is coming!" guy.

3) There's no sense of danger in any of this, and since there aren't even any other actors, or sets, it feels small, like a play.

4) There's lots of boring archaeology and symbol analysis.

5) Musaka, when he/she finally shows up, is a big letdown, simply Data with a goofy mask on his face.

6) Picard also wears a goofy mask and recites goofy alien Shakespeare, giving us a boring talk talk talk solution.

How it could have been better:

Have an alien entity who takes over Data have special powers--telekinesis, lightning bolts, etc. Have the crew fight and try to subdue him, and then figure out how to purge his system of the alien influence.

Eye of the Beholder

The plot:

Someone kills himself in a power chamber and Troi has to figure out why, even as she feels like killing herself as well.

What works:

1) After sex with Worf, Troi says, "Why didn't we do this a long time ago?"

2) When Troi catches Worf boning some other woman, Worf laughs at Troi. The laughter is entirely inappropriate and makes no sense, but at least, for once, we see Worf showing some emotion, even if for no reason.

What doesn't work:

1) Once again, instead of having a *real romance* between Troi and Worf, we have a *dream sequence* which, when concluded, allows everyone to hit the reset button *so nothing has changed*. Every time I see one of these cowardly substitutions for a real world romance I groan at the cowardice of the writers.

2) Troi wears two different wigs in this episode, a dark and a light colored one, apparently coordinated with her Starfleet uniform and yoga/sex/counseling outfit. It looks very phony to see her hair change color several times in a single episode.

How it could have been better:

Stop with the dream sequences and parallel dimensions. Have things happen in our dimension. Show Worf trying to bone Counselor Troi. Have Riker get jealous and get involved in a three way contest. It may not be as convoluted as this episode, but it would be a lot more dramatic.

Genesis

The plot:

The crew turns into different kinds of animals, and Picard and Data have to de-animal-ify them.

What works:

1) Riker gets dumb like a cave man! I love it when he has trouble concentrating and tells Geordi, "You'll take care of that... security thing?"

2) A great scary episodes filled with monsters on the Enterprise!

3) They find a dead crewman gored on the bridge!

4) Picard is attacked by grunting caveman Riker!

5) I loved the reaction on Picard's face when Data tells him he will become a lemur or pygmy marmoset!

6) Picard was chased by the growling Worf monster! It created some danger, some drama.

What doesn't work:

1) Picard takes a shuttle to retrieve a lost photon torpedo? Isn't a photon torpedo, once fired, pure energy? Why is Picard going, why will it take several days, and why would Picard volunteer to be on a shuttle for several days? I understand they are setting up the story so Picard will be off the ship when everyone turns into animals, but it is lazy writing.

2) Barclay has a lot more hair than last time. All from the back, 6 inch strands combed to the front. A very weird wig.

3) Troi wears an enormous bushy reddish brown wig that looks very fake.

4) Worf sprays Crusher with venom, but it looks like a green light! Crusher screams "Oh no, oh no, oh no!" Her bad acting is funny here.

5) When Crusher is sprayed, Nurse Ogawa says "get a hypospray". A hypospray? Filled with what? Ogawa doesn't know or care.

6) Why is Crusher fine in stasis, but no one else on verge of death in any other episode is ever put in stasis?

7) Why is Nurse Ogowa advising Riker--are there no other doctors on the ship, like the episode "Remember Me" where everyone disappears?

8) The non-romance between Worf and Troi continues, but only in monster form. Enough already.

9) At the end of the episode, we hit the reset button. There is no discussion of who killed the guy who had his guts torn out on the bridge, nor any discussion of anyone else who was killed by other crewmembers in monster form, no repercussions, just a few extra empty quarters on the ship. Crusher, who caused it all by giving Barclay the wrong medicine which caused the virus to mutate, is not held responsible for all the deaths.

10) Crusher looks completely unchanged after her "reconstructive surgery".

How it could have been better:

It was an average monster story, but it would have been more interesting if the monsters talked and had personalities.

Journey's End

The plot:

While on the planet of the American Indian stereotypes, Wesley discovers he has magical powers to control the passage of time and to travel in different dimensions.

What works:

1) This is the last time we ever see Wesley on Star Trek: The Next Generation.

What doesn't work:

1) Wesley's entire life has been geared to a career in Starfleet. Remember the Traveler said he was the Mozart of starship operations? Now he throws that entire storyline for 7 years in the toilet to become some kind of intergalactic dimensional space being. Wesley. This makes his entire storyline feel like a waste.

2) At one point, when Crusher is surprised to learn Wesley is unhappy with Starfleet, she says, "Why didn't you ever say anything?" Exactly. He never did. There was never any foreshadowing. After 500 episodes featuring Wesley the starship genius, at the 501th episode, Wesley suddenly changes his mind without warning. It's called lazy writing.

3) How did Crusher know that the Traveler called Wesley Mozart? The Traveler told this to Picard and made him promise not to tell Crusher.

4) The scene where Picard tries to curry favor with Admiral Nechayev is ridiculous. By now he should know that all Starfleet admirals are evil.

5) This was a ridiculous episode about political correctness for American Indians, *on an alien planet*. Indian calls Picard their historical oppressor. Wesley starts dressing like an American Indian.

6) Most of the episode features Wesley being rude to the crew, but not in a funny way.

7) An Indian guy with a giant wart stares at Wesley like a pedophile, and gets Wesley hooked on drugs. He manipulates the image of Wesley's dead Dad to get Wesley to do what he wants.

8) Wesley can stop the flow of time? What????

9) The Indian guy with the giant wart turns out to be the Traveler. I still wonder if he had pedophiliac designs on Wesley.

"I've waited a long time for this moment, Wesley."

10) Most ridiculous line: "You are a very spiritual person, Wesley"

11) At the end, Wesley is going to travel to other dimensions. But first, he is going to study American Indians, because the two are closely related. What?

12) The Indians agree to live under Cardassian rule, and we are given a happy ending. What happens after the Cardassians start slaughtering them?

13) Second most ridiculous line: "Wesley, be sure and dress warmly on those other planes of existence". Instead of trying to talk sense into him, or exploring the danger of what he is attempting to do, Crusher simply waves goodbye like an absentee Mom.

How it could have been better:

Have a dimensional rift open in the American Indian settlement. Have hostile aliens emerge who consume the American Indians. Have Picard figure out a way to fight the aliens and close the rift, perhaps with the help of Wesley and the Traveler.

Or, if Wesley can really stop time, have him use it in service to the Enterprise on a dangerous mission.

Firstborn

The plot:

A future version of Alexander comes back into Worf's present to try to prevent Alexander from growing up to be such a pussy.

What works:

1) The scene where future-Alexander convinces Worf that he is Worf's son is very dramatic.

What doesn't work:

1) Future-Alexander never reveals how he travels back in time, simply explaining he found a guy to time travel him. At the end of the episode Future-Alexander simply leaves, presumably to find his time travelling friend... or not. It's all written very vaguely and unconvincingly.

2)Worf, upon learning that Alexander is going to grow up to be a pussy who will get him killed, is not worried at all. That's a very dumb reaction.

3) Most of the episode features Alexander whining that he doesn't want to become a warrior. Alexander irritates me. Why must we have so many episodes focusing on little boys?

How it could have been better:

Show Future-Alexander going back in time to an actual event in Worf's present where Worf is assassinated. Prevent the assassination, but then have him block secondary attempts to have Worf killed, using his future knowledge.

Bloodlines

The plot:

An evil Ferengi makes Picard think he has a son so the evil Ferengi can then torture the son, or something.

What works:

Nothing.

What doesn't work:

1) Family family family family family. Star Trek is in love with episodes about family. However, because the writers are too lazy to write about *actual* family members and establish the relationships over 7 years, they just create unlikely family members and have them *parachute in for an episode*. Here Picard's son isn't even his son. It's not compelling at all.

How it could have been better:

It might have been better if Picard had a real (grown up) son and had a real relationship with him over the past 7 years, as an occasional guest star. When the son gets in trouble Picard can help him. Create an emotional bond over several episodes with a real relative. What we got here was mush that viewers had no reason to care about.

Emergence

The plot:

The Enterprise computer becomes a sentient train on the holodeck.

What works:

Nothing.

What doesn't work:

1) Most of episode is padding, filler, as the crew very slowly tries to figure out what is going on. The crew go on the holodeck train several times and talk to the odd people there. Nothing much else happens. Once again, there is no real antagonist in this story.

How it could have been better:

Have the Enterprise computer malfunction, become sentient, and try to kill the crew. At first, not in an obvious way--an accident here, an accident there. But as Picard figures out what is happening, he has to find a way to shut down the computer. The ship's computer is located in a very heavily protected vault. Data and Riker have to fight their way past the ship's defenses. Meanwhile, the rest of the crew has to survive the ship's booby traps.

Preemptive Strike

The plot:

Ensign Ro is given a mission to betray the Maquis but she decides to join them instead.

What works:

1) Ro grew some hair for this episode, almost looks like a woman again.

2) There's a great scene where Ro pretends to be a prostitute for Picard.

"Hello, are you alone? Why don't we get more acquainted?"

And then Picard tells her she charges too much for her services.

3) At the end, Riker is dressed like a Bajoran, with a crinkly nose and an earring that reminds us of his Angel One gigolo days.

What doesn't work:
1) They painted Ro's chin wart white! It looks huge.

2) The entire story is basically Ro feeling torn between wanting to please Picard and wanting to work for the Maqui. It's boring because Ro, who disappeared from the show about a year ago, hasn't been shown to have any relationship with Captain Picard, so why do we care if she lets him down?

3) In this episode, everyone is sensitive, and there is no antagonist, and thus no real drama.

How it could have been better:

1) Have Ensign Ro decide to betray the Enterprise, helping the Maqui to capture it. Have Picard retake the ship but in the process killing Ensign Ro. That would be real drama.

All Good Things

The plot:

Picard finds himself travelling in the past and future as well as the present, and has to figure out why an energy thing in outer space is going to destroy the Earth, and how to stop it.

What works:

1) It's interesting watching Picard jumping from time to time and trying to figure out why he is time travelling. It is also good, for nostalgia, to see the ship and crew as it was in the very first episode, with the old uniforms, with Tasha, with Data acting more whimsical, etc. They even have a scene where Picard talks to Riker without a beard, and they use a clip from "Arsenal of Freedom" to show a beardless Riker.

2) Q is revealed to be a good guy in this episode, who is actually helping Picard, and Picard actually thanks him! Their relationship has certainly evolved.

3) It's great seeing Troi in her first season gogo boots, miniskirt, and frizzy hair.

4) It's funny watching Q's midgets making obscene gestures at Picard.

5) When Beverly learns Picard may get Alzheimer's, she gets sexually aroused and kisses him on the lips, However, she kisses like a wooden mannequin, telling him "A lot of things can happen", as if she is trying to extend the 7 year cock tease she has been leading Picard on

6) Q allowing Picard to ask 10 questions with yes or no answers is cute.

7) Data observes: "Q's interest in you has always been very similar to a master and his beloved pet."

What doesn't work:

1) Finally Worf bones Troi, not in an dream sequence, not in an alternate reality, and not as a monster. Unfortunately, it's too little too late, as this is the last episode, nor does it make any sense--Worf and Troi are totally incompatible for each other.

2) Future Geordi has a big belly, looks like a panda.

3) It is hard making Picard look old when he already looks old, so all they can do is give him wild hair and a big beard.

4) When Picard learns he is going to get Alzheimer's, he is totally unconcerned. Totally unrealistic.

5) Q is supposed to be judging Picard but in the process gives Picard nearly all the answers, raising the question of what was the point of this entire test?

6) Picard should have explained the situation to his Farpoint crew, it would be easy to prove he knew future facts, intimate details about the crew, but instead he asks them to risks their lives without apparent reason--more dramatic, but also more dumb and unrealistic.

7) The biggest cock tease: when Q starts to tell Picard the meaning of it all, and then stops.

8) They regularly play poker with Troi. She can read emotions. How can anyone bluff with her there?

How it could have been better:

1) The episode was an innovative idea, but it was slow, as two parters typically are. Most of the episode focused on realizing what the problem was and how to stop it, and that wasn't enough to fill up two episodes, even in three timelines. The episodes really needed more things for them to do, and more of a sense of immediate danger to work better.

2) The very last scene, where they are playing poker and Picard comes in, reminds me of the episode where Picard gets photocopied by aliens studying the concept of authority and have a Picard imposter see how many things he can get the crew to do. It would be funny if those aliens came back and replaced Picard again, and when the imposter Picard comes in to their card game, he orders Riker to purposefully lose. Then he orders Worf to stun Geordi. "That was an order, Mistar Worf!" Then he orders Dr. Crusher and Troi to disrobe and assume yoga stretching poses. That would be a lot more memorable than the last scene of Picard playing poker with the crew we were presented with.

3) Or, alternatively, make this entire two parter actually a holodeck episode, where the entire crew are holocharacters in a holostory which is being viewed by Captain Jonathan Archer, T'Pol, and Trip Tucker on their own ship, in order to study something or other. That would have been a great ending too.

****

To conclude:
There were a lot of good Star Trek: The Next Generation episodes. But also a lot of bad ones. The series had a lot of good ideas, but relied too much on technobabble, too much on natural disasters, too much on child rearing stories. Characters didn't always act like real people. But now you know how it could have been even better.

About the Author

Steven Gordon is the author of 30 books, including an analysis of all the Game of Thrones books. You can see some of his books at CliffordCroft.com, and send feedback through http://cliffordcroft.com/feedback.asp

****

****

****

****

If you liked this book, please go online and give my analysis a good rating. I spend many, many months watching all the episodes and thinking of ways to analyze and improve upon them and it would really make me feel good to hear from people who like my book. Thanks!!!!

You can write a review by going to Amazon, searching for

"Making Star Trek: The Next Generation Even Better" :

and entering a review on the product page.

****

****

****

****

22384391R00159

Printed in Poland
by Amazon Fulfillment
Poland Sp. z o.o., Wrocław

THE UNPUBLISHED MARILYN

The Unpublished
MARILYN

JAMES HASPIEL

MAINSTREAM
PUBLISHING

EDINBURGH AND LONDON

First published in Great Britain in 2000 by
MAINSTREAM PUBLISHING COMPANY (EDINBURGH) LTD
7 Albany Street
Edinburgh EH1 3UG

ISBN 1 84018 170 2

A catalogue record for this book is available from the British Library

Typeset in Van Dijck
Mono and colour separation by Inside Image Ltd, Edinburgh
Printed and bound in by Butler & Tanner Ltd, Frome and London

DEAN EDMUND HASPIEL, you with the charisma of a youthful Brando, on the night you were born I walked through the silent, early-morning streets shouting aloud with joy. Decades have passed and the joy remains. From *The Verdict* to *Billy Dogma*, you've made me one proud papa!

ACKNOWLEDGEMENTS

For contributing images to this effort, much appreciation to Bud Barnett; without you this would be a thinner volume! To John Guzman, Frieda Hull, the late Paula Klaw and Jimmy Leggi, to Jerry Ohlinger and his Movie Material Store, a treasure palace to all those who collect star photos; Neil Rodgers, Ray Zweidinger and George Bailey, and a special thank you to Seth Dinnerman for the portrait of my son.

Thank you also to my good friend Denis Ferrara for appreciating what I do here; to the guys at Panda, especially Robert Thompson; to Jimmy Ziakos and his American Restaurant for allowing me my 'office' space; to my agent Robert Smith; may we never run out of projects MM! Love to Mike and Barbara and Cathy and JFS.

And just because, to . . . Tom Smalley.

INTRODUCTION

For me, what began in the *reel* world on 8 August 1952, and continues to this day, began in the real world on 9 September 1954 and ended in the early-morning hours of 20 May 1962. In both worlds her name was Marilyn Monroe. On that day in 1952, I looked up at her from my seat in a local cinema. Twenty-five months and one day later, I looked at her in the flesh for the first time, as I would continue to do for the remainder of her life. During that eight-year interval, I would progress in age from sixteen to twenty-four, while she would transcend into an agelessness all her own. At our first encounter on a New York street, I asked her for a kiss and she responded, her lips landing on this admirer with an impact that was destined to last a lifetime. Following that event, everywhere she appeared, I showed up, and before long she was calling me 'Jimmy'. The journey that took place between us was charged with happiness and, on my part, wonder, sensuality, outrageousness, even anger. Marilyn was friend, sister, mother and the one soul around who gave me the strength to meet another day. For all of it, I owe her. This book is a payment against the debt.

'Give him milk, he's a growing boy,' she called out to the waiter as we sat together just like ordinary people, at a drugstore counter. I was ordinary enough for the two of us. She was an *artiste* who, from time to time, allowed me to share time with her. The remaining memories of those moments still result in profound feelings. I'd felt the need to protect her, and it became a matter of concern: 'You don't have to defend me, Jimmy,' she urged, taking my hand in hers. Even as I recall that long-gone gesture, I *still* feel the need.

She could be the most vulnerable of all the kids on the block, even at thirty! And she could get tough, too. 'I could have slapped your face last night!' she admonished me for one of my indiscretions. For sure, there were times she should have. 'Jimmy, I remember when you were seventeen,' she whispered to me on my twenty-first birthday. A year later, she inscribed on a photo: 'For the one and *only*, *Jimmy*, my friend, Love you, Marilyn.' There could be no doubt that I loved her, too. Still do.

Marilyn was not my only love, so it was with some interest that I recently read a batch of letters I'd written around the mid-fifties to my first love, Reha, who'd saved the missives which document events of that time.

14 DECEMBER 1956
'Dear Reha
I went to the *Baby Doll* première party last night and in the midst of a crowd, MMM [Marilyn Monroe Miller] shouts "*Hi, Jimmy.*" I nearly passed out!'

And in that same letter:

'On a huge (& gorgeous) picture MMM wrote, "To Jimmy, Thanks for your friendship and devotion, Marilyn."'

2 MARCH 1957
'I've seen myself on television several times, in news films with Marilyn.'

14 AUGUST 1957
'I had a terrific time last weekend – visited Marilyn in the hospital – spent a half-hour with Kim Novak in her suite and spent loads of time with Jayne!'

The hospital visit with Marilyn followed the loss of her unborn son; I'd been a guest of Kim's at a party in her suite in a New York hotel; and Jayne Mansfield and I had become close friends in recent years.

16 OCTOBER 1957

'Everything is a little mixed up with me at present and I don't know when I'll get untangled. [Sounds like another romance.] Marilyn is back in our city again and that makes me feel a little better anyhow.'

16 DECEMBER 1957

'I'm going uptown to meet my friends and Marilyn in a short while, and I can't wait. By the way, MMM's next picture is *The Blue Angel*, maybe with Spencer Tracy. She'll be singing some new and some old songs in the picture, and I can't wait for the soundtrack album.'

When this remake of Marlene Dietrich's film arrived in cinemas in 1959, May Britt and Curt Jurgens were the co-stars; Monroe had passed on the project.

A letter written on 20 January 1958 summed it up: 'Always find MMM just *wonderful*!'

Indeed, for every time we met, I would move on, bursting with pride. She had ethics I wanted for myself. She was a pleasure to observe, to study, to *know*. Once, when my demand was more than she could give, she chose the very next time we met to make a public spectacle of her approach to me and, with all eyes about glued to her, asked, 'Did I pay enough attention to you today, Jimmy?'

Love is an enriching thing. When she was near, I felt like the wealthiest man alive.

I was not alone. There she was at that circus benefit in 1955, an already inebriated gent sitting in an aisle seat one row behind mine in the packed upper balcony, his girlfriend to the right of him and his six-pack of beer sitting on the steps to the left of him. All through the evening he continued to imbibe the contents of the beer cans. Finally, MC Milton Berle announced to the waiting audience: 'Now here comes the only girl in the world who makes Jane Russell look like a boy!' The now drunken fellow leaves his seat and his girlfriend behind and stumbles down the steep steps to wind up hanging dangerously over a railing high above the object of his desire, hollering out, 'Marilyn! Up here, Marilyn!'

Shortly after meeting Marilyn Monroe in person, it struck me that she was so utterly different from the image on celluloid: she was not unlike a clown at the circus, so completely covered by their performance make-up that virtually nothing of the person underneath that make-up is visible to the audience. And so it was with Miss Monroe. When she applied both the material and emotional layers of 'Marilyn' in order to meet the camera and the public, her real self – Norma Jeane – all but vanished. Off screen, you would more likely encounter Norma Jeane.

Once, I was standing near the corner of 46th Street and Broadway in New York City one late afternoon. In front of me, already off the kerb, waiting for the traffic lights to change, stood a cluster of citizens, all of them gazing up at the four-storey figure of actress Marilyn Monroe – then adorning the front of the Loew's State Theater building – advertising the movie playing inside, *The Seven Year Itch*. What none of the onlookers realised was the identity of a woman standing among them, *not* looking up at the icon on the building's façade, but hailing a taxi instead – the real Marilyn Monroe. The cab stopped, she entered it, and the vehicle took off. The lights changed to green and the people went on their way, several of them walking straight over to the box-office of the Loew's State Theater. Despite her make-up-less-but-fabulous face and the tousled blonde hair, Norma Jeane had managed to keep 'Marilyn' her secret on that crowded corner in Times Square.

In time, both the woman in the cab and the woman on the façade would rise to mythological heights in all areas of the arts, including the written word. Book-wise, if author Anthony Summers' *Goddess: The Secret Lives of Marilyn Monroe* (Macmillan, 1985) remains the definitive biography of MM, the *best* book still, has to be the one written during her lifetime by an author who actually met his subject, Maurice Zolotow's *Marilyn Monroe* (Harcourt, Brace & Company, 1960), a work in which I can recognise the woman I knew on many of its pages. While neither Summers nor Zolotow delivered unflawed books, nonetheless their biographies of my friend are yet imbued with integrity. Like the victory of Monroe's image over that of the Jayne

was her picture. I have never been anywhere in my life – yet – that she doesn't turn up, without my quest for her image. It cannot be said of the others of her time.

'You knew Marilyn Monroe?' said an impoverished woman to me while hanging out the washing. 'May I just touch you?' With this book, I want to touch *you*. The intention of this effort is to recall her with dignity and a genuine sense of kindness. After all, what did she do here on earth but make the rest of us smile a lot.

There are *artistes* who have celebrated her, and I have culled from their words for you. What can we say about the images that accompany the words? Nothing, other than to express a genuinely grateful *thank you* to each and every photographer who pointed a camera in her direction. Marilyn Monroe's images supply their own captions! Words can offer only mundane details, the where-and-when information that will cease to be important as the decades move on.

Hielke Jan Welling wrote to me from the Netherlands: 'I read your book – after looking at the pictures again and again of course – when I read your story everything seemed to have happened only yesterday,' referring to my first book, *Marilyn: The Ultimate Look at the Legend* (Smith Gryphon Ltd and Henry Holt and Company, 1991). Wasn't it only yesterday that Marilyn had said to me, 'Don't get so excited, Jimmy'? But how could she possibly ever actually know what it was like to see her in real life? Her own mirrors were but two-dimensional, after all.

There were the walks, the talks, the hugs and kisses, all of it now long gone, but most of all, I miss her personal presence among us. With that itself gone, *Life* magazine opined: 'Her death has diminished the loveliness of the world in which we live.' Others have flared up white-hot and then fizzled, while Marilyn's light continues to embellish our universe.

JAMES HASPIEL

'I'm a Christian Scientist. I work for the
church. My work is diametrically opposite to
what she was doing in the moving-picture
industry. I never wanted her to be in that
business. Of course, I never told her one
way or the other; I never told her a word.'

Gladys Eley, Marilyn Monroe's mother, to author
James Haspiel in 1972.

RIGHT: *With her mother taken away, the child Norma Jeane would spend the period from 13 September 1935 to 26 June 1937 as a ward of the Los Angeles Orphans' Home Society (now called Hollygrove), as well as in a number of foster homes. 'I could read . . . I saw "Orphan", and I put my foot down on the sidewalk. They had to drag me in. I said, "I'm not an orphan!" I used to sit up in the window and cry, because I'd look over and I'd see RKO, and I knew my mother had worked there, she'd been a cutter there.'*

BELOW RIGHT: *In addition to her work as a film cutter at Columbia Pictures, RKO Radio Pictures and Consolidated Film Industries, mother Gladys spent a considerable portion of her life in mental institutions. She died from heart failure in Gainesville, Florida, aged eighty-three, on 11 March 1984.*

FACING PAGE: *Architect of an icon: Gladys Pearl Monroe was born in C.P. Diaz, Mexico, on 24 May 1900. Wed three times (to Jasper Baker, Martin Edward Mortenson, John Eley), but not to her daughter Norma Jeane's real father, C. Stanley Gifford, Gladys listed the name 'Mortenson' on the baby's birth certificate, 1 June 1926. Norma Jeane Mortenson was to become known to the world as Marilyn Monroe.*

ABOVE: *Norma Jeane on her wedding day, 19 June 1942. Bridegroom James Edward Dougherty eventually became a Los Angeles policeman, recalling: 'You know, I never knew Marilyn Monroe. I knew Norma Jeane Dougherty. But Marilyn Monroe and Norma Jeane were two different people. Norma Jeane was my wife, Marilyn Monroe was a glamorous movie star. I don't know anything about her life. I never talked to her. I just didn't know her.'*

Dougherty was one of the policemen assigned to crowd control at the 1950 Hollywood première of MGM's The Asphalt Jungle, *a film in which his ex-wife played a featured role. Marilyn Monroe did not attend the opening.*

FACING PAGE, TOP: *A lifelong lover of animals, Norma Jeane – after becoming Marilyn Monroe – had a number of house pets, including a basset hound named Hugo during her marriage to playwright Arthur Miller, and a poodle named Maf (short for Mafia) during the last year of her life.*

FACING PAGE, BOTTOM: *Little could the young girl know what dizzying heights of fame lay ahead when she posed for this routine snapshot during a happy 'family' outing circa 1938.*

Mrs Jim Dougherty strikes
a pin-up-style pose at a time
when the only movies in her
yet-to-be sex-symbol life
were still only on screen at
the local drive-in. Norma
Jeane divorced husband Jim
in 1946.

FACING PAGE: This close-
up of Norma Jeane as a
model was culled from
16mm film of the young
beauty circa 1945. It was
over the next year that she
– as Jean Norman, et al.
– began appearing on
numerous magazine covers.

'This girl had something I hadn't seen since
silent pictures. She had a kind of fantastic
beauty like Gloria Swanson and she radiated
sex like Jean Harlow. She didn't need a
soundtrack to tell her story.'

Leon Shamroy, the cinematographer who shot MM's
first screen test in 1946.

Success as a model led Norma Jeane to an acting contract at 20th Century-Fox on 26 August 1946. Newly blonde, she posed for this studio portrait. On screen, she appeared as an extra in several of the studio's productions, finally playing very small roles in Scudda-Hoo! Scudda-Hay! *and* Dangerous Years, *both filmed in 1947. 'I didn't have an opportunity to do anything, actually, during the year that I was there at 20th Century-Fox the first time . . . and then they dropped me.' The newly named Marilyn Monroe moved on to a Columbia Studios contract in 1948, playing a co-starring role in* Ladies of the Chorus. *Her refusal to become intimate with studio boss Harry Cohn quickly ended her days at Columbia.*

Freelancing, the budding actress made the rounds in the Hollywood of 1948, appearing next in Love Happy, *a United Artists release in which she received 'Introducing . . . Marilyn Monroe' billing. Her next appearance - stark naked – resulted in her famed calendar photos, shot on 27 May 1949.*

MM appeared with an assortment of movie starlets in the 20th Century-Fox production, A Ticket to Tomahawk, *filmed in August of 1949.*

The issue of Life *magazine on 10 October 1949 carried a picture spread featuring the current crop of Hollywood starlets. The 31 October edition of the magazine carried a letter to the editor from a Mrs Sakakeeny of Massachusetts: 'Marilyn Monroe is not only the most beautiful, but the one who will no doubt make a name for herself in Hollywood.' And so it was.*

Marilyn Monroe next appeared in her first important film, MGM's The Asphalt Jungle, *followed in 1950 by roles in 20th Century-Fox's* The Fireball, *an unbilled cameo in MGM's* Right Cross *and a highly visible role in the 20th Century-Fox release* All About Eve, *then in another MGM release,* Home Town Story. *Still in 1950, MM filmed a television commercial for Union Oil of California, plugging their Royal Triton motor oil product.*

'I knew I belonged to the public and to the world – not because I was talented, or even beautiful, but because I had never belonged to anyone else. The public was the only family I had ever dreamed about. I didn't go into movies to make money. I wanted to become famous so that everyone would like me and I'd be surrounded by love and affection.'

Marilyn Monroe.

'Marilyn Monroe was one step from oblivion when I directed her in *The Asphalt Jungle*. I remember she impressed me more off the screen than on . . . there was something touching and appealing about her.'

John Huston, who also directed MM in her last
completed film, *The Misfits*.

'I used to think as I looked out on the Hollywood night, "There must be thousands of girls sitting alone like me, dreaming of becoming a movie star. But I'm not going to worry about them. I'm dreaming the hardest."'

Marilyn Monroe, 1953

Marilyn is seen here in a portrait sitting that resulted in her appearance in Life *magazine January 1951, on the pages of which she was dubbed a 'Busty Bernhardt'.*

In December 1950,
Marilyn Monroe was
signed to a seven-year
contract with 20th
Century-Fox. Her first film
under the long-term pact
was As Young As You
Feel, *starring Thelma*

Ritter, who would – a
decade later – share scenes
with Monroe in her final
released film, The Misfits.
Also starring in As Young
As You Feel *was David*
Wayne, an actor who would
later appear in three more

MM films, We're Not
Married, O. Henry's
Full House *and* How to
Marry a Millionaire.
Here, Marilyn models
costumes for her featured
role in As Young As You
Feel.

'Marilyn Monroe! She's a gal with a big future behind her.'

Constance Bennett, MM's co-star in the 1951 film, *As Young As You Feel*.

In *Fox's* Love Nest, *Monroe played scenes with June Haver, the actress she'd made her actual movie debut with in Scudda-Hoo! Scudda-Hay!* five *years earlier. Here, MM models costumes for* Love Nest, *in which the sarong was replaced by a two-piece bathing suit.*

FACING PAGE: *Fox next cast Monroe in* Let's Make It Legal. *In the summer of 1951, Marilyn was finally on display in cinemas across the United States. Here, she heralds her 20th Century-Fox debut in* As Young As You Feel.

'I was driving somebody to the airport, and
as I came back there was this movie house,
and I saw my name in lights. I pulled the car
up at a distance down the street – it was
too much to take up close, you know – all
of a sudden. And I said, "God, somebody's
made a mistake." But, there it was, in lights.'

Marilyn Monroe, on the early years of her career.

'There was a sort of magic about her which we all recognised at once . . . she seemed just a carefree kid, and she owned the world.'

Barbara Stanwyck, MM's co-star in the 1952 film, *Clash by Night*.

On loan to RKO Radio Pictures, MM made a film called Clash by Night, *in which she played a character unlike any other before or after in her entire film career. Finally* not *playing a showgirl-type, as Peggy – through Monroe's delicately crafted performance in this Clifford Odet's drama – she not only tugged at audiences' heartstrings, but Monroe also supplied the mostly dramatic* Clash by Night's *brighter interludes.*

In December of 1951, Fox cast Monroe in Don't Bother to Knock. *Here, she models costumes for the production, in which she played a deranged babysitter.*

'AMERICA'S MOST EXCITING PERSONALITY . . . MARILYN MONROE. EVERY INCH A WOMAN . . . EVERY INCH AN ACTRESS! . . . [watch] AS THE MOST TALKED ABOUT ACTRESS OF 1952 . . . ROCKETS TO STARDOM,' *announced theatrical coming attractions for Fox's release of* Don't Bother to Knock.

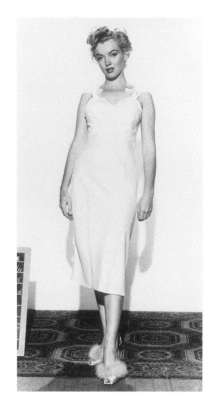

'I liked Marilyn Monroe. She was a vulnerable kid. Murder to work with, because she was scared to death of acting – even when she had become big. She was a movie animal. Something happened between the lens and the film. Nobody knew what the hell it was. On the set you'd think: "Oh, this is impossible; you can't print this." You'd see it and she's got everyone backed off the screen.'

Richard Widmark, MM's co-star in the 1952 film, *Don't Bother to Knock*.

'On *Don't Bother to Knock* I worked with another newcomer, Marilyn Monroe. It was a remarkable experience! Because it was one of those very rare times in Hollywood when I felt that give and take that can only happen when you are working with good actors. Marilyn played a babysitter who has done some very destructive things to this child, and everyone in this hotel had become aware of it. It was the scene where they were bringing her down to the lobby to be held for the police. I was just somebody in the lobby; and I was to walk over to her and react, that's all; and there was to be a close-up of her and a close-up of me – you know, to show my reaction. Well, I moved toward her, and I saw that girl – of course, she wasn't the big sex symbol she later became, so there was nothing I had to forget or shake off. There was just this scene of one woman seeing another who was helpless and in pain. It was so real, I responded; I really reacted to her. She moved me so much that tears came into my eyes. Believe me, such moments happened rarely, if ever again, in the early things I was doing out there.'

Anne Bancroft, MM's co-star in the 1952 film.

Soon to become every man's dream girl, Marilyn exchanges an affectionate embrace with an unidentified male, circa 1952.

At the onset of 1952, Monroe was cast in Fox's We're Not Married, *in which actor David Wayne played her husband. Wayne would again wed Monroe in the 1953 Fox production of* How to Marry a Millionaire. *Here, MM models costumes for* We're Not Married.

 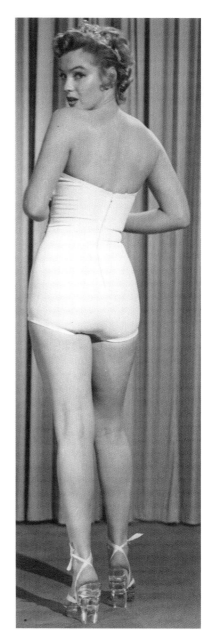

Monroe dons her costumes for the 1952 Fox production, Monkey Business (*not to be confused with the 1931 film of the same name starring the Marx Brothers*).

FACING PAGE: *Playing Hollywood's sell-the-movie game, Marilyn poses with an unknown actor for publicity fodder for the Fox release,* Monkey Business. *MM next played a cameo role in the studio's production of* O. Henry's Full House.

'She seemed very shy, and I remember that when the studio workers would whistle at her, it seemed to embarrass her.'

Cary Grant, MM's co-star in the 1952 film, *Monkey Business*.

Dropping by a local
drugstore in Hollywood . . .

Monroe holds a copy of her
first Life *magazine cover,*
7 April 1952. MM went
on to appear on a record
fourteen Life *magazine*
covers (counting the
magazine's European
edition cover for The
Prince and the Showgirl
in 1957) between 1952
and 1996. In fact, seven
MM covers have appeared
since her death in 1962.

*Birth of a sex symbol.
This candid pin-up shot on
a California beach leaves no
doubt as to the future
status of the budding
thespian.*

*While her now-and-future
admirers across the land
sleep soundly, actress
Marilyn Monroe begins her
day with a sunrise date
under a hairdryer at the
Fox studios, camera and
crew awaiting her on a
nearby movie set.*

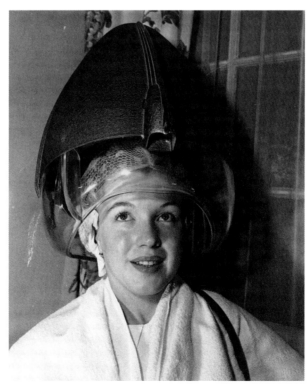

'I owe Marilyn Monroe a real debt. It was
because of her that I played the Mocambo
[an important nightclub in the Fifties]. She
personally called the owner of the Mocambo
and told him she wanted me booked
immediately, and if he would do it, she
would take a front table every night. The
owner said yes and Marilyn was there, front
table, every night. The press went overboard.
After that, I never had to play a small jazz
club again. She was an unusual woman – a
little ahead of her times. And she didn't
know it.'

Ella Fitzgerald, singer.

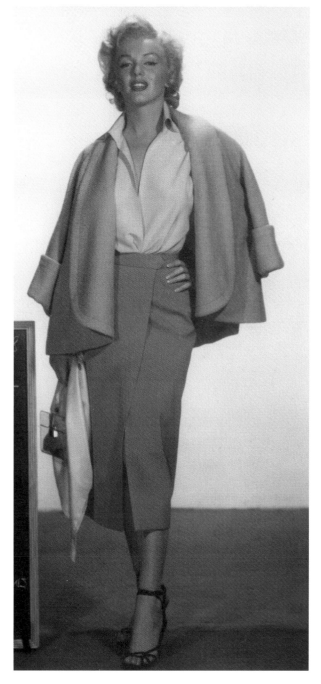

Monroe models costumes for the 1952 Fox production of Niagara, *the film that – along with 1953's* Gentlemen Prefer Blondes *– virtually guaranteed Marilyn's movie stardom.*

'NIAGARA AND MARILYN MONROE — THE TWO MOST ELECTRIFYING SIGHTS IN THE WORLD!' announced theatrical coming attractions for Fox's release of Niagara *in 1952.*

'I did *Niagara* with her. I found her marvellous to work with and terrifically ambitious to do better. And bright. She may not have had an education, but she was just naturally bright.'

Henry Hathaway, director of the 1952 film.

With co-stars Jean Peters (the future Mrs Howard Hughes) and Casey Adams, MM rehearses a scene for Niagara.

Director Henry Hathaway advises his star, Marilyn Monroe, on the set of Niagara.

FACING PAGE: *Wildly beautiful, beautifully free, Marilyn is seen here while on location in Canada for the filming of* Niagara, *as photographed by Dr Thomas H. Morton*

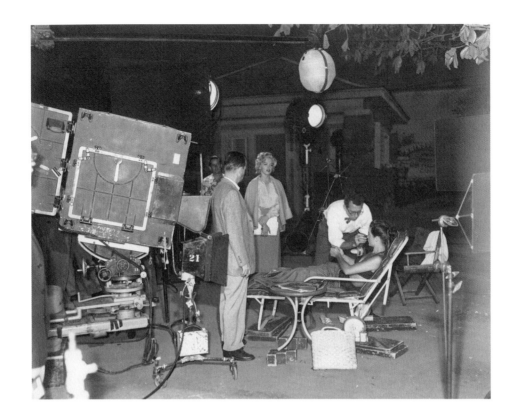

'She does two things beautifully: she walks
and she stands still. She's the only actress
who makes her greatest entrances when she
exits.'

A Hollywood press agent.

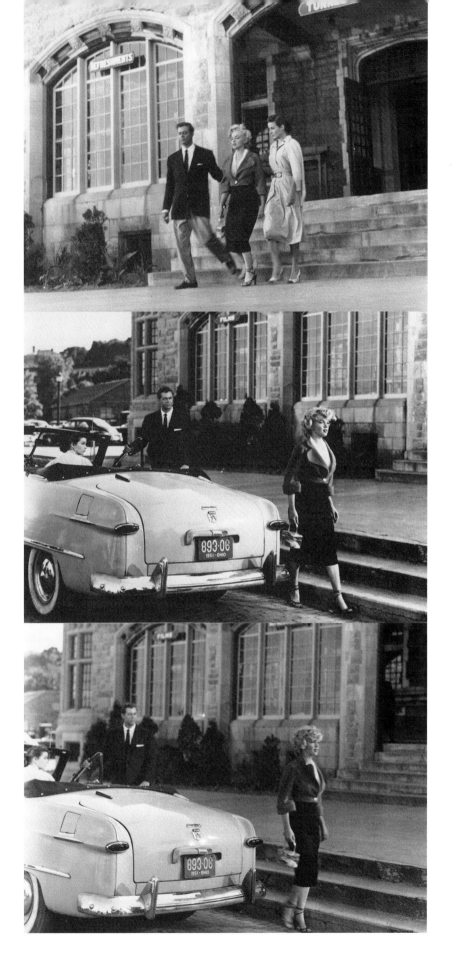

On location at Niagara Falls, Canada, co-stars Jean Peters and Casey Adams film the onset of a Niagara *sequence in which Marilyn Monroe would then take the longest on-screen walk in cinema history.*

FACING PAGE: *Star Monroe stands by patiently while co-star Jean Peters' make-up is retouched on the* Niagara *set.*

Filming on location in Canada, a terrified Monroe attempts to escape her would-be murderer in 1952's Niagara.

Co-stars Joseph Cotten and Marilyn Monroe pose for publicity fodder for the 1952 release of Fox's Niagara.

FACING PAGE: A dynamic-looking Marilyn Monroe poses with an unidentified man on location at Niagara Falls, Canada.

In 1952, columnist Sidney Skolsky wrote of Monroe: 'I think she's going to be one of the most popular actresses the movies have ever known.' Here, Marilyn poses with Sidney's daughter, Steffi.

FACING PAGE: *Helicopter pilot Lt Jimmy Mann of the US Navy delivers MM to musician Ray Anthony's lawn party to launch his new record, 'Marilyn', on 3 August 1952.*

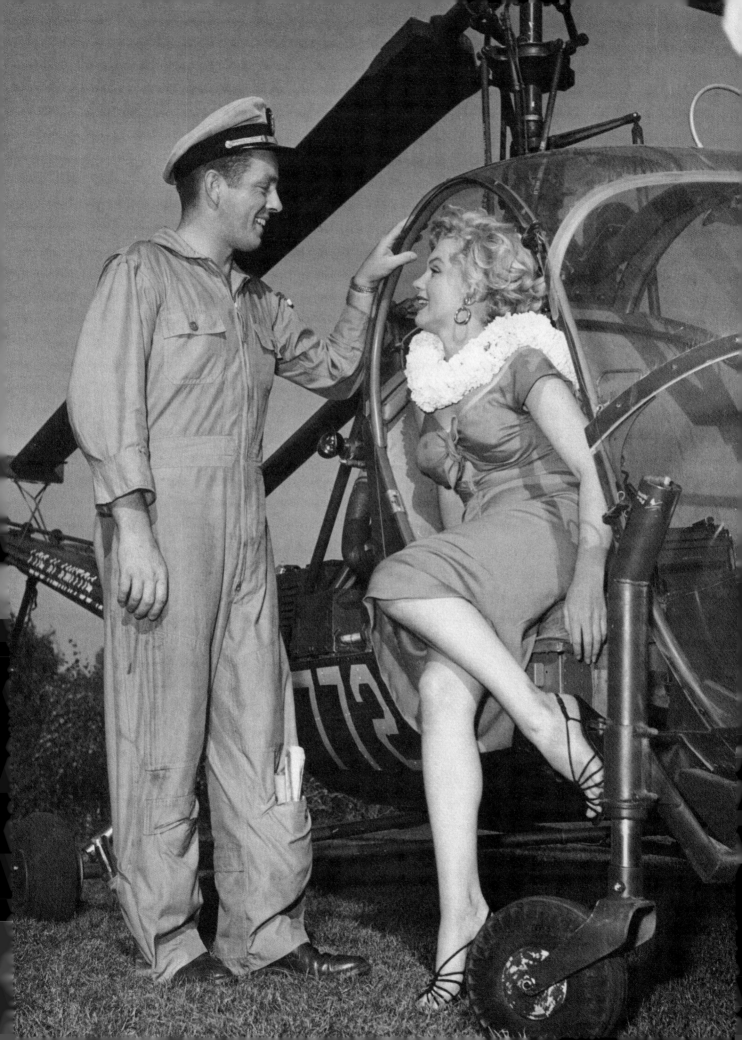

FACING PAGE: *Ray Anthony – soon to become the husband of 'Universal Pictures' answer to Marilyn Monroe', starlet Mamie Van Doren – poses with the real article, on 3 August 1952.*

Anthony and Monroe check out the lyrics ('An angel in lace, a fabulous face, that's no exaggeration, that's my Marilyn') to the Capitol Records tune written by Ervin Drake and Jimmy Shirl.

'She is a beautiful child. What she has – this presence, this luminosity, this flickering intelligence . . . It's so fragile and subtle, it can only be caught by the camera. It's like a hummingbird in flight; only a camera can freeze the poetry of it. But anyone who thinks this girl is simply another Harlow is mad.'

Constance Collier, actress and acting teacher.

MARILYN MONROE INHERITS HARLOW'S MANTLE headlined the New York World Telegram & Sun *on 5 August 1952 – an exact decade before the date of*

MM's death – to which Erskine Johnson added: 'Hollywood took 14 years, three-score screen tests and a couple of million dollars to find a successor to Jean Harlow, who melted movie

celluloid from 1927 to 1938.'

On 2 September 1952, MM turned up in New Jersey to promote the release of Fox's Monkey

Business. *Among the festivities, her appearance as Grand Marshal in the Miss America Parade, where she greets fans along the world-famous boardwalk in Atlantic City.*

Grand Marshal Monroe poses with Miss Alabama, a contestant in the 1952 Miss America Pageant.

FACING PAGE, TOP: *In New York City in September of 1952, Marilyn poses for a cover shot for the* Sunday News. *A portrait from this sitting (with MM wearing another dress) appeared in the 30 November edition of the newspaper.*

FACING PAGE, BOTTOM: *Here, Marilyn is seen receiving a marriage proposal from a famed puppet when she guest-starred on radio's 'Edgar Bergen–Charlie McCarthy Show' in November 1952. Bergen's daughter Candice would later achieve her own fame in the world of show business.*

Between 31 October and 31 December 1952, Marilyn Monroe models costumes for the film that would once and for all establish her as a major star with movie audiences across the land and beyond: Fox's 1953 release of Gentlemen Prefer Blondes.

On the verge of her superstardom, MM is seen here at her dressing-room door on the Fox lot during the filming of Gentlemen Prefer Blondes.

FACING PAGE: Designer William 'Billy' Travilla shows MM his sketch during a costume test for Gentlemen Prefer Blondes.

'Marilyn and I often used to lunch at the Café de Paris commissary at 20th Century-Fox. I can still see us walking in there, and here's Bette Davis, Tyrone Power, Susan Hayward with their forks frozen halfway to their mouths as they gaped at her. All these stars with their press people and agents and all the background of a studio going on and it all just stopped dead when Marilyn appeared. It was awesome – and she wasn't even trying.'

William 'Billy' Travilla,
MM's dress designer on several films.

ABOVE LEFT: *On 25 November 1952, MM modelled this silk robe – which she'd worn the previous year in Fox's* Love Nest *– for a scene that was filmed, then later cut from the release prints of Fox's* Gentlemen Prefer Blondes, *in 1953.*

ABOVE MIDDLE: *On 31 December 1952, MM posed in this costume for* Gentlemen Prefer Blondes. *It was not to be seen in the finished film.*

ABOVE RIGHT: *On 13 January 1953, MM modelled a costume to be* used on screen at the start *of* Gentlemen Prefer Blondes. *The feathers were not used in the finished film.*

FACING PAGE, TOP: *Sidney Brownstein, president of the Jewelry Academy, presents Fox's new star with an award: 'To Marilyn Monroe – the best friend a diamond ever had.'*

FACING PAGE, BOTTOM: *Wearing a costume from* Gentlemen Prefer Blondes, *Marilyn poses for publicity fodder with an unknown male contract player at Fox.*

'Marilyn Monroe and I got along great. Marilyn was very shy and very sweet and far more intelligent than people gave her credit for . . . I had a ball on *Gentlemen Prefer Blondes*.'

Jane Russell, MM's co-star in the 1953 film.

'Marilyn Monroe and I were very close. Once, when we were doing *How to Marry a Millionaire*, I got a call on the set. My younger daughter had had a fall. I ran home. And the one person to call was Marilyn. She did an awful lot to boost things up for movies when everything was at a low state. There'll never be anyone like her for looks, for attitude, for all of it!'

Betty Grable, MM's co-star in the 1953 film.

'One afternoon we were doing a silent shot for *How to Marry a Millionaire* of Marilyn Monroe asleep, dreaming. She was covered with a rich, shiny silk sheet. Her eyes were closed. I couldn't miss the opportunity to lean over the bed and fix the folds a little closer to her body. After all, I was the director. As my knowledgeable painter's hands were doing the required job, gently folding and pushing the silk sheet under her, I realised that she was completely nude. "Marilyn, are you nude?" I whispered. "What if there is a fire and you have to run out of bed?"

'She opened her eyes. "The script says nude. So I am nude."

'By the camera, two young priests, visitors on the set, their eyes bulging out of their heads, were leaning forward out of their shoes towards Marilyn. And certainly thinking, this is better than heaven!'

Jean Negulesco, director of the 1953 film.

(Note: MM wore a nightgown in the finished film.)

Betty Grable — Fox's main attraction for a decade — to Marilyn Monroe: 'I've had mine, honey. Now go get yours!' The co-stars are seen here on the set of their 1953 film, How to Marry a Millionaire.

'I couldn't dislike Marilyn. She had no meanness in her – no bitchery.'

Lauren Bacall, MM's co-star in the 1953 film, *How to Marry a Millionaire*.

'She represents to man something we all want in our unfulfilled dreams. A man, he's got to be dead not to be excited by her.'

Jean Negulesco, who directed MM in the 1953 film, *How to Marry a Millionaire*.

'Marilyn's a phenomenon of nature, like Niagara Falls and the Grand Canyon. All you can do is stand back and be awed by it.'

Nunnally Johnson, who produced the 1953 MM film, *How to Marry a Millionaire*. Johnson is buried near MM's crypt at Westwood Memorial Park.

On 9 April 1953, MM models a swimsuit to be worn on screen in How to Marry a Millionaire.

FACING PAGE: *Marilyn Monroe, Betty Grable and Lauren Bacall film a scene from* How to Marry a Millionaire.

Multiple Marilyns are on display in this pose taken on the set of Fox's How to Marry a Millionaire *in 1953.*

Marilyn Monroe and Betty Grable flank columnist Walter Winchell at a party for columnist Louella Parsons, held at Ciro's nightclub in Hollywood on 13 May 1953.

FOLLOWING PAGES: *In these rare shots, taken* circa *1953, Marilyn is seen promoting lawn furniture; the print layouts and commercials never appeared publicly. The man with Monroe is unidentified. Several years later, Jayne Mansfield – along with her hubby Mickey Hargitay – posed for the same layout, also unseen by the public.*

It was said that a man lost in the wilds of Africa came upon a tribe of primitive natives. Pointing at himself, the man announced: 'American.' To which the tribal chief responded: 'America. Coca-Cola, Marilyn Monroe.'

On 8 June 1953, Monroe donned her costumes for wardrobe tests for the film that was to become her least favourite cinema venture, River of No Return. (Said MM: 'We won't talk about that!') A 1954 Fox release directed by Otto Preminger.

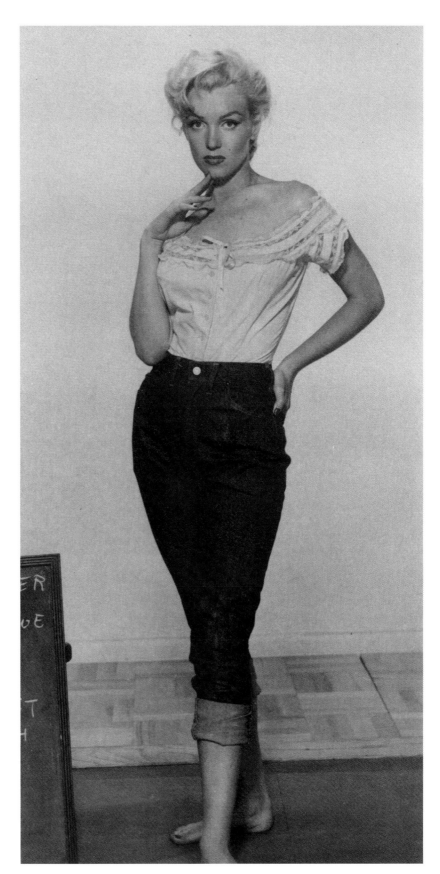

Marilyn at home in her apartment at 882 North Doheny Drive in Beverly Hills, California, in June 1953. Monroe returned to this address in 1961, once again to apartment No. 3.

Currently Hollywood's resident 'bubble-head', Marilyn Monroe poses off screen, at home with her collection of books — she was an avid reader — in June 1953.

FACING PAGE: *The star all of Hollywood wanted to duplicate. At this interval, Universal Pictures was serving up starlet Mamie Van Doren, and studios would offer the likes of Sheree North, Diana Dors, Jayne Mansfield and a clutch of lesser lights — Leigh Snowden, Kathleen Hughes, Cleo Moore, et al. — all of them riding the trail of Fox's Marilyn Monroe.*

'It's a toss-up whether the scenery or the adornment of Marilyn Monroe is the feature of greater attraction in *River of No Return*. The mountainous scenery is spectacular, but so in her own way is Miss Monroe.'

Bosley Crowther, movie critic for *The New York Times*.

THIS PAGE AND OVER:
*Marilyn films her '. . .
bath in the waterfall' scene
for* River of No Return.
*The sequence was cut from
1954 release prints of the
film.*

FACING PAGE, TOP: *With
co-stars Tommy Rettig and
Marilyn Monroe looking
on, Robert Mitchum ropes
a deer for the location
filming* of River of No
Return.

FACING PAGE, BOTTOM:
*Monroe – with Mitchum
and Rettig – rides the
rapids in a tank back on the
Fox lot, filming additional
scenes for* River of No
Return.

'She had a great natural dignity (I cannot imagine anyone who knew her trying to take a liberty with her), and was extremely intelligent. She was also exceedingly sensitive.'

Edith Sitwell, poetess, 1965.

And of a previous meeting with MM:

'In repose her face was at moments strangely, prophetically tragic, like the face of a beautiful ghost – a little spring-ghost, an innocent fertility-daemon, the vegetation spirit that was Ophelia.'

Monroe is seen here in the final moments of River of No Return, *singing the title song, which rose to number one in the record charts in Italy. Under contract to RCA Victor Records, Marilyn was by now becoming something of an international sensation.*

Benny and Monroe consider
Benny's sidekick Rochester,
in a scene not used during
the live telecast.

FACING PAGE: *Marilyn
Monroe at an airport,
during the filming of*
River of No Return.

RIGHT: *MM's career-long
(1946–62) make-up man,
Allan 'Whitey' Snyder,
retouches the star's face for
her television debut on* The
Jack Benny Show *in
1953.*

FACING PAGE: *Marilyn Monroe and Jack Benny during her live appearance on* The Jack Benny Show, *telecast over the CBS network on 13 September 1953. For her television debut, Benny gave MM a black Cadillac convertible as a gift.*

On the evening of 4 November 1953, Marilyn – escorted by the film's producer, Nunnally Johnson – attended the Hollywood premiere of Fox's How to Marry a Millionaire. *Since 1977, Johnson's final resting place has been only yards away from Monroe's at Westwood Memorial Park in Westwood, California.*

Marilyn Monroe is greeted by actor Jack Carson at a Hollywood event circa *1953.*

BELOW: *Marilyn with new husband Joe DiMaggio on their wedding day, 14 January 1954. The ceremony took place at City Hall, in San Francisco, California, Joe's home town. While the marriage came apart in a mere nine months, Joe's love for Marilyn was to endure for his lifetime.*

FACING PAGE: *On stage in Korea, Marilyn – wearing a skin-tight cocktail dress – sang 'Diamonds Are a Girl's Best Friend', 'Somebody Loves Me', 'Do It Again' and 'Bye Bye Baby'.*

'The highlight of my life was singing for the soldiers there. I stood out on an open stage and it was cold and snowing, but I swear, I didn't feel a thing except *good*.'

Marilyn Monroe, recalling her experience in Korea.

*On 19 February 1954,
Mrs DiMaggio arrived in
Seoul, Korea, to entertain
the troops.*

FACING PAGE: *On 15
February 1954, MM
signed autographs for
airmen of the US Air
Force 315th Troop Carrier
Wing at Brady Air
Installation in Japan, while
on her honeymoon with Joe
DiMaggio.*

On 9 March 1954,
Marilyn Monroe, flanked
by Photoplay *magazine's*
editor-in-chief Fred
Sammis and actor Alan
Ladd, receives the
Photoplay *Gold Medal*
Award 'as the selection of
all of the moviegoers of
America, who have voted
you the most popular
actress of the year'.

Yet another award is
bestowed upon Marilyn
Monroe in the Hollywood of
1954 (the presenter and
the award are
unidentified).

FACING PAGE:
Hollywood's 'most popular
actress' on the evening of 9
March 1954. At the
DiMaggio home, 508
North Palm Drive in
Beverly Hills, things were
not as positive.

From 23 May through to 28 June 1954, Marilyn Monroe appeared in these wardrobe tests for her next Fox feature, There's No Business Like Show Business.

'You can figure a Monroe picture is going to run an extra few hundred thousand dollars because she's coming late. I don't think Marilyn is late on purpose and it's not because she oversleeps. It's because she has to force herself to come to the studio. She's scared and unsure of herself. I found myself wishing that I were a psychoanalyst and she were my patient. It might be that I couldn't have helped her, but she would have looked lovely on a couch.'

Billy Wilder, having directed MM in 1955's *The Seven Year Itch*.

Marilyn did this wardrobe test for her newest Fox film, The Seven Year Itch, *on 28 August 1954.*

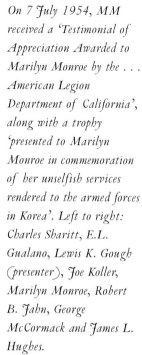

On 7 July 1954, MM received a 'Testimonial of Appreciation Awarded to Marilyn Monroe by the . . . American Legion Department of California', along with a trophy 'presented to Marilyn Monroe in commemoration of her unselfish services rendered to the armed forces in Korea'. Left to right: Charles Sharitt, E.L. Gualano, Lewis K. Gough (presenter), Joe Koller, Marilyn Monroe, Robert B. Jahn, George McCormack and James L. Hughes.

Human art (MM!) checks out some canvas art in New York City circa September 1954. The woman on the left is the wife of actor Edward G. Robinson.

FACING PAGE: Marilyn at the Stork Club, New York City, on the night of 12 September 1954, three days before she filmed the famed 'skirt-blowing' scene for The Seven Year Itch.

'This is a little kid who wants to be with the other little kids. She's frightened to death of that public which thinks she is so sexy. My God, if they only knew.'

Allan 'Whitey' Snyder, MM's make-up man.

'I've made five transcontinental tours in the past five years, ninety cities. And you know, they still want to know about Marilyn Monroe. It's like the great American dream blew up in their faces when she died. I only worked with her in *The Seven Year Itch*, but we had lunch together every day. Sometimes she wanted to talk; sometimes she didn't. I found her delightful. And I remember when we first met she stood up and a book fell on the floor. An Italian–American cookbook. She was still married to Joe DiMaggio. I liked her, because I knew she was trying.'

Tom Ewell, MM's co-star in *The Seven Year Itch*.

Alongside co-star Tom Ewell, a pensive Marilyn rests between takes of her skirt-blowing scene for The Seven Year Itch, *a sequence destined to make film history as the most famous image ever captured by a motion-picture camera.*

104

A rare close-up view of
Marilyn Monroe as she
shot the famous scene. A
displeased Joe DiMaggio,
watching from the sidelines,
departed the area early.
There were reports of an
argument when MM
returned to their hotel
suite.

FACING PAGE: Monroe's
skirts fly high on the night
of 15 September 1954.
The scene was filmed
outside the Trans Lux
52nd Street Theater, on
New York City's Lexington
Avenue.

Allan 'Whitey' Snyder makes up the face of Marilyn Monroe, while Gladys Rasmussen, MM's hairdresser at Fox, awaits her turn with the star in these rare and candid shots taken circa *1954.*

FACING PAGE: *Marilyn Monroe on the set of* The Seven Year Itch.

*Marilyn Monroe at work
on the Fox lot in sequences
for* The Seven Year Itch,
co-starring Tom Ewell.

Tom Ewell joins Marilyn Monroe in a test being filmed for The Seven Year Itch. *By the time of the film's release in June of 1955, the intended sequence had been cut from the movie.*

'It's no fun being married to an electric light.'

Joe DiMaggio, MM's second husband.

'The real marvel lies in the paradox –
somehow we know that this extraordinary
performance is pure charade . . . Miss
Monroe is a make-believe siren . . . an urchin
pretending to be grown up . . . sipping ginger
ale as though it were champagne. This then
is the wonder of the age – like Giradoux's
Ondine, she is only fifteen years old; and she
will never die.'

Cecil Beaton, designer and MM photographer.

*A devastated Marilyn
Monroe departs 508 North
Palm Drive, Beverly Hills,
in October 1954, on the
day the DiMaggio
marriage fell apart once
and for all. Monroe's
divorce lawyer, Jerry
Giesler, stands to her left.
The divorce took place in a
Los Angeles courtroom on
27 October 1954.*

Marilyn examines Monroe. Looking in a mirror at photographer-friend Milton H. Greene's studio on New York City's Lexington Avenue, 28 January 1955.

112

*Marilyn Monroe rides a
pink elephant at Mike
Todd's Circus Benefit.
Milton Berle introduced
MM as 'the only girl in the
world who makes Jane
Russell look like a boy!'.*

'Marilyn was history's most phenomenal love
goddess.'

Philippe Halsman, photographer.

Two legends, Edward R. Murrow and Marilyn Monroe, meet prior to her appearance on his Person to Person *CBS television show in April 1955.*

Monroe poses for the CBS television camera on 8 April 1955, the night on which she appeared live on Edward R. Murrow's Person to Person *programme. MM was visited – along with Milton and Amy Greene – at the Greenes' home in Connecticut. On Murrow's death, it was revealed that the only programme he had saved for his personal collection from the long-running series was the MM episode.*

FACING PAGE: East of Eden *actor Richard Davalos chats with Marilyn Monroe at the première of the James Dean film, held at New York City's Astor Theater, in Times Square, on the evening of 9 March 1955.*

The real Marilyn Monroe – caught walking without make-up along East 50th Street in New York City, circa *April 1955* – pauses to oblige an admirer with an autograph. As seen here, the off-screen 'sex symbol' preferred simple clothing, favouring high-necked blouses etc.

FACING PAGE: *The man on the street is asked his opinion about the four-storey-high 'Marilyn Monroe' being hoisted above Times Square's Loew's State Theater for the world première showing of* The Seven Year Itch. *The reply: 'I think it's wonderful, I think it's wonderful, wonderful, wonderful!'*

'She saw herself drowning in Hollywood in 1955 and told her studio, "I'm not going on just wiggling my behind." Marilyn is not any one thing; she's multi-dimensional. As an actress, she has lots of imitators – but only Marilyn survives.'

Eli Wallach, MM's co-star in the 1961 film, *The Misfits.*

VELL in the seven yea

LOEW'S STATE

121

MM is seen here in Times Square on the night of 12 December 1955, attending the première of the Anna Mangani film, The Rose Tattoo. *Other celebrities present included actor Marlon Brando, and at the post-première party, Broadway star Jayne Mansfield.*

'I saw that what she looked like was not what she really was, and what was going on inside her was not what was going on outside, and that always means there may be something there to work with. In Marilyn's case, the reactions were phenomenal. She can call up emotionally whatever is required for a scene. Her range is infinite.'

Lee Strasberg, creator-director of the Actors Studio.

Artist's services herein contracted for are of a special, unique, unusual, extraordinary and intellectual character and of great and peculiar value to Fox, and Artist's talent and services cannot be replaced by Fox.

20th Century-Fox motion picture studio contract, 31 December 1955.

Marilyn defines the word beauty in this commanding image captured circa *1955.*

Having just attended the Broadway opening of Paddy Chayefsky's play, Middle of the Night, *Monroe is seen here at the doorway to Josh Logan's apartment building on the evening of 8 February 1956. Logan was set to direct MM in her next film,* Bus Stop.

FACING PAGE: *9 February 1956 at New York City's Plaza Hotel, Sir Laurence Olivier and Marilyn Monroe meet the press to announce their upcoming production of* The Sleeping Prince. *Warner Brothers released the finished film in 1957 under its new title,* The Prince and the Showgirl.

'She is a brilliant comedienne, which to me means she also is an extremely skilled actress.'

Sir Laurence Olivier who co-starred with and directed MM in the 1957 film, *The Prince and the Showgirl*.

Monroe's adoring gaze at Olivier was destined to turn into something of a frown months later when working on their joint film venture. The soon-to-be cinema duo are seen here in New York City, 9 February 1956.

Author James Haspiel (far left) — Jimmy to MM — just turned eighteen years old, joins others seeing Marilyn off to Hollywood on 25 February 1956 to begin filming Fox's Bus Stop.

Photographer, friend and vice-president of Marilyn Monroe Productions, Milton H. Greene, and president Monroe arrive in Hollywood on 25 February 1956 to begin filming Bus Stop.

FACING PAGE: *The star of* Bus Stop *arrives in Phoenix, Arizona, in March 1956 to film location sequences for the Fox production of William Inge's Broadway play.*

'One evening I chanced on a television trailer for *Bus Stop*, and there she was. I'm not even sure I knew whom I was seeing on the screen, but a light had gone on in the room. Where everything had been grey there was all at once an illumination, a glow of something beyond the ordinarily human. It was a remarkable moment, of a kind I don't recall having had with any other actress, and it had its place with certain rare, cherished experiences of art.'

Diana Trilling, critic, 1963.

Describing Marilyn Monroe's live performance in the title role of *Anna Christie* on stage at the Actors Studio in February 1956:

'She was wonderful. We were taught never to clap at the Actors Studio – it was like we were in church – and it was the first time I'd ever heard applause there.'

Kim Stanley, the actress who originated MM's *Bus Stop* role on stage.

'She probably knows more about acting in films than anyone in the world.'

Joshua Logan, after directing Monroe in *Bus Stop* in 1956.

'I had no idea she had this incandescent talent. She made directing worth while. She had such fascinating things happen to her face and skin and hair and body as she read lines, that she was – it's a cliché – but she was inspiring. She got me all hot and bothered just with her acting. Sexually it went way beyond that, *ça va sans dire*. She was gorgeous to look at, to get close to, to smell and feel – that, with her talent, too, I was a goner for her. I still am.'

Joshua Logan, who directed Monroe in 1956 in *Bus Stop*, to author Anthony
Summers – *Goddess: The Secret Lives of Marilyn Monroe*.

'She is luminous and completely desirable. Yet naive about herself and touching, rather like a little frightened animal, a fawn or a baby chicken.'

Joshua Logan, who directed MM in *Bus Stop*.

'Marilyn is as near a genius as any actress I ever knew. She is an artist beyond artistry. She is the most completely realised and authentic film actress since Garbo. She has that same unfathomable mysteriousness. She is pure cinema.'

Joshua Logan, the director of *Bus Stop*.

Following a 1970 screening of *Bus Stop* at the Museum of Modern Art:
'This is her performance – I gave her the freedom to improvise. It is one of the rarest and most perfect performances ever given by an actress. She was an *acting genius*.'

Joshua Logan, director of the 1956 MM film.

*On the evening of 29
October 1956, Mr and
Mrs Arthur Miller arrive
at London's Empire Theatre
to attend the Royal
Command Film
Performance of* The
Battle of the River
Plate. *Others present at the
gala included France's
Brigitte Bardot and
America's Joan Crawford.*

'Her work frightened her, and although she had undoubted talent, I think she had a subconscious resistance to the exercise of being an actress. But she was intrigued by its mystique and happy as a child when being photographed; she managed all the business of stardom with uncanny, clever, apparent ease.'

Sir Laurence Olivier, who directed MM in the 1957 Marilyn Monroe Production of *The Prince and the Showgirl*.

'A couple of my Hollywood friends, as a sort of joke after a dinner party, ran this now old picture, *The Prince and the Showgirl*. At the finish everyone was clamorous in their praises. I was as good as could be and Marilyn Monroe was quite wonderful, the best of all.'

Sir Laurence Olivier, MM's co-star.

'Her quality when photographed is almost of a supernatural beauty.'

Lee Strasberg, creator-director of the Actors Studio.

Awaiting her presentation to Queen Elizabeth II on 29 October 1956, Marilyn Monroe is flanked by American actor Victor Mature and British actor Anthony Quayle.

As Marilyn Monroe adjusts her glove, Anthony Quayle takes a moment to check out her décolletage.

With Victor Mature looking on, the United Kingdom's Queen Elizabeth II greets Hollywood queen, Marilyn Monroe.

FACING PAGE, TOP: *Two worlds join hands: Queen Elizabeth II meets America's Marilyn Monroe on 29 October 1956.*

FACING PAGE, BOTTOM: *Princess Margaret chats to Marilyn Monroe, as actors Victor Mature and Anthony Quayle look on, on the evening of 29 October 1956.*

MM laughs with members of the press on 4 December 1956, while publicising the upcoming première of Elia Kazan's film, Baby Doll, at which she would play the role of 'usherette' at New York City's Victoria Theater in Times Square.

At New York City's Actors Studio on 4 December 1956, famed party-giver Perle Mesta – 'the hostess with the mostest' – and Marilyn Monroe publicise the première of Baby Doll.

FACING PAGE: A lush-looking Marilyn arrives at the post-première party for the Carroll Baker film, Baby Doll, on the evening of 18 December 1956. MM is wearing a dress she'd bought off the rack only hours before attending the première.

Marilyn Monroe – with husband Arthur Miller – 13 June 1957, at New York City's Radio City Music Hall for the world première showing of her own production of The Prince and the Showgirl, *released by Warner Brothers. MM would win both the French and Italian equivalent of the Oscar for her performance in the film.*

FACING PAGE: *Without any of her movie-star glamour, Mrs Arthur Miller is captured by a hidden camera as she and her husband consider the front yard of their new home in Roxbury, Connecticut, in 1957.*

'I've learned about living from her. I took her as a serious actress even before I met her. I think she's an adroit comedienne, but I also think she might turn into the greatest tragic actress that can be imagined.'

Arthur Miller, writer and husband of MM, 1957.

Lady on the beach: Monroe is seen here with some unidentified people at the shore in Amagansett, Long Island, in the summer of 1957.

'Her beauty and humanity shine through . . . she is the kind of artist one does not come on every day in the week. After all, she was created something extraordinary.'

Arthur Miller, writer and husband of MM.

*Marilyn Monroe at a
March of Dimes fashion
show benefit held at New
York City's Waldorf
Astoria Hotel on 28
January 1958.*

'An apparition in white materialised in the doorway, white hair aswirl in the propwash of another plane; white silk shirt open at the powdered white throat; white, tight, silk skirt; white shoes; white gloves. Marilyn Monroe blinked big, sleepy eyes at the world . . . began descending – slowly and wickedly – down the steps. "I'm so sorry," she cooed, "I was asleep."'

Reporter for the *Los Angeles Times*, describing MM's arrival in Hollywood to begin filming *Some Like It Hot*.

Monroe sips champagne at the launch party for the film that would later be considered her greatest cinematic success, Some Like It Hot.

With his soon-to-be announced disdain for his co-star well hidden, a smiling Tony Curtis introduces his mother and father to Marilyn Monroe at the door to her dressing-room on the set of Some Like It Hot.

FACING PAGE: *Marilyn Monroe boards a TWA flight to Los Angeles, 8 July 1958,* en route *to Hollywood and the filming of Billy Wilder's classic,* Some Like It Hot.

'There are certain wonderful rascals in this
world, like Monroe. She's *zaftig*, as the
Germans say. She has breasts like granite,
she defies gravity. God gave her everything.
The first day a photographer took a picture
of her, she was a genius.'

Billy Wilder, while directing MM in *Some Like It Hot*,
1958.

Marilyn Monroe films scenes for the United Artists 1959 release, Some Like It Hot.

'She was an absolute genius as a comic actress, with an extraordinary sense for comic dialogue. It was a God-given gift. Believe me, in the last fifteen years there were ten projects that came to me, and I'd start working on them and I'd think, "It's not going to work, it needs Marilyn Monroe." Nobody else is in that orbit; everyone else is earthbound by comparison.'

Billy Wilder – who directed MM in *Some Like It Hot* in 1958, and before that in *The Seven Year Itch* in 1954 – speaking about her *circa* 1984.

Monroe and Lemmon rehearse a scene on the beach for the location shooting of Some Like It Hot.

When questioned about Tony Curtis's comment that 'kissing Marilyn was like kissing Hitler', Monroe allowed, 'It was out with him and in with the character; he was never *there!'*

Reel females Tony Curtis and Jack Lemmon check out the real Marilyn Monroe filming a scene for Some Like It Hot.

'She had flesh which photographs like flesh.
You feel you can reach out and touch it.
Unique is an overworked word, but in her
case it applies. There will never be another
one like her, and Lord knows there have
been plenty of imitations.'

Billy Wilder, director, upon hearing of MM's passing.

'She has a certain indefinable magic that comes across, which no other actress in the business has.'

Billy Wilder, while directing MM in *Some Like It Hot* in 1958.

'They've tried to manufacture other Marilyn Monroes and they will undoubtedly keep trying. But it won't work. She was an original.'

Billy Wilder.

In 1959, an incredibly beautiful MM poses for publicity for the release of Some Like It Hot.

159

Stepdaughter Jane,
Marilyn Monroe and
stepson Bobby.

FACING PAGE: *A very*
candid Marilyn is seen here
relaxing with her
stepdaughter Jane Miller.

'She was alive in a way not granted the rest of us. She communicated such a charge of vitality as altered our imagination of life, which is the job and wonder of art. Hollywood, Broadway, the nightclubs all produce their quota of sex queens, but the public takes them or leaves them; the world is not as enslaved by them as it was by Marilyn Monroe, because none but she could suggest such a purity of sexual delight. The boldness with which she could parade herself and yet never be gross, her sexual flamboyance and bravado which yet breathed an air of mystery and even reticence, her voice which carried such ripe overtones of erotic excitement and yet was the voice of a shy child – these anomalies were integral to her gift. And they described a young woman trapped in a never-never land of unawareness. Even while she symbolised an extreme of sexual knowingness, she took each new circumstance of life like a newborn babe. And this is what made her luminous. The glow was not rubbed off by the ugliness of life because finally in some vital depth, she had been untouched by it.'

Diana Trilling, author.

A delighted and delightful Marilyn arrives at 135 Central Park West for the Lee and Paula Strasberg-hosted post-première party following the showing of Some Like It Hot.

Wearing the same off-the-rack evening gown she'd worn to the 1956 première of Baby Doll, *MM raises a toast at the April in Paris Ball held at the Waldorf Astoria Hotel in New York City in 1959.*

FACING PAGE, TOP: *On 13 May 1959, Marilyn was presented with the David di Donatello Award as Best Actress for her performance in* The Prince and the Showgirl. *The ceremony, held in New York City, was attended by Italy's Anna Mangani, pictured here with Monroe and Dr Filippo Donini.*

FACING PAGE, BOTTOM: *Having received Italy's most prestigious acting award, MM departs the Italian Embassy in New York City with Arthur Miller, while author James Haspiel – seen with an 8mm movie camera in the upper right-hand portion of the picture – shoots home movies of the event, 13 May 1959.*

'Marilyn always dreamt of being an actress. She didn't, by the way, dream of being just a star. She dreamt of being an actress. And she had always lived somehow with that dream. And that is why, despite the fact that she became one of the most unusual and outstanding stars of all time, she herself was never satisfied. When she came to New York, she began to perceive the possibilities of really accomplishing her dream, of being an actress.'

Lee Strasberg, creator-director of the Actors Studio.

'The legend is that Marilyn Monroe was a movie star driven to despair by the obliterating glare of fame. The truth about Marilyn Monroe is that she was *saved* by Hollywood. Fame saved her. The spotlight beating on her twenty-four hours a day made the world seem liveable to her. She lived in the midst of her fame as if she were more a poster than a woman, but the unreality never hurt her. It was the only world in which she could thrive. The real world held only hobgoblins for her, terrors that harried her nights. The movies did not destroy Marilyn; they gave her a long and joyous reprieve from the devils which hounded her in earlier years.'

Ben Hecht, writer and friend.

'I was [am] a poet, who knew another poet when I saw one. I enjoyed her beauty. She enjoyed my poems. We were mostly off-stage friends. When she was the star, I moved away, uncomfortable. At film openings or official receptions, she wore her mask. I knew her without it. I re-read a postcard she wrote to me years ago. On one side, a large American Airlines jet in a blue sky. Her message, a single sentence: "Guess where I am? Love, Marilyn."'

Norman Rosten, poet and friend of MM.

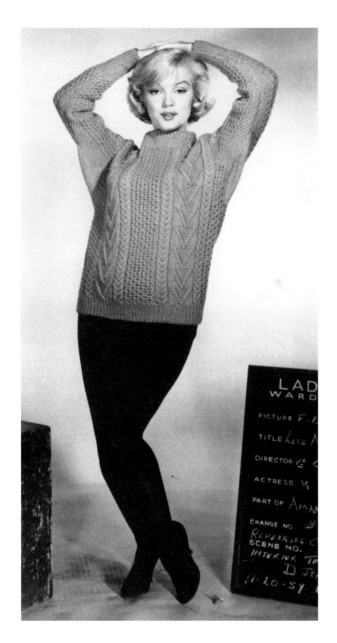

Some of Monroe's costume and hair tests for her 1960 release, Fox's Let's Make Love. *The film was directed by George Cukor, who would later helm the production of MM's final movie at Fox, 1962's ill-fated* Something's Got to Give.

FACING PAGE, RIGHT: *Marilyn Monroe and Judy Garland walk towards the Café de Paris commissary at 20th Century-Fox, en* route *to the luncheon being held for Russian Premier Nikita Khrushchev on 19 September 1959.*

'She treated me more like a friend than a
studio associate. Before I would go into a
scene to stand in for her, she would come
over and fix my hair and my clothes and
she'd give me the motivation for the scene,
so I would know what I was doing. She was
my Paula Strasberg.'

Evelyn Moriarty, MM's stand-in, *circa* 1959–62.

*Marilyn in her show-
stopping number – 'My
Heart Belongs to Daddy' –
in* Let's Make Love.

*Monroe lands a friendly
kiss on the forehead of*
Let's Make Love *co-star
Frankie Vaughan.*

*Choreographer Jack Cole
coaches Marilyn for her
'Specialisation' number in*
Let's Make Love.

A sexy Monroe vamps her way through the song 'Specialisation' with co-star Frankie Vaughan in 1960's Let's Make Love.

FOLLOWING PAGES: *At last, the never-before-seen photos of Marilyn Monroe and Elvis Presley, or, if you like, Elvis and Marilyn.* Not! *The young hunk in these rare pictures shot on the set of* Let's Make Love *is actually the fledgling actor, John Gatti, who portrayed Elvis Presley in the film's 'Specialisation' number.*

*MM meets MM.
Hollywood columnist May
Mann visits Marilyn
Monroe on the set of* Let's
Make Love. *Ms Mann
would later write a
biography of Ms Monroe's
shadow at Fox – Jayne
Mansfield.*

'What am I afraid of? I know I can act. But I'm afraid. I am afraid and I should not be and I must not be. Shit!'

Marilyn Monroe, *circa* 1960.

'The last time I saw Marilyn was in late 1959, when I appeared in *Let's Make Love* at Fox. The wide-eyed naïve Marilyn I had first known was gone. This Marilyn was more beautiful than ever.'

Milton Berle, comedian.

*Legendary dancer Gene
Kelly and MM take a coffee
break on the set of* Let's
Make Love, *as co-star
Yves Montand looks on.*

FACING PAGE: *Yves
Montand, Tony Randall,
Marilyn Monroe, Wilfrid
Hyde-White and David
Burns in the finale of*
Let's Make Love.

'Marilyn Monroe is the greatest farceuse in
the business, a female Chaplin.'

Jerry Wald, producer.

'She listens, wants, cares. I catch her laughing across a room and I bust up. Every pore of that lovely translucent skin is alive, open every moment – even though this world could make her vulnerable to being hurt. I would rather work with her than any other actress. I adore her.'

Montgomery Clift, MM's co-star in the 1961 film *The Misfits*.

Marilyn is seen here with friend (and author) James 'Jimmy' Haspiel on 8 July 1960, in frames culled from an 8mm home movie of the two subjects, who first met in September of 1954 and who knew each other until MM's demise in 1962.

*The very candid, off-screen
Marilyn is seen as she
makes her way around New
York City, circa 1960.*

'She was not the usual movie idol. There was
something democratic about her. She was
the type who would join in and wash up the
supper dishes even if you didn't ask her. She
was a good talker . . . she spoke well on the
national scene, the Hollywood scene, and on
people who are good to know and people
who ain't.'

Carl Sandburg, poet and friend.

'Marilyn is a kind of ultimate. She is uniquely feminine. Everything she does is different, strange and exciting, from the way she talks to the way she uses that magnificent torso. She makes a man proud to be a man.'

Clark Gable, MM's co-star in the 1961 film, *The Misfits*.

Marilyn Monroe arrives in Reno, Nevada, in July 1960, to begin location filming on The Misfits.

FACING PAGE: *First there were the nude calendar shots in 1949, then there was the nude swim scene for* Something's Got to Give *in 1962. In between those events, Monroe was caught off guard on the 1960 set of* The Misfits *as she prepared to film a scene in which co-star Clark Gable wakes her up following their first night together.*

MM on the set of The
Misfits *in 1960.*

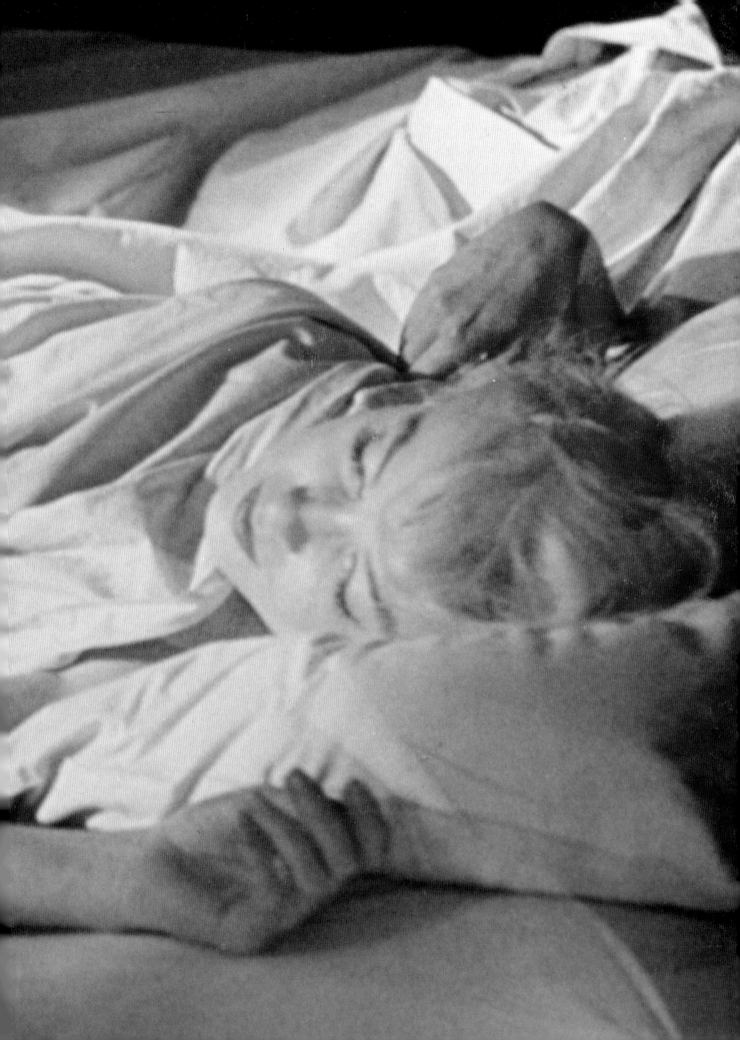

'She is capable of sensitive concentration . . . always the secret of making any talent work, which hers does.'

Truman Capote, writer, now buried near MM's crypt at Westwood Memorial Park.

'She went right down into her own personal experience for everything, reached down and pulled something out of herself that was unique and extraordinary. She had no techniques. It was all the truth, it was only Marilyn. But it was Marilyn, plus. She found things, found things about womankind in herself.'

John Huston, in 1984.

'It's a terrible pity that so much beauty has been lost to us.'

John Huston, who directed MM in 1950's *The Asphalt Jungle* and in her last completed film, *The Misfits*, 1961.

Following gallbladder surgery, Marilyn arrives home to her New York City apartment at 444 East 57th Street on 11 July 1961. Monroe's press agent, John Springer, can be seen on the extreme right in this picture.

Following Marilyn Monroe's divorce from Arthur Miller on 20 January 1961, ex-husband Joe DiMaggio came back into her life. The famous pair are seen here as they take a stroll in Florida in March 1961.

FACING PAGE: *Marilyn's famed childlike quality is on display in this candid image shot during the making of* The Misfits.

'I based a lot of Roslyn, the girl in my *Misfits* screenplay, on Marilyn. Her extraordinary embrace of life is intermingled with great sadness. To understand Marilyn best, you have to see her around children. They love her; her whole approach to life has their kind of simplicity and directness. She can imply the world in a look. Marilyn has become a sort of fiction for writers.'

Arthur Miller, writer and husband of MM.

*Marilyn Monroe at the
Golden Globe Awards on 5
March 1962.*

FACING PAGE: *The woman
with the 'great future
behind her' walks away
from the camera on a
Florida beach in February
1962.*

'I want to say that the people – if I am a
star – the people made me a star. No studio,
no person – but the people did.'

Marilyn Monroe, speaking just weeks before her
untimely death.

'She would have interested me even if she
had had no record as a great actress. Gosh,
there were a lot of people who loved her.
There were no pretences about Marilyn
Monroe. She gave me an impression of
happiness. I remember Marilyn sitting two or
three feet from me on the sofa when we
met in New York. I didn't rise and escort her
to the elevator when it was time for her to
leave. I hope she forgave me.'

Carl Sandburg, poet.

*On 5 March 1962,
Marilyn Monroe received
the Golden Globe Award as
the World's Favourite
Female Star. To MM's
right is actor Rock Hudson
and just behind the two
stars is her Los Angeles
press agent, Patricia
Newcomb.*

'Marilyn had the power. She was the wind,
that comet shape that Blake draws blowing
around a sacred figure. She was the light and
the goddess and the moon. The space and
the dream, the mystery and the danger. But
everything else all together, too, including
Hollywood and the girl next door that every
guy wants to marry. I could have hung up
the camera, run off with her, lived happily
ever after . . .'

Bert Stern, who photographed Monroe little more
than a month before her death, speaking *circa* 1982.

Marilyn Monroe arrives at Madison Square Garden in New York City on the evening of 19 May 1962, to sing 'Happy Birthday' to President John F. Kennedy.

Marilyn Monroe, wearing a kerchief and sunglasses, is seen backstage at Madison Square Garden in New York City on the afternoon of 19 May 1962, at a rehearsal for that night's performance. MM's press agent, Patricia Newcomb, is to the left of the star.

'Thanks, Mr President, for all the things
you've done, the battles that you've won, the
way you deal with US Steel and our
problems by the ton, we thank you so much.
Everybody – "Happy Birthday!"'.

Marilyn Monroe, singing to President John F. Kennedy
at New York City's Madison Square Garden on 19
May 1962.

'I can now retire from politics after having
had "Happy Birthday" sung to me in such a
sweet, wholesome way.'

John F. Kennedy, President of the United States,
following MM's rendition of the classic song at
Madison Square Garden in New York City on 19 May
1962.

'I know people who say, "Hollywood broke her heart," and all that, but I don't believe it. She was very observant and tough-minded and appealing, but she adored and trusted the wrong people. She was very courageous – you know the book *Twelve Against the Gods*? Marilyn was like that, she had to challenge the gods at every turn.'

George Cukor, MM director.

'She was the *realest* person I ever met.'

Evelyn Moriarty, MM's stand-in, *circa* 1959–62.

'After a short life, during which she succeeded in giving this none-too-happy world a great deal of pleasure, Marilyn Monroe is dead. Our hearts go out to her and to any who truly loved her. May she rest in peace.'

New York Daily News newspaper editorial.

'The tragic death of Marilyn Monroe shocked and unsettled the serenity of a summer sabbath for many people in this country and all over the world. She was recognised and applauded sincerely by those who respected her quality as a remarkably able comedienne and a developing dramatic star.'

New York Times newspaper editorial.

'We are writing to your paper to tell how much we loved Marilyn Monroe. She was so beautiful she made our hearts tingle.'

Betty Spink, 11, and Laurie Turner, 9, schoolgirls in 1962, in the *Utica Daily Press.*

In this final image, a candid shot taken by my life-long friend Lou Valenti, the icon is on public view on a New York City street, the evening wind caressing her, the loveliness of her smile eternal . . . Marilyn!

'Nobody discovered her, she earned her own way to stardom.'

> Darryl Zanuck, president of 20th Century-Fox, buried today only yards from Marilyn Monroe's crypt at Westwood Memorial Park.

'Anyone who has ever felt resentment against the good for being the good, and has given voice to it, is the murderer of Marilyn Monroe.'

> Ayn Rand, novelist.

'A profoundly beautiful, profoundly moving young woman – she has given warm delight to millions of people, made them smile affectionately, laugh uproariously, love her to the point of caring deeply – the waste seems almost unbearable. The magnificent blonde image in the American memory-stream, in the great film collections, in movie houses as unlikely as Tehran's.'

> *Vogue* magazine.

'Her soul will always be restless, unquiet.'

Maurice Zolotow, ending his 1960 biography, *Marilyn Monroe*.

'Her death has diminished the loveliness of the world in which we live.'

Life magazine, 17 August 1962.

'Marilyn Monroe . . . the most fragile and lovable legend of all.'

Look magazine; *The Look Years 1937–1971*.

'She was probably the last of the big stars. Whether or not she knew that is debatable – but then we ourselves didn't realise it at the time. Ten years ago . . . long enough for a cult to fade, a myth to evolve. Time to realise how timeless she really is.'

Daily Girl magazine, June 1972.

'She was so beautiful and untouched, it was as though she were just beginning.'

Bert Stern, photographer.

A poem written in 1957:

Here goes –
Good nite
Sleep
and sweet repose
Where ever you lay your head –
I hope you find your nose –
Marilyn.